Studia Fennica
Ethnologica 9

The Finnish Literature Society (SKS) was founded in 1831 and has, from the very beginning, engaged in publishing operations. It nowadays publishes literature in the fields of ethnology and folkloristics, linguistics, literary research and cultural history.

The first volume of the Studia Fennica series appeared in 1933. Since 1992, the series has been divided into three thematic subseries: Ethnologica, Folkloristica and Linguistica. Two additional subseries were formed in 2002, Historica and Litteraria. The subseries Anthropologica was formed in 2007.

In addition to its publishing activities, the Finnish Literature Society maintains research activities and infrastructures, an archive containing folklore and literary collections, a research library and promotes Finnish literature abroad.

OA.FINLIT.FI

Editorial Office
SKS
P.O. Box 259
FI-00171 Helsinki
www.finlit.fi

Passages Westward

Edited by Maria Lähteenmäki & Hanna Snellman

Finnish Literature Society • Helsinki

Studia Fennica Ethnologica 9

The publication has undergone a peer review.

VERTAISARVIOITU
KOLLEGIALT GRANSKAD
PEER-REVIEWED
www.tsv.fi/tunnus

A digital edition of a printed book first published in 2006 by the Finnish Literature Society.

Cover Design: Timo Numminen
EPUB: Tero Salmén

ISBN 978-951-858-065-5 (Print)
ISBN 978-951-858-067-9 (PDF)
ISBN 978-951-858-066-2 (EPUB)

ISSN 0085-6835 (Studia Fennica)
ISSN 1235-1954 (Studia Fennica Ethnlogica)

DOI: http://dx.doi.org/10.21435/sfe.9

A free open access version of the book is available at http://dx.doi.org/10.21435/sfe.9 or by scanning this QR code with your mobile device.

Contents

The Making of New Finland

Deep Roots

Crossing Borders

The Finns living on the northern edge of Europe have always had close contacts with the western world. From the arrival of the Swedes to Finland in the 1150s up until 1809, Finland was part of Sweden. Learned people, savants and the clergy were in the vanguard of westernization. Since the Middle Ages, the Finns have crossed borders in search of western ideas from universities in Europe. For example, there were Finnish students at the University of Paris already in 1313. The universities of Prague, Leipzig, Heidelberg, Cologne, Rostock, Greifswald and Frankfurt all attracted Finnish students early on. In 1530 the father of the Finnish language and a key person in the Reformation, Mikael Agricola enrolled at the University of Wittenberg. The University of Leuwen was also a destination for several students of theology from Finland.

Crossing borders has not necessarily involved Finns leaving Finland; western ideas were also brought to Finland. As the eastern part of Sweden, "Eastland", Finland received a great number of visitors such as explorers and merchants. German merchants in particular took up residence in Finland at an early stage. With them they brought not only ideas, but also artefacts, which had an effect on the material culture of Finland in those areas where German burghers had settled. The first Finnish students at the universities of Central Europe were, in fact, descendants of these merchants. In addition to religious institutions and values, trade relations played a major role in westernizing. Works of art should also be mentioned; not only artists but also their works traveled.

However, the Finns were not only just attracted to Western Europe, the East also exerted a certain fascination. Russia and the Baltic received a Finnish population at an early stage. Tallinn was already a center of trade in the Middle Ages, and as such interested Finnish merchants. The founding of St. Petersburg at the beginning of the 1700s led to an extensive migration of Finns to the growing metropolis. In general, Finns have traveled because of war, famine, work and in search of scientific or artistic development.

In the nineteenth century, early Finnish nationalism came to rest on a particular movement within Western European ideology, namely German Romanticism. Science and the arts were harnessed to serve the formation of the nation. The World Fair in Paris in 1900 was a triumph for Finnish artists

– and the self-esteem of Finns, as it confirmed their sense of belonging to the West. Romanticism aroused interest amongst Finns in their own language and popular culture. As a consequence, the foundations of academic disciplines such as ethnology, Finnish history, folklore studies and Finnish literature were laid.

Finland's geopolitical location between East and West has caused a lot of tension in Finland over the past two hundred years. In particular from the nineteenth century onwards it has been argued that the Finns are European, not Asian or Slavic. The fact that the Finnish language belongs to the uralic language group, led the Finns to argue for their westerness. Finland was part of the Russian empire between 1809 and 1917, which also had an effect. The wish to distinguish itself from Russia, which had gone "Red" with the Bolshevik revolution, and the declaration of independence in 1917 only accelerated the urge to present Finland as an outpost of the West. In the 1920s the Pan-European movement extended to the north of Europe. For example, a well-known Finnish author demanded the "opening of windows to Europe". During the Second World War, Finland for one became a brother in arms alongside Hitler's Germany, against the "Giant of the East", the Soviet Union. Even genetics has been recruited to the cause of arguing for Finland's westerness: in the 1960s it was announced that Finns were genetically at least half European. In the 1990s, the European ancestry was proved to be seventy five.

A Pedagogical Experiment

Bringing out this anthology has involved crossing borders in many senses. It is the offspring of our joint PhD seminar between the disciplines of ethnology and history at the University of Helsinki. The seminar was a part of our ongoing projects at the Academy of Finland (project numbers 1211043 and 211152). The idea of the seminar was to give PhD students of ethnology, Katri Kaunisto, Leena Louhivuori, Leena Paaskoski, Terhi Willman, and history, Oona Ilmolahti, Tarja Kytönen, Päivi Maria Pihlaja, a chance, at an early stage of their research, to present their research results to an audience who do not share the same academic background. In addition, salient concepts frequent in today's academic discussions were analyzed. Visitors from the Universities of Gothenburg and Amsterdam contributed to the group. One aim of the seminar, which met for three years, was to write an anthology of ongoing projects. This book is the result. In addition, we invited scholars, not only, from different disciplines: applied linguistics (Lotta Weckström) and literature (Minna Aalto), but also, different corners of the world: a historian from the University of Canberra (Katri Tanni) and two ethnologists from the Universities of Gothenburg (Marja Ågren) and Linköping (Mirjaliisa Lukkarinen Kvist), to contribute to this book.

This study presents and evaluates Finnish people's relationships and links with the West with the help of fourteen case studies. For the Finns the West has provided new ideological and financial resources, fresh ideas, schemes of things and operational models. The West has also absorbed Finnish expertise. Throughout the centuries, the West has attracted scholars and artists. Furthermore, Finns were a part of the great conquest of the West when they migrated to America at the turn of the century. Canada and Australia received their share of Finnish migrants during the twentieth century. Labor migration to Finland's neighbor, Sweden, in the 1950s, 1960s and 1970s is a special case of its own. New generations of Finns are living in all these countries. Finland after the Second World War faced new challenges in its westernization.

In 1995 Finland joined the European Union, which has increased contacts between Brussels, Central-Europe and Finland. Because of the European Union's Bureaux and the common market area, more and more Finns are spending at least some of their working life outside Finland, for example, somewhere in Europe. Finns are free to seek employment in the countries of the European Union. The concept of a migrant has, therefore, gained new meanings.

The Faculty of Arts at the University of Helsinki gave us financial support for publishing this anthology. We want to thank the faculty and especially Aili Nenola, the Dean, and Petri Mirala, PhD, for the support. The Finnish Literature Society accepted our manuscript for its series. We want to thank the editorial staff of the Finnish Literature Society, for their excellent co-operation. Departmental amanuensis of Ethnology Katarina Koskiranta has acted as the sub-editor for this book. She and the authors of this book deserve our warmest appreciation. We are deeply indebted to the Research Council for Culture and Society at the Academy of Finland for giving us this opportunity to work on such an interdisciplinary and international pioneer project.

Helsinki May 4, 2006
Maria Lähteenmäki   *Hanna Snellman*

New Places, New Spaces

MARIA LÄHTEENMÄKI

Finnish Expatriates in Brussels

It was a sunny Saturday evening, the last day of April. The crossroads of Rues de l'Etuve and du Chêne in the lower town of Brussels was thronged with dozens of people whose noisy laughter and eager talk was audible a long way off. Every now and then champagne corks popped and festival trumpets tooted. Precisely at 6 o'clock a young man in a black suit and a young woman in a tiny dress climbed up to the side of the small pool. They both were white student caps on their heads. Most of the audience had similar hats. The man had a bigger cap in his hands and, carrying it solemnly, he placed it on the head of the Manneken Pis to loud applause. The ceremony had reached its traditional climax. Again, on the eve of the first of May the Manneken Pis had been crowned with his white student cap: the symbol of Finnishness. At the very same time in Helsinki, students were capping the beautiful statue of a naked woman, called Havis Amanda, and in Rovaniemi in Finnish Lapland, they capped the statue of a timber worker. In Brussels, the small statue of a little boy from the seventeenth century is, therefore a very suitable object for this ritual spring celebration of Finnish students.[11] The first time the statue in Brussels was given its Finnish student cap was in 1993.

In this article, I will present and analyze the experiences of Finns living in Brussels. Belgium is the latest notable destination for Finnish migration; it began to attract a few Finns in the 1950s, and after Finland joined the European Union (in 1995) the number of Finns has increased especially in Brussels. In 1991, the number of Finnish citizens living in Belgium was about 600, by 1999 it had risen already to 2,800, and by 2005, to approximately 3,500. During the twentieth century the most attractive destination for Finnish migrants has been Sweden. The next most popular destinations have been Germany, Great Britain and Norway.[22]

Brussels is one of the most international cities in Europe.[33] In the region of Brussels there are about 270,000 foreigners out of a population of one million. This means that about one-third of the inhabitants of the region have citizenship other than Belgian. The biggest foreign communities in Brussels are the Italian, French and Dutch. Next come the Moroccan, Turkish, German, British and Portuguese. Together these groups make up almost 80 per cent of the foreign population in the region. Of the three regions of Belgium (Brussels, Flemish and Walloon) Brussels is the most cosmopolitan. Of the

13

French speaking population of the Walloon region about nine percent were foreigners and of the population of the Flemish region about five percent (in 2002).[44] The Finnish community is concentrated in the city Brussels although some Finns live in other parts of the country, like Antwerp and Ghent. Although the Finnish colony is not the biggest, it occasionally makes its presence felt, as the Manneken Pis celebrations indicate.

The history of Finnish migration can be divided into three main waves. The old (great) migration of the nineteenth century took Finns mainly to the USA and to Canada but at the beginning of the century, also to northern Norway and Russia, especially to St. Petersburg. The second important migration wave took place in the 1960s and 1970s: the main direction of migration at that time was Sweden. The third wave, the "new migration", began in the 1990s and the destination countries for Finnish migrants were member countries of the European Union. The difference between the old and the new migration is so clear that the terms *"migration"* (siirtolaisuus) and *"migrants"* (siirtolaiset) are nowadays often replaced in Finnish discussions by the terms *"expatriation"* and *"expatriates"*. Expatriates are workers sent abroad by the national governments or companies. There is no exact Finnish translation for the term "expatriates" – Finns use a mixed English-Finnish word *ekspatriaatit*. The term of *ulkosuomalaiset* is normally used when discussing *Finns living abroad*. Later in this article, I will analyze the differences between the old migration and the new migration/expatriation. In this connection I will use the concept "expatriate". It is a concept most of my interviewees defined themselves.

The theoretical framework of this paper is linked to discussions concerning the future of a united Europe, cultural and economical diversity and new identities – the return of old ones and the transformation of existing ones.[55] The question of identities is at the same time a question of about similarities and differences between Europeans and "others". Identity became one of the unifying themes of social scientists during the 1990s. Everybody – anthropologists, geographers, historians, political scientists and sociologists – has something to say about this issue.[66] The famous cultural researcher Stuart Hall has stated that this is because western culture is in crisis. Also researcher Kobena Mercer has argued that identity only becomes an issue when it is in crisis, when something assumed to be fixed, coherent, and stable is displaced by the experience of doubt and uncertainty.[77] According to some researchers, a distinctive type of structural change is transforming modern societies in the late twentieth century and this is fragmenting the cultural landscapes of class, gender, sexuality, ethnicity, race, and nationality, which used to give us firm locations as social individuals. These transformations are also shifting our personal identities, undermining our sense of ourselves as integrated subjects.[88]

According to the textbooks, *identity* means "sameness" or "exact likeness"; by identifying somebody we try to discover or recognize who or what a particular person or thing is. The Oxford English Dictionary offers the following definition: "Identity is the consistency or continuity over time that is the basis for establishing and grasping the definiteness and distinctiveness of something." Sociologist Richard Jenkins has emphasized, as have many

14

other scholars, that individual as well as collective identities are systematically produced, reproduced, and implicated in each other.[99] According to Hall, identity bridges the gap between the "inside" and the "outside" – between the personal and public worlds.[10]

With this article, I want to turn a new page in the history of Finnish migration. Finland has been a member of the European Union since 1995, but there are no scientific studies about the experiences of Finns in Brussels. For other places – especially France (Paris, Bretagne and Provence) – there are some memoirs and travel books written by Finnish expatriates and travellers.[11] There are also lots of studies about the so-called old migration, for instance, to America and Sweden.[12] The main sources for this article are thirty interviews conducted in Brussels during May–June 2005.[13] Most of the interviewed persons are Finnish expatriates (sent workers or their family members), and only a few are immigrants living permanently in Brussels. Another source has been the newspaper *Parlööri* (1978–2005) which is published by the Finnish Club of Belgium (Club Finlandais de Belgique).[14] Whilst conducting my research, I lived in Brussels (in 2004–2005), so I was also part of the Finnish community.[15]

Early Contacts

The first image of Belgium which often comes to minds for Finns concerns the Walloons. Finns generally are eager to study their roots and quite a lot of families in Finland's iron working communities have French speaking ironsmiths among their ancestors. The Walloons came to Sweden and Finland in the seventeenth century to teach iron working skills and some of them stayed. When Finland declared its independence in December 1917, contacts with Belgium took on a official nature. Belgium recognized Finland's independence in June 1919 and diplomatic relations were established in July that year. Finnish Embassy was established in Belgium in 1938. Ten years earlier a Belgian Embassy had opened its doors in Helsinki.

The Finnish industry companies have been active in forming contacts with Belgium as well as other parts of Europe ever since Finland declared independence. Finnish companies became even more active in the 1970s: they opened own office in Brussels in 1974. Finnish industrial circles lobbied eagerly for Finland to join the European Union. Nowadays there are about 200 Finnish firms and 30 subsidiary companies active in Belgian market (2005). The biggest companies are Nokia (mobiles), UMP-Kymmene (paper, chemical pulp), Kemira (chemicals), Kone (elevators), and Valio (food products).[16] These companies provide work for many Finnish expatriates. The EU-Commission and the European Parliament are also important employers of Finns. In 2005 there were 615 Finns working in the Commission and 155 in the Parliament. Of those working at the European Parliament about one-third work in Brussels and the rest in Luxembourg.[17] In the last elections (2004) Finland sent fourteen members to the European Parliament. The Finnish government and individual ministries, national private organizations (like labor movement, employer's organizations, political parties), international

15

schools (The European Schools, the Scandinavian School) and the Finnish Seaman's Mission,[18] which has activities both in Brussels and Antwerp, are amongst the other employers of Finns. The Seaman's Mission opened its church in Antwerp in 1905. After the Finnish population in Belgium increased, a parsonage opened in Brussels in 2000. It is a very popular meeting place among Finns.

The areas favored by Finnish residences in Belgium have changed over time. The membership lists of the Finnish Club provide more information about the locations of the Finnish communities. In the 1970s the first members of the Finnish Club were living all around the country, for example in Waterloo, Antwerp, Overijsen, Zaventum, and Brussels. In the 1990s, members lived mainly in the region of Brussels, like in Rhode-St-Genèse, Uccle, Ixelles and in the center of Brussels. All in all, the city contains 19 independent municipalities around the center. At the beginning of the 2000s, the biggest Finnish communities are to be found in the eastern part of the city, in Woluwe St. Lambert and Woluwe St. Pierre. Nowadays, the nearby regions, Etterbeek and Kraainem, are also popular residential areas for Finns.[19] This is mainly because of the European School II: Finnish classes are available at that school. The metro line and the nice surroundings have also affected the decisions to settle in these areas – and, of course, the other Finns already living there. Finnish families want to live near other Finns because they want friends for their children and social activities for themselves. It is interesting that although Finns in Brussels can speak several languages they still choose to live regions where there are other Finns. The same phenomenon was found in Sweden in the 1960s and 1970s: Finns went to live near other Finns.[20] Single Finns prefer to live near the EU-buildings, in downtown Brussels, and in the Merode and Schuman areas. One of the interviewed Finns said that the areas in the East of Brussels are boring: "Middle class civil servants live there!" She herself lives near the center in the St. Gilles district, which is a popular area among artists and people with an alternative life style.[21]

Better Work, Better Wages

The most important reason for moving to Brussels for Finns has been work: work that is more interesting, more challenging, and better paid than in Finland. If we compare the new migrants/expatriates with the old migrants who moved to Sweden in the 1960s and the 1970s, fundamental differences are evident. First of all, expatriates are highly educated: the Commission, the EU-Parliament, international schools and private organizations require a university degree for most of their positions. The old migrants, on the contrary, were often uneducated and without foreign language skills. Most of the expatriates spoke at least three languages (Finnish, Swedish, English) when they arrived in Brussels. The cultural background is also different between these two groups: the old migrants come from the peripheral northern and eastern agrarian regions of Finland. Most of the expatriates come from the urban southern regions. The alternatives available to these Finns and their future plans regarding Finland reveal often differences between these two groups.

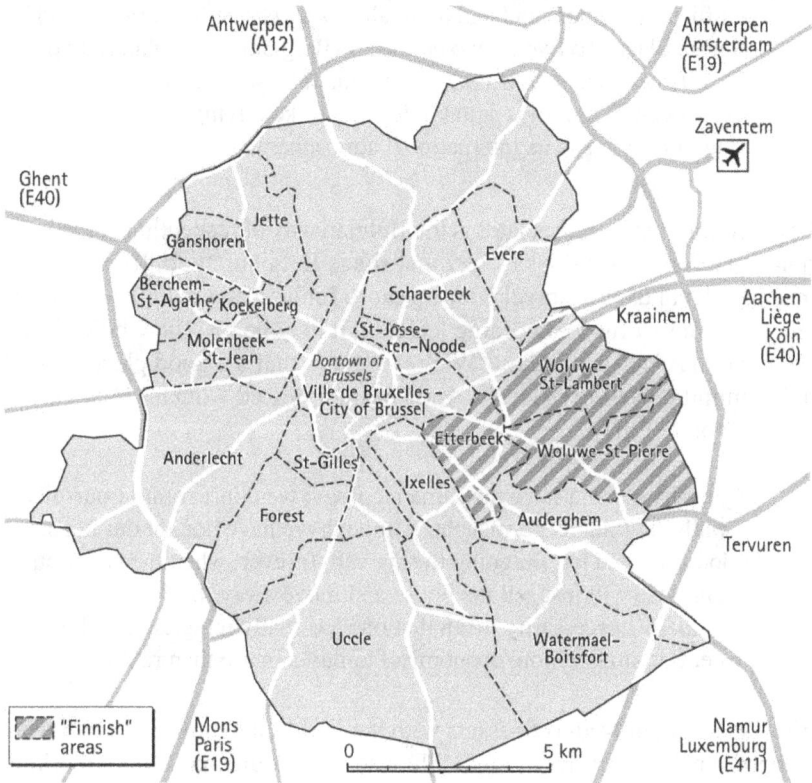

Municipalities of Brussels.

Although higher wages and new career opportunities are very important factors for the expatriates, many interviewees wanted to emphasize that it was "not just the work" but "the idea of living abroad" which lay behind the idea of living in Brussels. Jenni is one of the Finnish workers in the European Parliament. She moved to the city in 1999 with her two children from Luxembourg where she had worked one year. Her African husband stayed in Finland. The third child of the family was born in Brussels. Jenni rents a house near the European School in the Wezembeek–Oppem area. One of her children is in a Flemish school: "To learn Flemish is more practical because the municipality workers in this area are Flemish." Jenni enjoys her work and has arranged childcare with the help of Finnish au pairs. To have au pairs is very common among Finnish expatriates. Jenni has integrated well into the city. She has an international network of friends and speaks many languages.

It was much more difficult to adjust to the mentality of Luxembourg: it is so hostile to foreigners, their language is a strange dialect which

17

is difficult to understand and all in all it is a very petit bourgeois and cliquish place. To live in two countries (Belgium and Finland), two cities (Brussels and Helsinki) and within at least three cultures (Finnish, African, Belgian) is suitable for me. I liked living abroad. The best thing in Brussels is its international atmosphere.

The other thing Jenni appreciates is the Belgian way of respecting someone's privacy. However, she doesn't feel that she is Belgian: "I don't know what it means." Jenni used to travel once a year to Finland and her husband visits in Brussels more often. According to Jenni, it may be that the whole family will move to Africa some day. "Wherever I am, that's a good place to be! I don't commit myself to place."[22] Another interviewed woman, Mia, agreed with this point of view:

> My husband and I have the same ideology: we don't commit ourselves to walls. Nothing is permanent. Although we have bought our house, it doesn't mean we are going to stay here forever: when the situation changes we will just sell the house and move away. Buying a house here doesn't necessarily mean that one has really integrated to this place. It is simply more economical to buy a house than rent it.[23]

Arja, like Jenni, moved to Brussels with her child. She moved in 1995 from southern Finland after her divorce. She had always dreamed about working abroad and now in her new circumstances her dreams came true: Arja had been in the Central Europe several times, especially in France, when she was a language student. She works for a private Finnish organization in the middle of Brussels. Her first home in Brussels was in Etterbeek and the next in Woluwe St. Lambert. Arja moved to Brussels because the work was more interesting and had a more international dimension to it:

> I like the atmosphere of the city, you make friends easily – there are so many singles in the city. However, the worst thing is loneliness: when my child passed the examination in the European School and moved to England to study at the university, it was horrible for me. Nowadays she is in Finland and I have wondered if I should also move back to Finland. It is not easy to do that kind of solutions. And otherwise, I like this city and the people here. What would happen if I didn't enjoy my work in Finland?

Arja travels to Finland approximately three times a year.[24]

The other Finnish woman, Lotta, said also that work is very important for her: it was her job that made her family move to Brussels. She moved to Brussels in 2003 from Asia, where she had lived several years. Lotta is a cosmopolitan: "I was born to travel in exotic countries and continents!" Like Arja, Lotta lives also in Etterbeek:

> The first few months I thought that this city was too boring for me, too European – you know, too familiar, too dark, too rainy. I worked

Manneken Piss with Finnish student cap. Photo: Maria Lähteenmäki.

in this city before and that's why I thought that this city had nothing to offer me. But, after a half a year I began to see the town in a better light: it's very green, the food is very good and the children enjoy their school.

Lotta feels herself to be very Finnish: abroad the feeling of Finnishness is more emphasized. The white-blue national flag, the unusual language, Finnish food and the annual festivals – like the First of May celebration (where I met Lotta for the first time), Christmas and the Midsummer Party – are the important signs of national identity among expatriates. These national symbols unite almost all Finns living abroad. When I visited the homes of the Finns, in almost every place there was a small Finnish flag in the corridor. In the street you can often identify Finns by their Marimekko-shirts or Kalevala-jewelry.

To Lotta and to many other Finns living abroad, Finnishness is a valuable quality in multicultural communities. However, a very strongly emphasized national or patriotic ethos could prevent the integration process. In Brussels there are Finns who, for instance, don't want to learn French or make contacts with local people. As there are so many Finns that one can communicate using one's mother tongue. Mia, who has lived in Brussels with her family since 2001 and before that in Luxembourg, said that these kinds of people "open a window and have a glance to see what Belgium looks like – and then close the window!"[25] However, it would appear that this group represents only a minority of Finnish expatriates. To leave one's home country voluntarily is, in any case, the first step to a more international way of life. People who move abroad are internationally oriented: they want a new way of life and new experiences. It is another question, whether all the family enjoys this kind of life or not. In some cases, the shock of being in a new country, the cultural shock and identity crisis – which always follow expatriates – is too strong. Expatriates can became frustrated, resist the integration process and return to their home country as soon as possible. Waiting only to return home they might turn their back on another culture.[26]

Housewives and "Homedaddies"

Because many Finns work in Brussels for between three to ten years, they often have their families with them. For families, the decision to move abroad is always a big challenge. It can be both mentally and practically difficult, although the decision to move has been made as a family together. In Finland, it is very common for wives to have their own careers, and if a husband gets a new job abroad it often means that the wife has to interrupt her career and stay at home in a new country – at least as long as the children are small. Most of the interviewed expatriates moved when their kids were very small (under 3 years old) or at school age. Wives or husbands who leave their job in Finland normally apply for leave of absence from their employer. However, they often get only a one year leave of absence and must then move back alone, or stay abroad as housewives or "homedaddies". Many of the Finnish expatriates with families have chosen to stay together.

Thirty-year old Teija moved to Brussels in 2004 with her husband and two small children. They rented a house from the municipality of Woluwe St. Lambert. Her husband got a job for four years and Teija stayed at home. She had been a housewife already in Helsinki because she had had children. "My career was not so excellent so I don't miss it much." Before having children she had worked outside the home, like most Finnish women. Having given birth, Finnish women usually return to work within a year; that is, when statutory maternity leave ends. According to Finnish law, it is also possible to stay at home until the youngest child is three years old. However, for many people this is impossible for financial reasons.

Teija has integrated well into the city. She went to French language courses as soon as she arrived and is an active member of the Finnish Club. Mothers with small children have organized a club for babies. In May 2005 the club met once a week at Teija's home. There are also other clubs held at the parsonage of the Finnish Seaman's Mission and lead by Finnish parents. Teija has also taken her kids to the local kindergarten once a week:

> I have got some local contacts there. I can't say that they are my
> friends but we know each other and say a couple words when we meet
> in the street. When you are living abroad it's important to learn some
> of the local language and other local customs. My eldest child is at
> the local part-time school but it is also important that Finnish children
> learn Finnish and that's why the clubs for babies and small children are
> necessary. They also give the mothers and fathers some social contacts
> with other adults.[27]

For Teija it was easy to adapt to the role of expatriate – she had been abroad during her school years as a trainee. Her husband had also worked abroad before Brussels.

Finnish expatriates in Brussels participate in many kinds of activities. Ladies are selling clothes on the street party in Merode. Photo: Maria Lähteenmäki, June 2005.

The homedaddy-institution is a very interesting phenomenon among expatriates. Although fathers in the Nordic countries have the opportunity to stay at home few weeks after child's birth, it is still uncommon for husbands to stay at home with older children. In Brussels, it is not so strange a situation, although in Belgium in general it is. Markku moved to Brussels in 2002 from southern Finland with his two children. His wife got a job with the Commission and moved to Brussels a little before the rest of the family. The EU-institutions provide a lot of jobs for women: many female expatriates work as translators or interpreters. The family rented a house in the Woluwe St. Lambert district and the children went to the European School. For Markku it was not so difficult to stay at home. He used to be at home with the children, so he had a homedaddy already been in Finland: "I think there is nothing special about being a homedaddy, it does not matter whether father or mother who takes care of the children or which one goes to work outside the home."[28]

The homedaddy-institution is not the only instance where men are crossing traditional Finnish male roles: in Brussels there are also Finnish male au pairs. When I interviewed Sari at her home, the male au pair was preparing food in the kitchen. Living abroad can result in more men staying at home and also encourage them to enter new fields of activity.

However, many homedaddies didn't want to give interviews: they can be homedaddies in Brussels but not in Finland. For many men it is as hard to live without one's own money, a reasonable occupation or adult contacts as it is for many housewives. For all family members it is important that housewives/homedaddies also enjoy the new way of life. The most common cause for cutting short a job abroad is a wife's/husband's difficulty in adapting to the new situation.

For these and other reasons, some of the families interviewed live in two cities. In Ella's family (two parents and three children), the mother and two children lived in Helsinki whilst the father and one child lived in Brussels. Whilst her husband was in Brussels, five years altogether, Ella lived in Brussels for two of the years. This was made possible by the fact that the children were already over fifteen years of age and their grandparents lived next door to their Helsinki home. During the school holidays the family used to be together in their Belgian home.

> It was a very enriching experience although it was quite hard for our family economy. Sometimes it was also hard mentally; my husband could not travel so often to Finland and it could be weeks before I saw him. Anyway, our children, and we parents as well, loved to stay in Central Europe. We made lots of journeys around the various countries by train or by car and we loved Belgian food and wines and also atmosphere. I suppose that for Finns it is quite easy to live anywhere in western countries. Our experience was so positive that it is possible that some day we will move abroad again. Actually, nowadays, here in Helsinki, we have a small society called "the Former Inhabitants of Brussels Society." There are about twenty families in the society. We have a party once a year just before Christmas.[29]

The European Schools

One of the most important factors for getting expatriates used to their new situation in Brussels is school. Choosing a school in one's new hometown is also the most important practical decision for Finnish families, even before they arrive in their new country. If Finns are going to work for the Commission or for the EU-Parliament this is not a problem: the children automatically get places in the European School (L'École Européenne). The European School institution was established in 1953: the idea was to open schools for the children of staff working in European organizations who came from the European Coal and Steel Community. The first European School opened its doors in 1953 in Luxembourg. In 2005, there are twelve European schools with 19,800 pupils and 1,400 teachers from all over Europe. The president of the European Commission (1985–1995) Jacques Delors has said regarding the purpose of the European School that instilling the European ideal in our children in such a way that it comes alive in their everyday experience is without doubt the finest and surest way to ensure lasting peace which alone can bring the Europe that so many before us have dreamed of and that we now have the opportunity to build.[30]

In Brussels there are nowadays three European Schools, but in 2009, a fourth European School will be opened in the city. The "mother" of the European Schools in Brussels is European School I, in the municipality of Uccle, which was established in 1957. The school's headmaster in May 2005 was a Finn. Finnish classes are in European School II, which opened its doors in 1974. Since 1997 it has been possible to take the Baccalaureate examination (EB) partly in Finnish. That means that the first language for Finnish pupils is Finnish. Half of the lessons are given in Finnish and second half of the lessons are in English or in French. The School is situated east of Brussels, in municipality Woluwe St Lambert.

Pia and Petra are young Finnish women who have passed their EB-exams in the European School II. Pia joined the school at the age of fourteen.

During the first term she was in an English class, but when Finnish classes were established she joined them. Pia's experiences from the school are very positive: the teaching was of a high-level, the Finnish classes were small, the pupils came from various cultural backgrounds and her skills in different languages got better. She thinks her school years in the European School also improved her choice of university studies: she has passed now her university studies in London. Also Petra's experiences from the European School are very positive. She was one of the first Finnish students who passed the EB-exam in the European School II. Petra also chose to study at a British university. The English language is much easier for Finns than French and that's why many choose English universities instead of French ones. Petra and Pia integrated rapidly into Brussels through their school friends and because of hobbies, like music and sports. After her studies in England Petra moved back to Finland, continued her law studies and is now working in Helsinki. Pia returned Brussels and is working in the European Parliament.[31]

Oona, a fifteen year old Finnish girl, is at the European School II. Her experiences from the school have been good. However, she differed from Pia and Petra by saying that she is not going to return to Finland to study or to work. She has lived in Brussels since she was six years old. Her parents have integrated into the town very well: both of them work in Brussels. In the case of Petra and Pia, their families lived partly in Finland and partly in Brussels. This was one reason why, for Pia and Petra, Finland was also a possible place to live: there had always been a home also in Finland. It is obvious that a child's age when she/he arrives in Brussels and the attitudes of one's parents dominates the adaption process and the level of satisfaction with their school of Finnish children.[32] Two Finnish boys, Hannu, twelve, and Teemu, sixteen, were at the European School II for a year. Although they considered the school in a quite positive way – it is international, there are good lessons and you make new friends – they, however, preferred schools in Finland. This is mainly because their best friends stayed in Finland. When their mother moved back to Finland to work, the two boys chose to go with her although they could have stayed with their father in Brussels. Their adaption was, after a year, still at the halfway stage.[33]

A City of Singles

According to the Finns interviewed, Brussels is a good place for singles: the EU-institutions are full of internationally oriented unmarried people. Besides, the town is very multi-cultural and tolerant. For many foreigners it is reassuringly small and safe, but it is also, however, near some of Europe's major cities: it is only 1,5 hours by train to the Gare du Nord in Paris and two hours to Waterloo station in London.

As for Finnish expatriates, there is now a new generation living in Brussels. Young Finnish people in Brussels are living a more international life than their parents and a more elitist way of life than most people their age back in Finland. This generation comes from middle or upper class families. Their parents have been abroad, speak many languages, and have enrolled their children at an early age in language courses and sent them to foreign universities.

One of the Finns interviewed, Kaari, belongs to this generation. She is 28 years old, a well-educated woman. She arrived in Brussels in 2003 to work at the European Commission. Before that she had graduated from London University. She has also studied in Sweden. Kaari analyzed her own position like this: "I have got everything that it is possible to get with money... so far my life has been full of language courses, journeys and parties." She has already lived eight years away from Finland but still feels very Finnish. She often meets her relatives and friends living in Finland. In spite of this, she didn't want to meet other Finns while living in Brussels. "My old friends are very important for me... I must say that we are still living like teenagers... maybe it is a fear of commitment... we don't want to give up our freedom." However, during the last couple of years she has thought a lot about the family life and having children: "Maybe, it is now time to have a family – I have seen everything already!" During her stay in Brussels she has had two African boyfriends. She met new friends through her hobbies: capoeira, reggae, and hip-hop. Kaari has also been eager to take part in concerts and "all kinds of city culture".[34]

One separate group of foreign "singles" in the coffee houses and clubs of Brussels are the au pairs. The Finnish-speaking au pair has been a very common phenomenon in Finnish families. Usually they are 18 to 25 year old women, but there are also some young men. The job of an au pair involves about 25–30 hours of work during the week, in return for which they have their own room, meals and some pocket money (about 300–400 euros per month). The work depends on the family but normally involves looking after the children, some cleaning, and some light cooking. Most of the Finnish au pairs study languages in their free time. It is one of the most important reasons for coming to Belgium. Demand for au pairs is big, especially in Brussels.[35]

The Finnish Club

One of the most remarkable actors in the adaptation process of Finnish expatriates in Brussels has been the Finnish Club. The club was established in the spring of 1978 in Waterloo by fourteen Finnish ladies. Nowadays (May 2005) there are approximately 2,000 members in the club. Most Finnish expatriates are members of the club. The structure of the members has changed since the 1970s. The first members were housewives, and the club was essentially a ladies society although "the doors were open also to men and children". Because ladies held their meetings – coffee parties – in the mornings it was impossible for men to take part in the sessions. In 2005 members come from all occupations and include men and women, old people and children. Female members of the club constitute now 57 per cent of all adult members. The other remarkable change in the membership structure to have occurred is that the number of single people has increased year after year. At the beginning of the 2000s about 55 per cent of member households of the Finnish club were childless. In 1994 the share of childless households

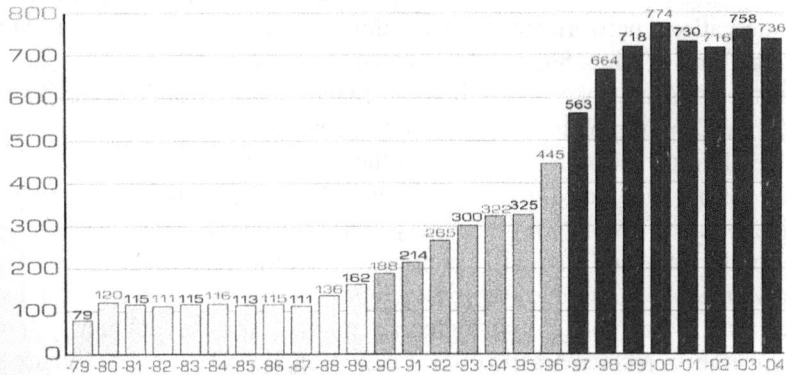

Members of the Finnish Club 1979–2004.

was 27 per cent. The number of club members rose dramatically after Finland joined the EU in 1995: in 1994 there were 320 households in the club, whereas in 2005 the number had more than doubled to 770 households.[36]

The first chairwoman of the Club has said that the idea of establishing the Finnish Club was taken from the Swedes, who have their own Swedish Club, *Svenska Klubben*. Most of the ladies (43 in May 1978) who were involved in the activity then, had met earlier at coffee parties and in other societies. They wanted to bring Finnish ladies living in Belgium together to discuss practical problems which occur when living in a foreign country, to help each other, to celebrate the traditional annual Finnish festivals and to share their experiences. The ladies began drawing up a list of Finnish people who lived in Belgium, organizing sports activities, arranging cultural visits and collecting a library of Finnish books. The members arranged cooking and make-up courses in their homes. The ladies studied together, played bridge, learnt Dutch, and ordered women's summer clothes from Finland.[37]

One of ladies at the first meeting of the Finnish Club was Stina: she was "the attaché for cultural relations" of the club. She moved to Belgium in 1956 from Helsinki at the age of 22 in order to work for a Finnish company. Her first residence was in the eastern part of Brussels, in Woluwe St. Pierre. She later married a Finnish man and they have three children. Two of the children went to the European School and one to the local French school. When the children were small, Stina stayed at home. She has been an active member of the Finnish Club since the 1970s. She established, for instance, "the garden circle" of the Finnish Club. She is also a member of the Women's International Club and the American Women's Club. Stina is "a typical" founder member of the Finnish Club. She has integrated perfectly into Belgian society and is going to stay in Belgium for the rest of her life. The family built their own house in the southern part of Brussels. According to Stina, the best things in Brussels are the standard of housing, the excellent food, the

25

international opportunities and it's location in the heart of Europe. Stina has an international network but still maintains contacts with her Finnish friends and the Finnish Club. She still has Finnish citizenship.[38]

In the 1990s a lot of new members joined the Club. One of them was Anna. She moved to Brussels in 1998 from Helsinki because of her husband's work. Three children of the family went to the European School II. The oldest child has now graduated from the school and is going to study at the British university. The first home of the family was in Woluwe St. Pierre where they are still living. Anna is an active member of the Finnish Club. She joined the club immediately after moving to Belgium. According to Anna, the Finnish Club was a very good way to integrate quickly into the Belgian system. The members receive practical information on almost all the problems to do with housing, rents, identity cards, taxation, schools, local customs, and language. All the other people interviewed shared this opinion: if you are going to move to Belgium, it is useful to visit the homepages of the club. Like Stina, Anna has also integrated well into her new hometown. Learning French is one indication of that. She is also active in the parents association and works as a voluntary library assistant at her children's school. Anna also supports the Finnish scout patrol in Brussels. She is going to stay in Brussels as long as the children are at school, and maybe longer. However, she and her husband are going to move back to Finland when they retire. Anna misses the "real" Finnish winter and her relatives back home. According to Anna, the early springs, long summers and the good health system are the best things in Brussels.[39]

Apart from the Finnish Club internet pages,[40] members are connected through the newspaper *Parlööri*. Its first numbers in the 1970s were circular letters but in the 1990s it took on the form of a newspaper. During the 1970s and 1980s, the newspaper was mainly used for advertising. Since then it has been edited more professionally, and, in 2005, there were a lot of articles and analysis on issues common among the members.

Supporting Institutions

In order to strengthen and, indeed, to ensure the survival of Finnish identity in Brussels the Finns need institutions. The most important organisation from this point of view is the Finnish Club. Richard Jenkins has argued that the activity of these kinds of organisations help construct "institutionalised identities". Institutionalised identities are distinctive due to their particular combination of the individual and the collective.[41] As far as the Finnish Club is concerned, this is very true. The club regularly reminds its members "how Finns used to do things". The club organizes all kinds of activity, the most popular events being celebrations, like the Manneken Pis party on 30 April or the Christmas and Midsummer holidays, and skiing competitions and tango dancing. The club has its own www-pages, its own newspaper and logos. All of these reinforce the idea of looking and behaving like a Finn. Richard Jenkins has observed that individuals seek to 'be' – and to be 'seen to be'– something or somebody, to successfully assume particular identities.[42] Members of the Finnish Club stress

Idyllic Woluwe St. Pierre is a popular residential area among Finns in Brussels. Photo: Maria Lähteenmäki, Spring 2005.

that Finnishness abroad is not the same as Finnishness in Finland. The Finns in Brussels may well share the same destiny as Finns in the northern Norway. Finns, mainly from Finnish Lapland,[43] moved to Norway in the nineteenth century and today have own habits, culture and even their own language – this is no longer Finnish, but *kven* language.[44] The same phenomenon is also found in northern Sweden: people in the Torne River Valley speak "meän kieli" (our language) and have a strong non-Finnish sub-culture.

When Finnish expatriates in Brussels move back to Finland, they continue to receive institutional support: "X-pat" club was founded in Helsinki in January 2003, and a newspaper called *Expatrium* was created in 1993. The X-pat club and the newspaper support Finns before, during, and after their move abroad. The main task of these institutions is to adapt Finns into "strange" cultures abroad, and help their readaption back into Finland. To many returning expatriates it is not at all easy to return to "peripheral" Finland.[45]

An organization called the Finnish Expatriate Parliament (Ulkosuoma-laisparlamentti) also strengthens Finnish identity. The Parliament was founded in 1997. In 2004 there were 408 member societies in the Parliament including four Finnish Clubs in Belgium. Sweden has the most Finnish Clubs (82), following by Germany (65), the USA (60), Canada (40) and Russia (31).[46] The purpose of the Parliament is to extent influence on the Finnish government on questions like dual citizenship (which was accepted in 2003), Finnish lessons abroad, social problems and interaction between Finland and other countries. Teaching Finnish abroad is an important part of the identity-building process. A Finnish school (Suomi-koulu) was established in Brussels in 1990. Somewhat earlier the first Suomi-koulu was founded in Antwerp.[47]

The Finnish-European Identity?

"Finns in Belgium are skilled survivors, full of ideas and eager to accept challenges." This is the optimistic statement of the previous chairman of the Finnish Club in January 2005.[48] No doubt, Finnish people have their own

27

Finns living in Brussels travel around Europe a lot. Here Finnish students from the European School are in the Alps. Photo: Tuomas Lähteenmäki.

specific character within a multi-cultural city like Brussels. Although I do not have comparable research on the subject, I suppose that, for instance, Swedes, Italians and Moroccans also have their strong sub-cultural communities in Brussels. It was also clear that Finnishness was important in same way to all the interviewed expatriates although not everyone wanted to live in Finland. This is because all identities are localized by language, culture and history. But what kind of things or phenomena are included in Finnishness?

In 1992, the year Finland celebrated 75 years of independence, the Finnish Club organized a writing competition for Finnish pupils in Brussels. About twenty girls and boys aged from four to sixteen years, wrote an essay on the theme, "What Finland and Finnishness means to me?" The four most popular subjects in the essays were (1) safety and freedom, (2) northern nature, (3) food and (4) relatives and families.

In most of the essays, the children wanted to emphasize that there is much more freedom to act and less control in everyday life in Finland than in Brussels. Juha (a four-year-old boy) said that, "It is not necessary in Finland to go to kindergarten. As I said, Finland is a good country!" Mari (16) wrote rather sadly that she had been taken to a completely different place, "to a place where not even sauna exist". For Mari, Finland is a place where she can go and stay whenever she wants. And she never gets sick or tired in Finland.

Being able to speak Finnish was also important for the children. Kaisa

(9) wrote: "I do miss Finland sometimes. My original friends are there and I can speak Finnish with them. I can take a bike and ride on my own alone to them." Being abroad meant that the children were more aware of their nationality. Fredrika (9) had noticed that in Brussels her family had become more important to her: "In Finland I never thought that I'm from Finland, now I'm doing that quite often." One child (11) wrote that "Finland and Finnishness are important for me here: Finland and its customs separate me from the mass, from the Walloons and the Flemish." Ari (5) simply said "I'm a Finn because I speak Finnish." Heidi (15) said "I'm proud of Finnish – it is such a difficult language and I can speak Finnish with my friends and be sure that nobody understands it!"

Children also wrote a lot about Finnish nature, blue lakes, white snow, light nights, as well as its cleanliness and the food. Noora (7) wrote "Finland is the best country because there is no dog excrement. There is snow, there is pea soup and granny and grandpa." One pupil (11) said "Here in Belgium it is stupid because you can not get a rye bread, sal ammoniac pastille (salmiakki) or real liquorice."[49]

A strong sense of national identity could also be seen at the beginning of the 1990s when Finns were considering joining the EU. In 1994, the Finnish people voted in favor of becoming a member of the EU. Linda, who was 15 years old at the time and had already lived in Brussels for ten years, said that she was very happy: "Finland got its place on the map of Europe at last." She was at the International school of Brussels where they had used an American textbook of geography. On the map of Europe, of the Nordic countries, only Denmark and the southern parts of Sweden and Norway were included. Finland was missing. "Sometimes you meet people who really think that we Finns live in the snow and ice like eskimos!" A Finnish student Kristoffer (19) was pleased that Finland had joined the EU. He was at the Scandinavian school and wanted to emphasize that Finland was one of the Nordic countries and most importantly, part of the "West".[50] One commentator from the newspaper *Parlööri* emphasized that in Brussels "our difference" offers the Finns a mirror for our self-awareness and that "membership of the EU is strengthening our national Finnish identity".[51] At least, the EU received its most northern point from Finland (Utsjoki) and also its most eastern point (Ilomantsi)!

The New Patterns of Migration

The integration process of Finnish expatriates in Brussels is a complex phenomenon. It means integration not only into the Belgian and Central European way of life but also integration into the Finnish community of Brussels. The degree of integration depends on many elements. First of all, it depends on the status of each migrant; whether he/she is an expatriate (sent worker) or an immigrant: whether he/she is working for Finnish employers or not; and whether he/she stays at home or works. If he/she has a good job and a good salary it helps him/her to enjoy life abroad. Secondly, the integration process also depends on the length of one's stay in the destination country:

whether the person is there for one year or for several years, and whether he/she knows about that in advance or not.

The third factor concerns the language and social skills of the migrant: whether he/she speaks many languages or not and whether he/she is socially active or not. Previous experience of living abroad also helps in the integration process. Marital status, attitudes of family members, and education level also affects the degree of integration.

As far as the persons interviewed were concerned, the majority of them were willing to return to Finland: 44 per cent were going to move back to Finland in a few years; 28 per cent were going to live in Brussels "so far"; 16 per cent were going to stay up to retirement and only 12 per cent wanted to stay in Brussels forever. Most of the Finns still dream about moving back to their own country.[52] All in all, most of the interviewed Finns regarded their stay in Brussels as positive experience. Their Finnish identity seems to have strengthened and the boundaries[53] between them and their Finnishness and other nationalities had become more clear. However, at the same time, they noticed that they shared, with the other inhabitants of the city, a common western way of life, with common values, ideologies and a common mentality. They are Finnish, but at the same time, West Europeans. They have many identities and sometimes dual citizenship. At least one of the people interviewed considered herself as global cosmopolitan.

At the beginning of the 2000s, global cosmopolitanism, multiculturalism, shared identities and shared citizenships – citizenships without borders – are more discussed than ever before.[54] In Europe, the globalization process has led researchers to re-evaluate the whole concept of migration. R. King has suggested that this new migration has five main features: (1) Migrants come from an ever more diverse range of cultural and ethnic backgrounds; (2) Migrants are more differentiated in terms of social class, with a greater variety of migrants; from those on long-term contracts to refugees, illegal migrants, highly skilled professionals, and commuting migrants who may stay a very short time; (3) Migration is accelerating, in terms of the sheer number of people crossing borders; (4) There is also a growing feminisation of migration; (5) Finally, the classic "push" and "pull" explanations of migration have changed.[55] In this diversity of cultures and with increasing migration, the Finnish expatrjates who celebrate their Finnishness on the eve of the First of May in downtown Brussels are a tiny minority, but in spite of that, their everyday life experiences tell us a lot about these new European citizens.

NOTES

1. The Finnish students' spring celebrations began in 1848 when the Finnish nationalist movement was taking its first steps. For the history of Finland see Facts about Finland 2002; Jussila & Hentilä & Nevakivi 1999.
2. Euroopassa asuneet Suomen kansalaiset maittain 1971–2002. Asuinmaiden tilastojen mukaan. Siirtolaisinstituutti. (Finnish Citizens living in European countries. The Institute of Migration, University of Turku). See http://www.migrationinstitute.fi/db/stat/fin/art.php?artid=56 (Accessed in May 2005).

3. On Brussels, see McNeill 2004, 21–25; Elmborn 2001.
4. See http://epp.eurostat.cec.eu.int/ (Accessed in May 2005).
5. For instance, Brysk & Shafir (eds) 2004; Rapport & Dawson 1998.
6. Jenkins 2004.
7. Mercer 1990, 43.
8. Hall 1992, 274–275.
9. Jenkins 2004, 4, 23.
10. Hall 1992, 276.
11. For instance, Nyytäjä 2004; Kunnas 2001; Petäistö 2001; Castrén 2001; Junkkari & Junkkari 2003.
12. For instance, Koivukangas 1998; Finnarnas historia i Sverige 1–3 1990–1996; Snellman 2003; Pynnönen 1991; Karisto 2000; Tuomi-Nikula 1989.
13. A total of 30 people were used for the research: 12 people were interviewed 1–3 times and filled in the questionnaire. 8 people filled the questionnaire and participated in discussions, and 10 people filled in the questionnaire without participating in discussions. The questionnaire asked for basic information like year of birth, sex, home area in Finland and place/district of residence in Belgium, marital status, family size, years of residence in Belgium, reason for moving to Belgium, school and work experiences in Belgium, hobbies, other activities, language skills and negative and positive experiences in Belgium. 80 per cent of the interviewed persons were female and 10 per cent were under the age of 18. The written material (the questionnaires and notes of the interviewer) are in the author's possession. The names of the interviewed persons used in the text are pseudonyms.
14. See Saastamoinen & Valtonen 2004.
15. During the spring of 2005, I was a visiting scholar at the Vrije Universiteit in Brussels. From this time, I would like to thank warmly Professor Alison Woodward from the Department of Women's Studies. During the year I was a member of the Finnish community in Brussels, I felt like "a marginal native". I belonged and yet did not belong at the same time. The concept of "marginal native" was introduced by Bronislaw Malikowski. See Freilich 1970, 530.
16. Http://www.finlande.be/doc/fi/belinfo/BelgiajaSuomi.html (Accessed in May 2005).
17. Http://dg5luxweb/statistic/data/2005_2/stat.htm; http://www.valtioneuvosto.fi/vn/liston/base.lsp?r=30780&k=fi; (Accessed in May 2005). My thanks to Jaana Ollila for this information.
18. Http://www.merimieskirkko.be (Accessed in May 2005).
19. Saastamoinen & Valtonen 2004, 18–21.
20. Snellman 2003, 93–97, 167–173.
21. Interview with Kaari on May 21, 2005 in Brussels by Maria Lähteenmäki.
22. Interview with Jenni on May 5, 2005 in Brussels by Maria Lähteenmäki.
23. Interview with Mia on May 10, 2005 in Brussels by Maria Lähteenmäki.
24. Interview with Arja on May 10, 2005 in Brussels by Maria Lähteenmäki.
25. Interview with Mia on May 10, 2005 in Brussels by Maria Lähteenmäki.
26. Junkkari & Junkkari 2003, 78.
27. Interview with Teija on May 15, 2005 in Brussels by Maria Lähteenmäki.
28. Interview with Markku on May 13, 2005 in Brussels by Maria Lähteenmäki; Interview with Heikki on June 15, 2005 in Brussels by Maria Lähteenmäki; See also Junkkari & Junkkari 2003, 91–97; *Suomen Kuvalehti* Sep 2002.
29. Interview with Ella on November 14, 2005 in Helsinki by Maria Lähteenmäki.

31

30. Http://www.eeb1.org/InfosGenerales/presentation_uccle_brochure.htm (Accessed in May 2005).
31. Correspondence with Pia on August 15, 2005/Maria Lähteenmäki; Correspondence with Petra on June 26, 2005/Maria Lähteenmäki.
32. See also Pirkola 1996. pro gradu -tutkielma. Käyttäytymistieteiden laitos. Oulun yliopisto.
33. Correspondence with Oona June 21, 2005/Maria Lähteenmäki; Interview with Hannu on June 2, 2005 in Brussels by Maria Lähteenmäki; Interview with Teemu on June 15, 2005 in Brussels by Maria Lähteenmäki.
34. Interview with Kaari on May 21, 2005 in Brussels by Maria Lähteenmäki.
35. *Parlööri* Jan 2005, 8–11.
36. Saastamoinen & Valtonen 2004, 20–21.
37. Circular letters Waterloo May 10, 1978 and Waterloo May 26, 1978. The Archives of the Finnish Club. Brussels.
38. Interview with Stina on May 10, 2005 in Brussels by Maria Lähteenmäki.
39. Interview with Anna on May 20, 2005 in Brussels by Maria Lähteenmäki.
40. Http://suomi-klubi.com (Accessed in May 2005).
41. Jenkins 2004, 23.
42. Jenkins 2004, 20.
43. On the history of Lapland, see Lähteenmäki 2006.
44. On the kvener, see Ryymin 2003; Anttonen 1999.
45. See www.ulkosuomalainen.com; www.xpat-klubi.fi; www.expatrium.fi (Accessed in May 2005).
46. *Suomen Silta* 6/2004.
47. *Parlööri* June 2000, 9; *Parlööri* Jan 2001; *Parlööri* April 2001, 8; *Parlööri* June 2001, 4–5.
48. *Parlööri* Jan 2005, 1.
49. *Parlööri* Dec 1992; *Parlööri* Jun 1992.
50. *Parlööri* Mar 1995, 20–21.
51. *Parlööri* Mar 1995, 15.
52. Snellman 2003, 223–233, 247–251; Tuomi-Nikula has observed that 60 per cent of Finnish migrants in Germany who had married German wanted to stay in Germany, but other wise most migrants were eager to move back to Finland. Tuomi-Nikula 1989, 160–161.
53. Fredrik Barth in his classic research has emphasized the importance of the social boundaries of ethnic groups as far as ethnic identity is concerned. See Barth 1970, 15–16.
54. On the concepts see Brysk & Shafir 2004, 213, passim.
55. King R. 1997, 22–23.

SOURCES

Unprinted sources

Circular letters and year reports of the Finnish Club of Belgium 1978–2005.
The Archives of Finnish Club, Brussels.

Interviews and questionnaires

12 interviews of Finns in Brussels/Interviewer Maria Lähteenmäki in May–June 2005.
30 questionnaires of Finns in Brussels/Made by Maria Lähteenmäki in May–June 2005.
Correspondence by Maria Lähteenmäki in 2005.

Newspapers/Magazines

Expatrium 1993–2005
Parlööri 1978–2005
Suomen Kuvalehti 2002
Suomen Silta 2004

Internet-pages

Http://dg5luxweb/statistic/data/2005_2/stat.htm.
Http://epp.eurostat.cec.eu.int/.
Http://suomi-klubi.com.
Http://www.eeb1.org/InfosGenerales/presentation_uccle_brochure.htm.
Http://www.expatrium.fi.
Http://www.finlande.be/doc/fi/belinfo/BelgiajaSuomi.html.
Http://www.merimieskirkko.be.
Http://www.migrationinstitute.fi/db/stat/fin/art.php?artid=56.
Http://www.ulkosuomalainen.com.
Http://www.valtioneuvosto.fi/vn/liston/base.lsp?r=30780&k=fi.
Http://www.xpat-klubi.fi.

BIBLIOGRAPHY

Anttonen, Marjut 1999. *Etnopolitiikkaa Ruijassa. Suomalaislähtöisen väestön identiteettien politisoituminen 1990-luvulla.* Helsinki: Suomalaisen Kirjallisuuden Seura.

Barth, Fredrik 1970. *Ethnic Groups and Boundaries. The Social Organization of Culture Difference.* Bergen: Universitetets Forlaget.

Brysk, Alison & Shafir, Gershon (eds) 2004. *People Out of Place. Globalization, Human Rights, and the Citizenship Gap.* London: Routledge.

Castrèn, Anna-Maija 2001. *Perhe ja työ Helsingissä ja Pietarissa.* Helsinki: Suomalaisen Kirjallisuuden Seura.

Elmborn, Camilla 2001. *Brussels, A Reflexive World City.* Almqvist & Wibell.

Facts about Finland 2002. Helsinki: Otava.

Finnarnas historia I Sverige 1–3. 1990–1996. Helsingfors & Stockholm: Finska Historiska Samfundet & Nordiska museet.

Freilich Morris 1970. Towards a Formalization of Field Work. Freilich Morris (ed.), *Marginal natives: Antropologists at Work.* London: Harper & Row.

Hall, Stuart 1992. The Question of Cultural Identity. Hall, S. & Held, D. & McGrew A. (eds), *Modernity and Its Futures.* Polity Press & Open University.

Jenkins, Richard 2004. *Social Identity.* London: Routledge.

Junkkari, Kaija Maria & Junkkari, Lari 2003. *Nykyajan paimentolaiset. Työ ja koti maailmalla*. Helsinki: Otava.

Jussila, Osmo & Hentilä, Seppo & Nevakivi, Jukka 1999. *From Grand Duchy to a Modern State. A Political History of Finland since 1809*. London: Hurst & Company.

Karisto, Antti 2000. *Suomalaiselämää Espanjassa*. Helsinki: Suomalaisen Kirjallisuuden Seura.

King, R. 1997. Migration, globalization and place. Massry, Doreen & Jess, Pat (eds), *In A Place in the World? Places, Culture and Globalization*. Oxford: Oxford University Press.

Koivukangas, Olavi 1998. *Kaukomaiden kaipuu. Suomalaiset Afrikassa, Australiassa, Uudessa-Seelannissa ja Latinalaisessa Amerikassa*. Suomalaisen siirtolaisuuden historia 4. Turku: Siirtolaisuusinstituutti.

Kunas, Tarmo 2001. *Elämäniloa Pariisissa*. Helsinki: WSOY.

Lähteenmäki, Maria 2006. *Terra Ultima. A Short History of Finnish Lapland*. Helsinki: Otava.

Mercer, Kobena 1990. Welcome to the jungle. Rutherford, J. (ed.), *Identity*. London: Lawrence & Wishardt.

McNeill, Donald 2004. *New Europe: Imagined Spaces*. London: Arnold.

Nyytäjä, Outi 2004. *Heinäpaalu roihuaa: näkymiä ja näkemyksiä Bretagnesta*. Helsinki: Gummerus.

Petäistö, Helena 2001. *Aamiainen Cocon kanssa: Brysselissä, Amsterdamissa ja Luxemburgissa*. Helsinki: Tammi.

Pirkola, Titta 1996. *Lapsen sopeutuminen uuteen kulttuuriin. Tutkimus perheidensä mukana vuosina 1992–1994 Suomesta Englantiin muuttaneista 9–12-vuotiaista lapsista*. Pro gradu -tutkielma. Käyttäytymistieteiden laitos. Oulun yliopisto.

Pynnönen, Marja 1991. *Siirtolaisuuden vanavedessä*. Helsinki: Suomalaisen Kirjallisuuden Seura.

Rapport, Nigel & Dawson, Andrew 1998. Migrants of Identity: perceptions of home in a world of movement. Oxford: Berg.

Ryymin, Teemu 2003. *"De nordligste finner". Fremstillingen av kvenene i den finske litteraere offentligheten 1800–1939*. Dr.Art.avhandling. Institutt for historie. Det Samfunnsvitenskapelige fakultet. Universitetet i Tromsö.

Saastamoinen, Salla & Valtonen, Anne 2004. *Puurojuhlia ja Parlöörejä. 25-vuotta Suomi-Klubin toimintaa ja tiedotusta Belgiassa*. Bertem: Drukkerij De Weide.

Snellman, Hanna 2003. *Sallan suurin kylä – Göteborg*. Helsinki: Suomalaisen Kirjallisuuden Seura.

Tuomi-Nikula, Outi 1989. *Saksansuomalaiset*. Helsinki: Suomalaisen Kirjallisuuden Seura.

KATRI KAUNISTO

Forest Expertise of Europe

On the 26 and 27 December 1999, storms Lothar and Martin caused a huge amount of forest damage in Denmark, France, Germany, Austria, and Switzerland. Hundreds of cubic metres of timber fell down and waited to be cut and transported for storage. The storm temporarily increased job opportunities in Central and Western Europe for forestry professionals. The timber in the damaged forests needed to be harvested and transported quickly before the hot season's weather conditions and insects added to the material damage. It was soon noticed that local forestry professionals did not have enough capacity to manage all the harvesting, logging, and transporting operations in the damaged areas by themselves. Therefore, qualified forestry workers, forest machinery operators from other European countries took part in harvesting the storm-damaged timber. Finnish forestry workers and forestry contractors had also the chance to work abroad.

Conditions in the storm damaged areas were difficult. Harvesting work was time-consuming and expensive; the work was demanding and dangerous and required an experienced work force. These storms resulted in enormous financial losses for forest owners. Additionally, there was no information about how the storm damage had affected the quality of the timber and the price of timber. This kind of uncertainty and lack of information in business in economic terms create transaction costs, which can be either concrete expenses or expences incurred due to the loss of time. These costs arise mostly in new situations, where the participants do not know each other. In these situations, planning and monitoring takes a lot of time, because trust among the participants has not been built up.[1]

Organisations and institutions have developed different kind of strategies to reduce transaction costs. The European Union for its part has tried to remove structures which prevent free competition, and the mobility of capital, commodities, and labor. Therefore the free movement of labor and "the right to take up and pursue activities as self-employed persons" was written in to the treaty establishing the European community.[2] Even though formal rules and norms may change overnight as the result of political or judicial decisions, policies, conventions, customs, and traditions change slowly.[3] The free movement of labor has increased international contacts and also highlighted difficulties in cross-cultural cooperation. Organisations and the behavior of people within organisations are culture-bound and have different work-related values, norms, and customs.[4] In modern relations, people must take risks and trust unknown experts on a day-to-day basis, which opens up a lot of opportunities for such experts.[5] In studies of social networks and labor migration, it has been shown that a network of relatives and acquaintances has an important role when a worker or an entrepreneur is trying to obtain information and economic support.[6] In the case of Finnish forestry professionals and their clients, both need to use their networks to obtain information about each other, their needs, their reliability, and also about arranging the work, and prices. There was also a question about their ability to negotiate and make profitable contracts and to control how the contracts will be fulfilled.

This article deals with Finnish forestry workers, forest machinery operators and forestry contractors experiences about working abroad. It provides an insight in to the free mobility of labor with in the European Union from the side of Finnish forestry professionals. This study is based on thirteen interviews with forestry workers and forestry contractors who have worked abroad or plan to work abroad.[7] These forestry workers and forestry contractors have worked abroad for a short time in Denmark, Estonia, France, Germany, Russia, and Sweden.[8] In the interviews they explained why they decided to work abroad, and what kind of difficulties and opportunities working abroad offered them. Simultaneously, they spoke about their experiences in Finnish forestry and compared it with their experiences abroad. In my analysis I will take advantage of the idea of transaction costs and studies on labor migration. My aim is to find out how Finnish forestry workers and forestry contractors adjusted to a new situation in the common European labor and business market.

Conventions in Finnish Forestry

Migration in search of work has been familiar to Finnish forestry workers for decades. During times of economic depression and unemployment, forestry workers were forced to find work abroad. For example, in the 1950s there was a lack of forestry workers in Sweden, and an opportunity to get better wages opened up for Finnish forestry workers who at the same time were suffering from unemployment and low wages in Finland. Migration in search of work reached a peak in the 1960s and 1970s when people from the countryside moved to urban areas within Finland and even to Sweden.[9]

In Finland, the forest companies and purchasers have traditionally organized the selling and transporting of timber. They have employed forestry workers for manual harvesting and forest management work. Nowadays, forest companies contracts harvesting companies and forestry workers, who sell their services to clients, such as forest owners, pulp and paper companies, and sawmills. Their main lines of business include harvesting, timber transport in forests, thinning, forest planting and making drainage ditches, preparation of the soil, and the construction of forest roads. Finnish forestry contractors are often small or medium size firms, or family

Finnish forestry contractors started to work in Russia with Finnish forest companies in the 1990s. Photo: Jarmo Saarela. Lusto/Jarmo Saarela's collection.

enterprises. The smallest enterprises, with one or two machines, often work as contractors and have no hired personnel. The largest firms of contractors have several *chains*, which include a harvesting machine, a forest tractor and a transport vehicle and employ several forest machinery operators.

Forestry workers and forestry contractors have often come from small farms from the countryside. Forestry contractors have also worked as forestry workers or in excavation work before they started their own enterprise. Contractors have not been eager to obtain a professional or business education, and they, as well as forestry workers have often learned their profession on the job. Additionally, they have been more work oriented than business oriented. Therefore, the development of economic thinking among these entrepreneurs has been low.[10] These entrepreneurs have not been used to defining their operational principles, because they have not been used to making strategies, or future business plans, which might have helped them in the marketing process. Actually, they did not spend much time marketing their enterprise; they usually mentioned that the quality of their work was the best way to market their firm and its services. Furthermore, they were not interested in, or do not have time to concentrate on, office work or bookkeeping, have usually bought in accounting services from company accountants. Consequently, their firms have depended on their bookkeepers' professional skills.[11]

Finnish forest companies have benefited from the forestry contractors' low interest in developing their business thinking. Certain conventions and customs

37

have developed over the decades, which have not always been profitable for the contractors. For example, forestry contractors have not been interested in developing their own price list for their clients or in billing systems.[12] Therefore, forest companies have developed their own systems for account transfers. Accordingly, every forest company has developed its own special computer programs and systems to, for example, gauge timber. Therefore harvesting companies have to buy certain expencive pieces of equipment and machines which are compatible with these programs. These are old and strong traditions, and are, therefore, difficult to change. All these different systems have meant that small harvesting companies have often been dependent on one big client's contracts and economic situation, because they cannot afford to operate simultaneously the different types of computer systems and machines used by different companies and buy expensive equipment and machines themselves.

The forestry contractor's relationship to a forest company has been quite solid and they have annually renewed the contracts about forest management services. However, competition between contractors has always caused uncertainty about the continuity of employment in the future. Recently, contractors have also suffered from their weak position in negotiations with forestry companies. There have only been a few big forest companies, and a few other employees who have been able to employ forestry workers and harvesting companies in Finland. The markets have been limited, and the contractors have found it difficult to broaden their working areas or get more clients.[13] According to these contractors, the forest companies have obtained such a strong position in Finnish forestry, that they are able to dictate prices and terms of work. The contractors' destiny has been to accept the unprofitable contracts or risk being unemployed. Therefore, working abroad has been seen as a good opportunity to broaden their business.[14]

Nowadays, there are several ways for forestry professionals to work abroad. Opportunities to work in Russia opened up for Finnish forestry contractors in the 1990s. In Russia, Finns have worked with local companies and with Finnish forest companies which have established enterprises in Russia for buying and delivering timber to Finland. In Central and Western Europe there have been international services and trading enterprises, which have operated between the forest owners and the forest industries. These kinds of enterprises employed entrepreneurs with their machines, forest machinery operators and forestry workers from Sweden, Scotland, Germany, Netherlands, Ireland, Norway, and Finland.[15]

Horizon of Opportunities

After the storm damage, information about the opportunities for working in Central and Western Europe spread rapidly through several sources. There were advertisements in newspapers where forestry companies searched for workers, entrepreneurs and their machines for subcontracting work.[16] The Trade Association of Finnish Forestry and Earth Moving Contractors gave information about working abroad to their members. The association's journal published articles about how French and German forest companies and forest owners were recruiting forest machines, operators and entrepreneurs for the storm disaster area. It also published entrepreneurs' stories about their experiences.[17] Information about the experiences of entrepreneurs helped other contractors to anticipate various difficulties. This kind of information was important, because it helped to save time and avoid unnecessary difficulties.[18] Several entrepreneurs also worked in Europe in the 1980s and 1990s in storm damaged forests.[19] These entrepreneurs and workers have also been important as models and advisers for those who were planning to go.

This kind of temporary labor migration has similar features to chain migration, where by those who emigrated first helped their relatives and friends to emigrate later and have also helped others to move abroad too. These kinds of social networks have helped immigrants in every step of the migration process. Social contacts have helped people to take the decision to emigrate and to integrate into the new way of life.[20] Official and unofficial information and social contacts have also been important for forestry professionals who planned to work abroad. Finnish forestry professionals who planned to work abroad formed groups with their workmates or relatives and traveled together and worked together as a team.[21]

> And then Tommi, he is now, he is twenty-two, but he is... Well, I can mention it here also, that I was in France one summer. We were work-ing there with one chain of machines and he stayed there. He wanted to be there one year, because that way he could get a benefit with taxes. He is still working there.[22]

Forestry contractors like other workers saw Europe as a potential market and, at least in theory, a place which offered better wages. According to the interviews, one reason for going abroad was the chance of earning easy money. With less work, they could earn more money and some could even take advantage of lower taxation.[23] When the economic situation was not so good in one's own country or when there was a clear risk of being unemployed in the near future, one did not have anything to lose and the decision to leave home was quite easy to make.[24] Although the better wages abroad and unemployment in one's own country may have been good reasons for employees and entrepreneurs to work abroad in general, it has been estimated that differences of language, culture, and bureaucracy among other things have also been sufficient obstacles to restrict cross-border mobility.[25] Family reasons often meant that it was not so tempting to work abroad for forestry professionals. Entrepreneurs who thought that they were too old to go wanted to encourage and give their sons and young drivers the chance to work abroad. Finnish entrepreneurs cooperated with each other and even let their own forest machinery operators work temporarily in other companies.[26]

According to interviews, forestry contractors, as well as entrepreneurs in general, balance a familiar and secure life with new and insecure opportunities. Usually, their first business idea was to be self-employed and to earn their living by having their own company. However, it is also

39

The lack of machines in storm damaged areas in Europe created opportunities to export the latest Finnish forest technology and knowledge. Photo: Jarmo Saarela. Lusto/Jarmo Saarela's collection.

important that entrepreneurs are eager to try something new, find new lines in business and take economic risk. For the forestry contractors, working abroad was a new step with new challenges.[27]

The following quotation shows what kind of economic risks forestry contractors were ready to take when planning to work abroad. This entrepreneur has not completed his studies in forestry school, because he did not pass the language courses for English and Swedish. At that time, he thought that he would not need those skills for his work in forestry. Forestry contractors and workers have usually not been interested in education and therefore the language skills were not well developed. However, language difficulties were not the reason why they had not tried to build up their business internationally:

> A year ago I planned to go to France after the storm disasters. They called me, because I belong to the association and because they needed machines. I was excited about it and we went there to look at it. Well, everything seemed so good, so I decided to continue to make more plans, and then we came back to Finland. Then I thought that we needed to buy a machine and send it to France, because it was urgent. So I bought a machine and I started to prepare it. At that time, the negotiations became difficult – we started to talk about money. I wanted to make sure that everything was alright. I sorted out things. I had one friend working in Switzerland in forestry work, who I could ask for

advice. Everything started to be complicated. It took a long time. We went there first in March, and they eventually called me at the beginning of May to tell me that "now everything is OK and now we can make a contract". But I said, "I do not come anymore." I started to think that it was too insecure. However, I kept the machine.[28]

This entrepreneur had bought this machine, which was better suited for forestry work in France than in Finnish forests, so nowadays he can only use it occasionally. Although he carefully prepared his new enterprise, his excitement turned to suspicion. The negotiations went too slowly and he changed his mind, because he did not want to risk being cheated. However, several forestry contractors who have been successful working abroad have usually wanted to work abroad again. It has been estimated that ten Finnish forestry contractors who have moved permanently to work abroad. It has also been suggested that the storm damage in Central and Western Europe secured the future employment of forestry contractors.[29]

Finnish forestry professionals not only exported their labor force but also their skills and their machines. For Finnish forest machinery manufacturers and entrepreneurs, this situation opened up an opportunity for exporting Finnish forest machinery. It provided an opportunity to export technical expertise, new machines, the modern Finnish forest technology, and knowledge.[30] Because of the lack of machines even old fashioned models were wanted for European forestry work and several entrepreneurs were delivering and selling old machines to European markets.

I have always bought used machines, and I try to sell them on to Europe. I have not succeeded in selling them to France, but machines have gone to Germany.[31]

A Fistful of Euros

The magazine of the Trade Association of Finnish Forestry and Earth Moving Contractors published an article at the beginning of 2000, where they gave a warning about dealers in Central and Western Europe who were not so respected and trustworthy. The situation in Europe's storm-damaged forest areas also tempted adventurers.[32] Rumours about unlucky contractors quickly spread among other contractors. The interviewees knew stories about people who had had economic difficulties and who had been short-changed.[33] Difficulties might have been expected especially if forestry professionals did not have enough practical information about local customs and established practices which differed from those they were used to in Finland. The long time it took to be paid was often a surprise to Finnish professionals.

As regard payment, it is quite normal for it to take about six months just to be paid a part of what one is owed. It is totally different here [in Finland] and what we have been used to. It is much more brutal than here.[34]

Usually, European clients stressed the fact that they did not have much time to wait. However, contractors who were already working abroad advised that it was important to make a contract as precisely as possible before leaving Finland. The entrepreneurs used to visit the area they would be working in before they made a contract. This was necessary because European forests differ from Finnish forests and they needed to use different kinds of machines and techniques there. Drawing up a contract was often a difficult process. Sometimes the contracts were so complicated that lawyers had to check the details of the contracts. Usually a forest work contract should include information about the price and wages, the duration of contract, and work descriptions, but sometimes contracts were not sufficiently specific. There was a lack of information about how the timber would be measured, and how the difficulties involved in harvesting would be taken into account, and the way the work should be done.[35] Forestry professionals were not used to this kind of bureaucracy or these kinds of tactics in negotiations.

> Well, at first, in Germany, there is a certain official bureaucracy when dealing with forests. There is a so-called *försterkultur* [forestry professional culture], stripes on a collar [uniform], and so on. Every *förster* [forestry official] has an opinion and of course it is the right one and nothing else will do. The culture of entrepreneurs in Germany is quite different to what we have here in Finland. Some contracts, for example, you can not trust oral contracts at all. If you make a deal, you should check with three lawyers that every comma is in the right place, if you want everything to go well there.[36]

In Finland, Finnish forestry professionals were used to trusting their business partners and believed they were reliable and that they could fulfil the contracts, because in Finland there is a strong norm about a contract's validity. Finns have often been accused of being over optimistic and of being naive in international business relationships.[37] It would appear that this has indeed led to unpleasant experiences for forestry professionals. Stories about unpaid work are the most common.[38]

> In other ways, it was fine, but I'm still waiting for my money, at least part of it. But no, I mean, I still trust it will be clear next week how it goes. Well, it is not such a huge sum of money, but anyway; some of money should still come.[39]

Also the contractors' experiences about working in Russia showed that working abroad could be a big economic risk for a contractor. According to forestry contractors, the working and living environment was unstable and sometimes even dangerous.[40] In addition, the language and cultural barriers were more difficult to overcome in Russia than in Central and Western Europe where you could cope with English. In 1995 the Trade Association of Finnish Forestry and Earth Moving Contractors provided some information for the contractors who were planning to work in Russia. Finnish forestry organisations also brought together important information about the constraints and opportunities involved in doing business in Russia to help Finnish forestry entrepreneurs.[41] This kind of information was not available for forestry professionals wanting to work in Central and Western Europe even though it would have been useful and necessary.[42]

Cultural Barriers and Gateways

After the storms, European forestry officials found themselves in a new situation; they needed to employ forestry workers and forest machine operators and forestry contractors from abroad. The committees which were set up after the storms in the 1980s and again in 2001 to make recommendations and produce manuals for harvesting timber in areas suffering from acute forest damage testify to the enormous difficulties involved.[43] These manuals set down principles about how to act before and after forest damage had occurred. International cooperation and an established network for the recruitment of professionals were important principles for finding qualified manpower and machines for harvesting work in time. It was also recommended that information about working and social conditions be given to forest workers and forestry contractors in connection with recruitment. These committees tried by producing these manuals to reduce uncertainty and increase stability and efficiency in an uncertain situation.[44]

However, Finnish forestry contractors found themselves in a new situation, where it was difficult to arrange a stable environment for doing business. The Trade Association of Finnish Forestry and Earth Moving Contractors was able to find out the average price level for services for contractors. But the association did not have enough resources to find detailed information about working conditions or clients in Central and Western Europe.[45] Finnish contractors had their own network for getting more information: other contractors gave them practical tips and passed on their experience of working abroad. They gave information about cultural differences and conventions which it was helpful to know before leaving Finland. However, it appeares that forestry contractors did not have enough advance information about local customs, rules, and business culture or about how to act in this new situation. Information was fragmented and difficult to find.

Uncertainty and lack of confidence were recurring themes in interviews and in newspaper articles. Forestry professionals had difficulties in being sure that they had negotiated profitable contracts. They were also concerned about the contract and how it would be fulfilled in practice. This kind of uncertainty strains the trust of a trading partner. Trust between negotiators is easier to achieve when the culture is familiar, and it is easy to find information about the reputation of the other negotiator.

> And one thing is obvious. You should follow the customs of the country you are in. And another thing is the language. I get along in English, but there the language was German, and you need to know German.[46]

Forestry professionals explained that the main reason for their difficulties was that they could not speak the language of the country where they were working.[47] Linguistic skills would have helped in their everyday life and in doing business in an international context. However, there were also other cultural barriers to overcome. Forestry professionals encountered local, and international customs and codes and business culture, which differed from that what they were used to in Finland.[48]

> In France, it was somehow difficult. It is the culture there, doing business. We negotiated there and we were prepared so to devote three days to these negotiations. So we discussed for two days, and on the third day, after the *siesta*, we were ready to talk about the price.[49]

Forestry professionals carry with them their own experience of, and traditions about, Finnish forestry. The work abroad was familiar, but the conventions, rules, and the way of working were different.[50] Forestry professionals looked at the different cultural environment from a professional point of view. When they compared the local forestry with Finnish forestry, they saw an undeveloped forestry management, old-fashioned machines and inefficient work. They assumed that they were superior in skills and in technical development. The tone of the stories gave us the impression that the Finns saw themselves as heroes who had the job of saving Europe's forests.

> There you can see how effective the French were. This tree was there on the roof about three months after the storm, and they have not got it off yet. We lived in these cottages and the tree was on the roof. [Laughing] Yes, things are not so well organized as they are here [Finland].[51]

> Yes, we could see a different way of life there. But still, even so there were several things more advanced than here in [Finland]. There were a lot of old fashioned things, too. Well, it might be the forestry, the mechanisation. If you think roughly, if you put things together, it is certainly still twenty years behind Finnish forestry.[52]

In the background of this kind of attitude, we can also detect a Finnish work oriented culture. According to cross-cultural business studies, Finns are more issue oriented, while the French, for example, are more people oriented. Finns usually pay more attention to professional and practical matters than social relations. Finns are confident when it comes to professional issues, but are too shy or aloof in social situations and in conversation.[53] Finnish workers have usually relied more on their professional skills rather than trying to develop social skills and cultural know-how.[54] Finnish forestry workers were convinced that they would be welcome in Central and Western Europe because they had the reputation of being skilful and efficient professionals. Furthermore, cultural differences were easily underestimated. For example, the working culture in Scandinavia was thought to be the same as in Finland.[55] Therefore, some forestry contractors went adventurously with their machines to Sweden to work on storm damaged areas in 2005 even though they did not have any specific information about a work contract.[56]

Finnish ethnologist, Hanna Snellman has studied Finnish labor migrants in Sweden and she has found out that Finns had difficulties in establishing social relations with Swedes and that they compensated the lack of social skills by working hard. Work may be the key to freedom, but it can also be a prison if one does not have social skills. Although Finns are famous in Sweden for being workaholics, the easiest way for a Finnish migrant to get a better job was to learn Swedish. Often, Finnish migrants did not plan to stay in Sweden very long, so they were not interested in integrating into Swedish culture or learning Swedish more than was useful for daily life.[57]

Finnish forestry professionals also did not plan to stay abroad very long. Usually, they planned only to work hard and earn some money. The work with storm damaged forests was only temporary, and they did not have time or interest to learn the culture or the language of the country where they were working. Forestry contractors and forestry workers were experts in their own field and they seemed to believe that their reputation as hard working and skilful professionals would convince everyone wherever they went. However, there were some forestry contractors who were fascinated by the cultural differences. Those who enjoyed and found positive elements in these differences were ready to go abroad again.

> During the weeks I spent there, I noticed that there is also life there. It is somewhat different. There is also a higher level of culture. It was somehow interesting, that if you saw a stranger on some local forest road in Switzerland, you could not just pass by without giving a greeting. It would have been odd behavior in Finland [to greet a stranger]. Additionally, when you lived downtown, you were expected to greet everyone you knew who lived there. And those greetings were different in a special way; you have to look at your watch to check what is the right way to greet someone at a particular time of day [Laughing].[58]

Conclusion

Although Finland belongs to the European Union and shares a modern western culture, there were differences between Finland and other European countries in bureaucracy, business culture, work-related values, and other conventions and traditions.[59] Finnish forestry contractors and workers were strangers and potential competitors in the labor market of Central and Western Europe.[60] However, the forestry contractors and workers were for the most part fascinated or amazed by the different customs; they used their professional experience and adjusted their behaviour according to the European clients' rules and conventions. Finnish contractors and workers took a risk when they made contracts in a new situation and in a new environment; they had to trust their new employers without knowing them. They used their own network, their relatives, and other entrepreneurs, to get information and avoid risks and costs. Additionally, the employers saw an opportunity and took a risk and trusted the expertise of Finnish forestry professionals.

After their work experiences abroad, these forestry professionals also started to see positive elements in Finnish forestry. Despite the difficulties, there was a close relationship between contractors and the forestry companies. They noticed that it has been easy to trust their clients and vice versa; they have usually fulfilled their contracts as promised. However, forestry professionals were still concerned about their weak position. These new experiences had not changed the basic problems affecting their profession in Finland.

In March 2000, Finnish forest machinery operators went on strike; they demanded better salaries and working conditions. It was a difficult situation for the forestry entrepreneurs because they were struggling to keep their enterprises profitable.[61] Gradually, the Trade Association of Finnish Forestry and Earth Moving Contractors has started to present stronger demands to the Finnish forest industry. They have regularly published announcements where they have demanded changes in the contractors' positions.[62] However, the Finnish forest companies have their own reasons for not paying more for the services of contractors. The Finnish forest industry nowadays depends on global markets, exports and the world economy. Competition in global markets has increased pressure in Finland to rationalise and increase effeciency, even though it has been estimated that Finnish forest harvesting work is the cheapest in Europe.[63]

According to sociologist Anthony Giddens, globalisation is a dialectical process where "local happenings are shaped by events occurring many miles away and vice versa."[64] Nowadays individual forestry professionals have international contacts and networks, and the opportunity to compare and observe positive and negative features of their own, and the foreign conventions and traditions. Additionally, several Finnish forestry contractors have decided not to stay in Finland and wait for changes in Finnish forestry; they have moved abroad more or less permanently to work in European forests.[65] Therefore, working abroad might be a key factor in promoting changes in Finland and in Western and Central Europe.

NOTES

1. Williamson 1987, 2, 20–22; North 1991.
2. Http://europa.eu.int/eur-lex/lex/fi/treaties/index.htm, (Accessed on September 22, 2005.)
3. Francis 1992, 63, 71; North 1991, 63.
4. Gahmberg & Alapiha 2002, 40–42; Hofstede 1984, 252–253.
5. Giddens 1992, 64, 147–148.
6. Granovetter 1973, 1370–1371; Sanders & Nee 1996, 232–233.
7. This research is based on my PhD thesis about how forestry workers, forestry contractors and forest machinery operators have experienced changes in Finnish forestry (Helsinki University, Department of Ethnology). This research is based on interviews carried out as part of a joint project with the Finnish Forest History

Society, the Lusto – Finnish Forest Museum, and the Ethnology Department of Helsinki University, called *Forestry Professions in a Changing Society – Oral History Project* 1999–2002. Docent Hanna Snellman was the leader of the project, and my role as project coordinator was to organise the interviews. Over one thousand forestry professionals from around Finland were interviewed in order to find out how changes in forestry have changed their work and lifestyle. Thirteen interviewees had experience on working abroad. Additionally, I have used, for this article, newspaper articles (*Maaseudun Tulevaisuus*) and the journal of the Trade Association of Finnish Forestry and Earth Moving Contractors (*Koneyrittäjä*) as an additional source to find out what kind of picture these forestry officials can offer about working abroad.

8. Lusto A02001: 735/55w, 774/48w, 849/54e, 855/42e, 866/52o, 899/28e, 906/61o, 919/49e, 928/59e, 963/35e, 965/62o, 967/45e, 973/56e, Forestry Professions in a Changing Society – Oral History project 1999–2002, Lusto – Finnish Forest Museum, Punkaharju. In the signum, the number '55' is the year of birth (1955) and 'w' means forestry worker, 'e' means entrepreneur and contractor, and 'o' means forest machine operator. Later in the text when I refer to these groups together, I use the term "forestry professionals".

9. Snellman 1996, 201–207; Snellman 2005, 97–101.

10. Hakkila & Kanninen & Mäkinen 1989, 53, 56–57; Koneurakoitsijain liitto r.y. 1980–1989, 52–57.

11. Mäkinen 1988, 32–34; Mäkinen 1993, 17–19.

12. Interview with an official of the Trade Association of Finnish Forestry and Earth Moving Contractors October 11, 2005, in the author's possession.

13. Mäkinen 1993, 17–18.

14. Lusto A02001: 855/42e, 917/63o, 919/49e.

15. *Koneyrittäjä* 5/2001. See also http://www.hedeselskabet.dk/ (Accessed on September 22, 2005.)

16. *Maaseudun Tulevaisuus* January 6, January 22, January 27, February 1, 2000; Lusto A02001: 913/71o.

17. *Koneyrittäjä* 2/2000; See also *Maaseudun Tulevaisuus* January 13, January 25, 2000.

18. See North 2004,16.

19. *Maaseudun Tulevaisuus* January 13, January 25, 2000.

20. Grieco 1996,72; Snellman 2005, 102–103.

21. Lusto A02001: 912/66e, 913/71e, 928/59e.

22. Lusto A02001: 928/59e.

23. *Koneyrittäjä* 5/2001; Lusto A02001: 735/55w, 906/61e, 913/71o.

24. Lusto A02001: 855/42e, 967/45e, 919/49e.

25. Employment in Europe 2001, 51; Kruse 2000, 288–289.

26. Lusto A02001: 866/52o, 906/61e, 917/63o.

27. See Hytti 2003, 35–40; Hakkila & Kanninen & Mäkinen 1989, 55, 62, 73.

28. Lusto A02001: 912/66e

29. *Koneyrittäjä* 1/2000.

30. *Koneyrittäjä* 1/2000; *Maaseudun Tulevaisuus* March 11, 2000.

31. Lusto A02001: 928/59e.

32. *Koneyrittäjä* 1/2000; See also *Maaseudun Tulevaisuus* January 25, 2000.

33. Lusto A02001: 963/35e; Interview with an official of the Trade Association of Finnish Forestry and Earth Moving Contractors October 11, 2005, in the author's possession.

34. Lusto A02001: 973/56e.
35. *Koneyrittäjä* 1/2000.
36. Lusto A02001: 973/56e.
37. Mikluha 1996, 74.
38. Lusto A02001: 849/54e, 919/49e, 967/45e, 855/42e.
39. Lusto A02001: 735/55w.
40. Lusto A02001: 855/42e, 967/45e, 919/49e.
41. Http://www.idanmetsatieto.fi, (Accessed on September 22, 2005.)
42. Vocational education has tried to satisfy this need by arranging a course on internationalisation in Oulu. *Maaseudun Tulevaisuus* January 20, 2000.
43. After the storm damage, the European Commission supported the STODAFOR project, which produced a Technical Guide on the Harvesting and Conservation of Storm Damaged Timber. Previous big storm damage occured in Europe during the 1980s and 1990s and led to similar discussions about employment and harvesting problems in storm damaged forests. A similar manual was produced in 1988. See http://www.ctba.fr/stodafor/technicalper cent20guide.htm (Accessed on September 22, 2005); http://www.unece.org/trade/timber/storm/manual.htm, (Accessed on September 22, 2005.)
44. See North 1991, 63.
45. *Maaseudun Tulevaisuus* January 13, 2000; January 25, 2000; Interview with an official of the Trade Association of Finnish Forestry and Earth Moving Contractors October 11, 2005, in the author's possession.
46. Lusto A02001: 735/55w.
47. Lusto A02001: 905/46e, 913/71w, 735/55w.
48. See North 1991, 6, 42–45.
49. Lusto A02001: 928/59e.
50. See North 1991, 13, 56–58.
51. Lusto A02001: 928/59e.
52. Lusto A02001: 913/71w.
53. Mikluha 1998, 16.
54. Junkkari & Junkkari 2003, 33–36.
55. Lusto A02001: 973/56e; *Koneyrittäjä* 5/2001; *Koneyrittäjä* 1/2000.
56. Interview with an official of the Trade Association of Finnish Forestry and Earth Moving Contractors October 11, 2005, in the author's possession.
57. Snellman 2003, 159–161.
58. Lusto A02001: 913/71w.
59. Hofstede 1984, 212–221; Grant 1998, 146–147.
60. See Hart 1998, 168; Hall 2002, 238.
61. *Maaseudun tulevaisuus* March 4, March 11, 2000; Särmä 2/2000, 3/2000.
62. Http://www.koneyrittajat.fi/?action=news&news_id=77, (Accessed on October 31, 2005.)
63. Donner–Amnell 2001, 87–88; *Maaseudun Tulevaisuus* March 4, 2000.
64. Giddens 1992, 64.
65. *Koneyrittäjät 1989–1999*, 36; *Maaseuden Tulevaisuus* January 25, 2000.

SOURCES

Newspapers

Koneyrittäjä 2000–2001.
Maaseudun Tulevaisuus 2000.
Särmä. Puu- ja erityisalojen liiton jäsenlehti 2/2000, 3/2000.

Interviews

Forestry Professions in the Changing Society – Oral History project 1999-2002, Lusto
    – Finnish Forest Museum, Punkaharju.
Interviews, in the author's possession.

Internet sources

Hedeselskabet
http://www.hedeselskabet.dk.

Idän metsätieto -internetpalvelu.
http://www.idanmetsatieto.fi.

Manual on Acute Forest Damage: Managing the Impact of Sudden and Severe Forest
    Damage. Http://www.unece.org/trade/timber/storm/manual.htm.

Technical Guide on Harvesting and Conservation of Storm Damaged Timber.
http://www.ctba.fr/stodafor/technicalper cent20guide.htm.

Treaty Establishing the European Community.
http://europa.eu.int/eur-lex/lex/fi/treaties/index.htm.

Koneyrittäjät
Tiedotteet:
Metsäalan urakointimalli on tullut tiensä päähän
Koneyritysten tuloskehitys vahvasti miinusmerkkinen vuonna 2004
http://www.koneyrittajat.fi/?action=news&news_id=77.

BIBLIOGRAPHY

Donner-Amnell, Jacob 2001. To be or not to be Nordic? How internationalisation has
    affected the character of the Nordic forest industry and forest utilisation in the Nordic
    countries. *Nordisk Samhällsgeografisk Tidskrift.* Nummer 33. Roskilde, 87–123.
Employment in Europe 2001. Recent Trends and Prospects. Luxembourg: Office for
    official Publications of the European Communities.
Francis, Arthur 1992. The process of national industrial regeneration and competitiveness.
    Strategic Management Journal, Vol. 13, 61–78.

Gahmberg, Henrik & Alapiha, Satu 2002. *Cross-Cultural Cooperation. Attitudes and Experiences – A Survey*. Proceedings of the University of Vaasa. Research papers. Tutkimuksia 242. Vaasa: University of Vaasa.

Giddens, Anthony 1992. *The Consequences of Modernity*. Cambridge: Polity Press.

Granovetter, Mark S. 1973. The Stregth of Weak Ties. *American Journal of Sociology*, Vol 78, No. 6. The University of Chigaco Press, 1360–1380.

Grant, Richard 1998.The political geography of European integration. *Modern Europe. Place, Culture and Identity*. Ed. Brian Graham. London: Arnold, 145–163.

Grieco, Margaret 1996. *Recruitment, reliability and repeated exchance: an analysis of urban social networks and labour circulation*. London: Routledge.

Hakkila, Pentti & Kanninen, Kaija & Mäkinen, Pekka 1989. *Metsäkoneurakoitsija*. Helsinki: Gummerus.

Hall, Stuart 2002. The spectacle of the 'other'. *Representation. Cultural Representations and Signifying Practices*. Ed. Stuart Hall London: Sage.

Hart, Mark 1998. Convergence, cohesion and regionalism: contradictory trends in the new Europe. *Modern Europe. Place, Culture and Identity*. Ed. Brian Graham London: Arnold, 164–185.

Hofstede, Geert 1984. *Culture's Consequences. International Differences in Work-Related Values*. Beverly Hills: Sage.

Hytti, Ulla 2003. *Stories of Entrepreneurs: Narrative Construction of Identities*. Publications of the Turku School of Economics and Business Administration. Series A–1:2003. Turku: Turku School of Economics and Business Administration.

Junkkari, Kaija Maria & Junkkari, Lari 2003. *Nykyajan paimentolaiset. Työ ja koti maailmalla*. Helsinki: Otava.

Koneurakoitsijain liitto r.y. 1980–1989.

Koneyrittäjät 1989–1999.

Kruse, Anders 2000. What will be the concrete meaning of citizenship. Nordic experience. *Thirteen years of free movement of workers in Europe*. Proceedings of the conference Brussels, 17 to 19 December 1998. Ed. Jean-Yves Carlier & Michel Verwilgnen. Luxembourg: Office for official Publications of the European Communities.

Mikluha, Arja 1996. *Työkulttuurit. Avain menestykseen kansainvälisessä liiketoiminnassa*. Helsinki: TT-Kustannustieto Oy.

— 1998. *Kommunikointi eri maissa*. Helsinki: Kauppakaari OYJ, Yrityksen tietokirjat.

Mäkinen, Pekka 1988. *Metsäkoneurakoitsija yrittäjänä*. Folia Forestalia 717. Helsinki: Metsäntutkimuslaitos.

— 1993. *Metsäkoneyrittämisen menestystekijät*. Folia Forestalia 818. Helsinki: Metsäntutkimuslaitos.

North, Douglass C., 1991. *Institutions, Institutional Change and Economic Performance*. New York: Cambridge University Press.

Sanders, Jimy M. & Nee, Victor 1996. Immigrant Self-Employment: the Family as Social Capital and the Value of Human Capital. *American Sociological Review*, Vol 61, No. 2, 231–249.

Snellman, Hanna 1996. *Tukkilaisen tulo ja lähtö. Kansatieteellinen tutkimus Kemijoen metsä- ja uittotyöstä*. Scripta Historica 25. Oulu: Pohjoinen.

— 2003. *Sallan suurin kylä – Göteborg*. Helsinki: Suomalaisen Kirjallisuuden Seura.

— 2005. *The Road Taken. Narratives from Lapland*. Inari: Kustannus-Puntsi.

Williamson, Oliver E. 1987. *The Economic Institutions of Capitalism. Firms, Markets, Relational Contracting*. New York: The Free Press.

MINNA AALTO

Finnish Immigrants in Provence

Travelling to the south is an essential part of Finnish culture. Frequent holidays to Southern Europe have been very popular with different population groups, especially in the late 1980s and early 1990s. "Etelänmatka" has also become a term in the Finnish language, which means taking a holiday in popular sun destinations favored by Finns. The traditional "south" for the Finnish tourist is the Spanish coast, but "south" is not a geographically exact term in this context. According to Tom Selänniemi, who has researched the subject, it is the "south" as found on an imaginary holiday map of the Finnish tourist.[1]

This article, however, discusses "etelänmatka" in the specific context of travel literature about southern France. My approach is that of the literary researcher, discussing three particular works of fiction about the region. The literature I have researched forms an interesting view of the traditional "etelänmatka", as favored by the Finnish tourist, as well as the fictional Provence of the books by Peter Mayle.

In fact, it would be difficult not to mention Peter Mayle's novels in the context of Provence. His worldwide best seller *A Year in Provence* (1990) has been translated into twenty-two languages. *A Year in Provence* was published in Finnish in 1992 and has gone through a number of editions. The television series based on the book was shown in Finland during 1993 and 1994. A combined edition of the three novels by Peter Mayle on Provence, *A Year in Provence*, *Toujours Provence*, and *Encore Provence,* was published in 2004. According to the publisher, the Finnish translation of Mayle's *A Year in Provence* has sold over 40,000 copies.

So, Mayle's books have a staunch following in Finland. Some Finnish travellers to France have followed suit and described life abroad with direct references to Mayle's novels. Both Aaro Vakkuri in his *Kylä Provencen taivaalla* ("The village on the sky of Provence", 1997) and Kari Kyrönseppä's *Provencen syleilyssä* ("On the arms of Provence", 2002) continue Mayle's style, and describe buying a holiday house and the life style it brings. Merja Tynkkynen, however, treats the subject slightly differently in her book *Valkoinen sohva Rivieralla* ("White sofa in the Riviera", 2003) where she analyzes her dream of having a holiday home in southern France.

Holiday Paradise

Finnish Tourism was born in Spain and the beaches of Spain have remained the holiday paradise for the Finnish tourist who wants to get away from everyday life in the north. A successful holiday in the sun requires certain conditions to be fulfilled: sun, sea, and a sandy beach are necessary for relaxation and idleness. The destination itself has little significance. It can be an environment specially created for this purpose, a destination where one wouldn't think of living on a permanent basis. Therefore, the destinations that fulfil the conditions of a holiday paradise are interchangeable.[2]

Merja Tynkkynen, in *Valkoinen sohva Rivieralla,* describes the French Riviera in much the same way as is seen to be typical for the holiday in the sun. However, her treatment does make a difference between Spain and the French Riviera. The author recounts that the family used to have holidays in Spain when their children were young and that therefore Spain was just a little bit too familiar. Additionally, she eschews the Finnish migrant population in Spain, which is constantly growing. In the 1990s, there were approximately 10,000 Finns who spent the winter season on the Costa del Sol, and around 3,000 Finns on the Costa Blanca doing the same. The majority of these are pensioners.[3]

The French Riviera differs from the tourist towns built on the Spanish coast in that the Riviera has a long history. Holidays in the sun were invented on the French Riviera, where sea-front boulevards were being built as early as the 1860s. Tynkkynen's travel book has some strong images about what is French, which add to the significance of the Riviera as a destination for local French culture. In the old town of Nice and on its sea-front boulevards, one can experience a life style that seems very congenial for somebody who has arrived from the depths of a harsh winter in Finland: "The Riviera isn't just any old place in the South. Once there, one really understands that behind the façade, there is a desire to embrace an easier life, just to walk around and sense the world around you."[4] This citation also reveals the reason considered paramount for travelling. According to Yrjö Sepänmaa, who has analyzed the aesthetics of travelling, the real motivation for travelling may well be the disassociation of the tried and tested, which also invokes the traveller to see everyday life – their own and others' – as something new and fresh in a more sensitive manner. The release from everyday life also affords the opportunity to pause and reflect.[5]

In *Kylä Provencen taivaalla*, Aaro Vakkuri concentrates on sightseeing and describing the environment. The book has the following dedication: "To my wife Madeleine, who took me to Provence". Aaro Vakkuri is both a fiction and non-fiction writer, who works as a construction engineer. Despite the fact that he has had to travel and live abroad because of his job, apart from Paris, France, was new to him. In the foreword, Vakkuri describes the somewhat negative expectations he had regarding Southern France. The book also conveys the sarcasm he feels regarding his wife. It is as if he was talking to male readers, assuming they understand how wives have a way of dominating their husbands.

The wife decided that we'd spend one week of our holiday just driving around Provence. I thought, maybe this holiday would be some kind of an endurance test of our marriage, characterised by the necessary "couch potatoing" in the front seat, and giving appropriate accolades for the marvellous sights found by competent map reading.[6]

It is difficult to define the books on Provence as just travel books because there is a lot more than travel in them. It would be more accurate to describe them as testimonies to the constant traffic between Finland and France. Many of the books discussing travel in Provence are memoirs, fragments of memories and events, which are woven into a story. Vakkuri's book gathers together memories of six years in Provence, beginning with the very first visit. It describes how a Finnish-Swiss couple settled in a small village in Provence.

As his wife's native tongue is French, her Finnish husband is often left out of conversations held in village cafés or hotels they visit on their journeys. The protagonist shows his sarcasm as, despite describing himself as a man of the world, he is led and dominated by his wife because she speaks the language. Vakkuri's travelbook contains a lot of inner searching about the significance of being fluent in French and of learning a foreign language in the first place. On the other hand, his role as a spectator, kept at arm's length, is amplified, although this of course is one of the vital elements that shape the experiences of a tourist.

Similarly, Kari Kyrönseppä describes seasonal life in France. *Provencen syleilyssä* comprises ten years of memories, events, and travel descriptions. Kyrönseppä is both a scriptwriter and a director working in TV and films. *Provencen syleilyssä* is his first book. As a travel book, it really describes a particular life journey in Provence: a beginning, a middle, and an end. Aesthetically, it describes both the physical and the spiritual experience of departure, stay, and return. It has a beginning and an end, which also structures the relationship between being somewhere and being away from somewhere.[7]

It is worth noticing that Tynkkynen's *Valkoinen sohva Rivieralla* describes the Riviera as the South of France. For both of the male authors, however, Southern France is personified by small villages surrounded by forests, which don't seem to have any significance for Tynkkynen. At the beginning of his book, Kyrönseppä describes the first impression of a tourist in Antibes, sitting on a terrace of a beach hotel, in a rather brusque way. The Provence of Kyrönseppä is that of small mountain villages. Then, the Mediterranean takes another form:

> The Mediterranean looks boring. When I look at a bay, it might as well be one in the Atlantic Ocean or the Gulf of Finland for that matter – there is no glimmering open sea. The scenery is closed. [8]

> The views as one approaches it are marvellous. It is as if the whole of Provence opened towards the Mediterranean. From up here, the waters seem enchanted, light as the clouds. The billowing ground, winding roads, and the cities on the hills shimmer in the mist. [9]

53

The travel books I researched often ascribe Provence an authenticity and reality in keeping with its thousand years' long history, its small villages, and relaxed life style. Provence is, therefore, the option for the traveller who dislikes mass tourism. Travelling to Southern France means that there are no hotels full of Finns, and there is little likelihood of meeting other Finnish travellers. Likewise, there are no Finnish guides, and no service in Finnish. This does not, of course, mean that the tourist who flies to the sunny beaches of Spain could not experience the local culture. As it is, the motives of both mass tourism and "alternative" tourism are the same: nostalgia for the ethnic, original, and untouched.[10]

The attraction of Provence, for the books mentioned, is very much about belonging to a small village community as a holiday resident. To the authors, Provence is about the inland scenery and participating in the local culture. In this sense, these books remind one of Peter Mayle's Provence. For Merja Tynkkynen, however, Southern France is much more about life on the beach boulevards of the Riviera, which can be seen as typical of the holiday in the sun.

The images we have of places and how we see them constantly evolve, and new ones are produced all the time.[11] However, even earlier Finnish travel literature has this two-sided view of Southern France. Eino and Katri Palola, a married couple, described in *Huoleton retki läpi Ranskan* ("Carefree trip through France", 1937) the sunny beaches of the Riviera as a tourist destination where the atmosphere was rather gloomy, especially out of season. As a counter point, they describe the mountains where one could enjoy marvellous scenery and have the opportunity to live in the past and experience both the politeness and the warmth of the people of Provence.[12]

Dreams and Reveries

Although the Finnish travel writers I studied are all active in the creative arts, they do not on the whole make references to the writing process even though one would assume it is an essential part of travel writing. According to Yrjö Varpio, travel and travel literature have always been closely linked. For instance, reading when travelling was regarded as so self-explanatory that it is rarely referred to. Alas, writing when travelling might be seen as self-explanatory too, an activity which by itself does not need describing.[13] Tynkkynen does not do this at all. Kyrönseppä and Vakkuri describe the writing process now and again, but for the most part, only as a prelude to something particularly typical of life in Provence. The actual holiday prose is about the holiday: the unhurried life style, visiting places, observing the local life, and doing up the holiday home.

As a literary works, travel books describe the journey more as a series of new impressions rather than an exact record of events. The handling depends on the ever changing rules that govern all literary works. Reading these Provence stories one can, however, ask whether the tradition of the travel book genre has changed in any significant way during its history. According to Yrjö Varpio, the first Finnish travel book by Adelaide Ehrnrooth (1890) was found by its reviewers to have concentrated on emotional experiences, just as we find in tourism today. It addressed the needs of readers who were getting used to travelling in an era of increasing international awareness. The reviewers praised the author's pleasing style, her ability to describe local customs and preferences through anecdotes, and her light, conversational style, and humour. The author openly admitted that she had wanted to impart some of the pleasure she had experienced on her travels to her readers.[14] This is still a central theme, in literature about Provence.

Kyrönseppä's book contains a considerable number of descriptions of the actual process of travelling. *Provencen syleilyssä* describes travelling from one place to another. Kyrönseppä discusses his journey from Finland to Sweden by car, the journey to Finland by his neighbour in France, and other such events by friends. Eeva Jokinen and Soile Veijola, who have researched tourism, say that the "lone rider" personification is typical for a male traveller.[15] The same phenomenon is apparent in Kyrönseppä's work as he describes his journey through Europe. Here is Kyrönseppä describing his impression and feelings en route to Southern France, on the Autoroute de Soleil:

> The Weekend movie by Godard becomes reality. I drive past three bad accidents during the night. Cars and caravans by the road side, the dead still not covered, surviving family crying by their side. – At the rest area people are in high spirits, somewhat macabre compared to the cruel realities of the road. At 4 am, everybody is awake, from baby to granddad, from dogs to turtles. A lot of eating, running, and noise. Maybe it is a celebration of the fact that they have made it so far? [16]

The lone rider experience should probably not be limited to men, as Merja Tynkkynen also describes a lonely journey by car which comes across as a brave, one-man effort, navigating the dark night without a map, which was still in a lost suitcase somewhere. Both authors refer often to popular culture and films, which signifies the importance of visual pictures in the narration. Tynkkynen's France relies considerably on the pictorial images of travel advertisements and magazines.

Tynkkynen describes her dream of a Mediterranean holiday home through everyday cultural images and fantasies from popular culture in a humorous fashion. As an advertising executive, and a first-time author, she dissects her needs in an intellectual way, needs that have been fuelled through advertising, magazines, films, and literature. "I had of course read all of Peter Mayle and Frances Mayes. I had read everything I could lay my hands on, about France, Italy or Spain."[17] The narrator is aware of the aesthetics of the consumer society, advertising, and fashion with which we are bombarded. She makes this clear through a poignant irony, which manifests itself as a parody of the reveries and dreams in her book. For example, the narrator fantasises how her long-standing marital relationship might change into a romantic affair with all the trappings. She is standing in a pink decorated flat in Nice and ponders: "I wonder now, how would our married life, so familiar now, change of something like this? – He would bring me breakfast in bed every morning and then we would walk on the beach, hand in hand, listening to the waves."[18] On the Riviera she watches an estate agent, whom she regards from the female point of view:

> I noticed his big brown eyes and his incredibly long eyelashes. His face bore the resemblance of Belmondo and Bogart. – I surprised myself imagining living with this embodiment of the French male. [19]

According to Yrjö Sepänmaa, one of the attractions of travelling is the very freedom it offers from one's self image in everyday life. One can start again, as a stranger, without any preconceptions or expectations, but – one is also without the benefits of what is familiar, without a social safety net.[20] *Valkoinen sohva Rivieralla* describes a woman's exodus of securing a time-share holiday home as a great adventure and a medley of minor complications. Additionally, the convention of the travel genre to describe what has happened already is well suited to the humorous approach. The narrator speaks today of the past, describing the journey as seen at the time of writing. Self-irony and humour is seen as particularly typical of women, as is the banter on important beliefs and life values.[21] When the narrator describes her colourful process of securing her time-share apartment, wondering how a family of four could possibly fit in to a small one bedroom flat, her story is filled with a humour that contrasts with the ambitious property escapades of many well-known Provence writers.

According to Ritva Hapuli, travel books don't tell us much about travel preparations, or the excitement before the journey or even why the journey is being undertaken.[22] Hapuli studied travel books written by Finnish women between the two world wars. In this respect Tynkkynen's book differs from the traditional approach as her thoughts before the journey are distinctly present. Motivation and arguments for and against are bandied about. In addition, Tynkkynen's work shows the importance of imaginary travel. The protagonist enjoys the holiday in advance in her imagination. [23]

Even if Tynkkynen describes her dream, a woman's dream of having a holiday home for the whole family in the southern sun, the travel description is still that of a middle-aged crisis. Social scientists and anthropologists have suggested that the mid-life phase is typically a time when women wish to loosen the bond of being "rationally responsible". This is understood as wanting to change the role given to and adopted by women, the role of caring and maintaining relationships.[24] The narrator turns her own experience into a universal one, which she treats in a humorous way. There is also the suggestion of self-irony as the narrator takes a step back thus distancing herself from the problem. Self irony often demands an outside view where the protagonist weighs her own characteristics as somebody else and puts it into wider perspective.[25] Tynkkynen writes: "I am sure I wasn't the first or last middle-aged woman who has fantasised about life in the Mediterranean where palm trees sway gently by the turquoise sea."[26]

The title *Valkoinen sohva Rivieralla* and the woman's dream of a white sofa induces various meanings throughout the text. The white sofa is a piece of furniture as seen in decorating magazines and the kind the writer would like to have in her own holiday home: "soft, clean, big and distinct". The sofa becomes a metaphor. It becomes a symbol of the independence of the mother and the wife. The white colour is chosen without children in mind, it is purely aesthetic. The colour white is also a metaphor for the wife's desire to give her relationship a new start, for a renewed closeness between husband and wife, which is not possible with all the pressures of everyday life.

The desire to have time for herself and to travel is very revealing and this is used as a vehicle in *Valkoinen sohva Rivieralla* to describe a woman's efforts to solve a potentially suffocating situation. So, Tynkkynen's travel book is a description of this process, which becomes a journey. The holiday dreams of the woman are part of a larger dream of life in general, and, as such, the white sofa takes central stage. As a travel book, *Valkoinen sohva Rivieralla* is the realisation of a woman's dream and her personal development.

The Provence of the Cultural Traveller

The origin of the title of Aaro Vakkuri's book becomes apparent as the story unfolds. There is a village in Provence, high on a mountain top, and the sign attached to the old ramparts reads, according to Vakkuri: "Doubletour, the village on the sky of Provence". In fact, the name of the village as used in the book is fictional; the author obviously does not want to reveal his secret. Vakkuri's book, comprising 24 chapters, was based originally on a series of 15 articles which he submitted to Helsingin Sanomat, a major Finnish newspaper. In the tradition of Finnish travel literature; the title pays reference to *Pariisin taivaan alla* ("Under the sky of Paris") by Irja Spira, published in 1924.

There is no doubt that Vakkuri is a cultural traveller for whom historic sights are an essential part of a holiday. It is almost obligatory to recount historical facts in travel literature.[27] In Tynkkynen's book this is displayed by a chapter on the history of Provence, which is slightly off the track of the story itself. Kyrönseppä does not concentrate on explaining historical sights. He is more interested in the everyday curiosities and complications which personalise the experience of historical sights. "Mentonista on moneksi" ("Menton has many faces") – is a chapter that relays the family's journey to Monaco and how they get lost and end up in Menton instead. They enthuse about Menton, believing it to be Monaco, before realising that it isn't. The chapter describing the sights of Avignon leaves the reader with an unforgettable impression of danger as the road was cut off by a storm and floods.

As historical and geographical information is just part of the convention of travel literature, the facts given are often haphazard, very superficial, and often taken straight from other guidebooks.[28] Vakkuri, for example, clearly states that his traveller uses the Michelin Guide and even recommends it to others. Travel guides and handbooks, which are studied carefully when travelling, have been part of Finnish travel literature since the 1800s.[29] Reading a guidebook is still part of the ritual of tourism.[30] Sometimes, Vakkuri makes a reference to his Michelin Guide and adds his own comments and views.

Other times, the protagonist is satisfied with quite a general description and adds an explanatory, self-reflective note about his own role as a tourist:

> When you are in Provence you can't help running into the "ancient Romans", who have built just about everything in whatever this province was then. In some ways it is difficult to understand how big the Roman Empire was 2000 years or so ago. – What business did they have being in every part of Europe? Apart from taxes, of course, to build more stone mounds. On the other hand, what on earth am I doing, wondering around somewhere in Provence in Southern France with a Michelin Guidebook, published by the tyre company? [31]

Vakkuri's cultural travelling is guided by a same desire that guides so-called "destination-bound" tourists. They go on holiday because they want to see the sights at particular destination.[32] For them, the reason is to avoid being idle, which is also apparent in Vakkuri's writings. The days that are not devoted to the renovation of his holiday home are spent seeing the sights. This travel book, written by a construction engineer, gives a lot of detail on architecture. This cultural traveller appreciates the vestiges of the old western civilisation and its vast cultural heritage so much that he recounts them in the fashion of travel guides.

As a rule, the cultural traveller has preconceptions and advance expectations regarding his destination. In Vakkuri's travel book the husband is described as having none of these, as his wife, who works in the travel industry, plans the holiday and its execution. Hence, the narrator is astonished and bewildered by his own role as a traveller and pontificates about his own status as he listens in silence as his wife reads the guide book. His role as the husband is also that of the chauffeur, navigating in a strange country, directed by his wife reading the map, and driving wherever his wife happens to think appropriate. The part of the nodding dummy is also his in restaurants and cafes where others decide what he has to eat or to drink.

> The Mrs asked what we would like to eat. Before we had a chance to respond, she continued and said that the *Chef* recommended something which I certainly didn't understand. – I agreed quickly with the *Chef's* recommendation, whatever it was.[33]

The books about Provence do not portray meeting an "untouched" world in the ethnographical sense. Rather, they discuss the experiences of the cultural traveller, not describing the destination as such, but the individual traveller's emotional experiences and thoughts. They represent a modern travel literature that does not seek to introduce unknown destinations per se. It is more a rendez-vous of the writer with his alter-ego. Even though Vakkuri's book can be used as a travel guide or a factual source, it is still a story of the survival of a Finnish man in a strange culture.

Cultural Pictures

Travel literature can be regarded as a common, wide playing-field for writers and readers alike, where new authors need to adhere to existing rules. As the genre grows, the authors who revisit popular destinations need to be aware of previous accounts and come up with a different angle. On the other hand, there is a certain expectation written the genre that reference, if not tribute, will be paid to earlier travel books on the same subject. Sometimes, a travel book is fashioned to fit the model of an earlier publication.[34]

Provencen syleilyssä by Kari Kyrönseppä is similar to Peter Mayle's books on Provence in terms of structure, as the individual chapters can be read alone, something which also contributes to the conversational style. Similarly, *Kylä Provencen taivaalla* by Vakkuri, based as it is on broadsheet articles, can also be read as individual chapters because the book has no particular plot which demands a chronological reading. Tynkkynen's book on the other hand has more of a plot. What is common to all three is the narrator's distance in time to the actual events described. This is one of the features of the travel writing genre. Sometimes the time span between the journey itself and the actual writing can be considerable, so the description of the journey knits together the time of writing and the actual events.[35]

In Kyrönseppä's work we meet an explorer who wants to experience something new and different or something familiar in a new environment. He describes the French versions of golf, randonnées, and downhill skiing through Finnish eyes. He introduces the reader to the secrets of buying a house, renovating and selling a property. Yvone Lenard's *The Magic of Provence* (2000) and the description of Provence by Kyrönseppä share a common thread in as much as they both explain how finding your own house in Provence is largely a risky game of chance.

There is also a cultural difference between the works written by the Finns, the American author Lenard, and the English writer Mayle. The Finns buy small houses inland. These do not usually have a garden let alone a swimming pool, so they do look very modest in comparison to luxurious villas. Kyrönseppä describes the economic issues and problems of house buying, which the other two internationally known authors of Provence do not: "The house, infused with memories of Fontbregouan, is beginning to feel more like an economic time bomb than a place of sunny, pleasant memories."[36]

Tynkkynen presents her story of wanting to buy a holiday home and ending up with a time-share largely in terms of economic necessity. Time-share as a word, *"holiday share"* in Finnish, also corresponds with the vision of the holiday expressed in the book: everyday is spent waiting for the holiday. The "holiday share" is a week's worth of the woman's own time: free time, not just from work, but also from the family.[37]

Vakkuri's book is especially keen on costs. The narrator is very aware of keeping within his budget and presents a number of estimates without fail, motivated by what he calls "the professional illness of the businessman".[38] Where the others get the builders in to do the renovation, the Finnish engineer is a do-it-yourself man. The wife's role is clear too:

My wife momentarily forgot scrubbing the floor tiles when I pushed her under the sink to screw in the door hinges of the kitchen cupboards. I could've done it myself, but I just couldn't fit in there. After I pushed my rather small wife onto a four inch tin of peas, cross-legged, head down with a Phillips screw driver in her left hand, the hinges were in place less than an hour. That was after I told her, of course, which way she should turn the screwdriver. [39]

In the travel literature I have studied the Finns do not, however, reflect about their role as tourists. This is, perhaps, because they travel alone. When Vakkuri describes his visit to Baux-en-Provence, he notices, as an elitist tourist, a group of foreign tourists. He joins them to inspect the ruins. This role as a tourist ends when he moves to a hotel. Similarly, Kyrönseppä describes Finnish guests being taken to see the sights. Tynkkynen does not consider herself as a tourist either. Although one would imagine there are lots of tourists on the sea front of Nice, the narrator only sees the French eating in the road-side restaurants: "Elegant, understated and stylish mademoiselles with French businessmen dressed in clean cotton shirts, and looking like French lovers."[40]

Cultural pictures of the French are found in Kyrönseppä's book too when he describes his neighbours in Provence. Sylvie in particular, with her high heels, lives up to the image of the elegant French woman, but descriptions of "French men looking like lovers" are not to be found in works by the male authors. It is interesting that Outi Nyytäjä, a Finnish woman who lives half of the year in Bretagne and half in Finland, comments on this clichéd view of French women being stylish. In her travel book, *Maailman laidalla. Kertomuksia Bretangesta* ("On the edge of the world. Stories from Bretagne", 2002), she describes how the women in Bretagne dress in quilted jackets just like their Finnish counterparts. She sees the myth of the elegance of French women as a literary image:

> Together with the vivacity and openness of the French, the elegance of the French woman is a myth which is questionable. The French woman does not walk daintily in a well cut-suit, clicking her high heels, as described in the books of Helena Petäjistö or the poet Björling or the statements by professor Klinge, where they are still convinced of the French woman's grace and beauty. [41]

Outi Nyytäjä is a scriptwriter, dramatist, and columnist whose interest in France was awoken some twenty years ago. Nyytäjä might be described as a Francophile with an interest in language and literature. Her two travel books, originally published as articles in women's magazines, seem relatively polemical when compared to other works of the genre. She is very aware of the cultural clichés attributed to the French, which dominate the Finnish view of the French. She attempts to find some common ground between the Finns and the French by describing Bretagne as a northern periphery at the edge of the world. According to Nyytäjä, however, the Finnish view of the French is that of Southern France:

It was sunny in the south. – Mountains rose around us, and, on the hill-sides, houses with the ochre coloured roofs. This was the Provence that the Finns knew as the real France. There were lots of Finnish people there, and when you come here to this paradise from the cabbage and potato fields of Bretagne, you feel you have come from far away, from the grim North. [42]

Although the descriptions of Provence are characterised by visual accounts, other senses are not excluded. The culture of food, so particularly French, is described by the Finnish authors of Provence. Vakkuri's *Kylä Provencen taivaalla* describes the adoption of the food culture. Throughout the story food is a frequent subject. Food becomes a prize for the cultural traveller gained after a well performed sightseeing-tour. Food itself becomes more central too. His wife describes the change she sees in her husband: "You seem to live here from one meal to another. Quite opposite to what you did in Finland, where you ate nothing at all."[43] To begin with food is irrelevant to the narrator but towards the end of the book he appraises the food served by a famous restaurant with culinary zest.

In terms of food, the availability of fresh and, from a Finnish point of view, exotic ingredients is a pleasure. Where Peter Mayle describes getting truffles, the Finnish Tynkkynen is satisfied just to admire the fact that you can get fresh berries during the winter. All three works describe visits to the market as an essential part of life in Provence, as well as fresh bread. Kyrönseppä even dedicates a whole chapter to praising the local *baquette* of his village. The Finnish writers are unanimous about the supremacy of French cooking, which is also apparent in Timo Tuomi's travel book *Jalan halki Ranskan* ("On foot though France", 2003). The author describes his journey on foot from Northern to Southern France. Tuomi stays overnight both in hotels and youth hostels. The meal at the end of a long day is nearly as important as the walk itself. Without exception, every meal is described in detail, often giving the menu of a number of courses.

Conclusions

The significance of travelling to Southern France varies widely in this literature. For Tynkkynen, the Riviera is the south where one escapes everyday life. The holiday makes a welcome break from normal everyday life, so *Valkoinen sohva Rivieralla* is also a treatise on a life crisis at a certain age. Vakkuri is a cultural traveller who attempts to describe Provence in the typical style of travel guides. His book also tells us of a man's survival in a strange culture. Kyrönseppä describes France as done and dusted, a period in life which is over. The author reflects on his views on Provence and contends that the attraction of Southern France "is largely due to the images already present in the mind".[44] The strength of ready-made cultural images is apparent in the Finnish books on Provence. In a way, they continue the internationally known series of descriptions about Provence. In their field, they repeat the familiar, cultural characteristics which are understood as "being French".

The descriptions of Provence have a connection to earlier Finnish travel literature but they also display a new Finnish phenomenon, the seasonal living abroad. Those Finns who live in Southern France during the winter do not regard themselves as tourists. They see themselves as travellers who are able to sense and know the special characteristics of where they live. The books are different in their approach, but they all have one common ingredient, humour. Vakkuri displays this humour with sarcasm, Tynkkynen with self-irony, and Kyrönseppä with situational comedy. Kyrönseppä's humour is also based on the way a Finn views a typical local feature.

Translated by Hannele Marttila

NOTES

1. Selänniemi 1996, 11,12.
2. Selänniemi 1996, 174.
3. Karisto 2000, 7.
4. Tynkkynen 2003, 38–39.
5. Sepänmaa 1998, 19.
6. Vakkuri 1997, 10.
7. Sepänmaa 1998, 13.
8. Kyrönseppä 2004, 7–8.
9. Kyrönseppä 2004, 9–10.
10. Jokinen & Veijola 1990, 33.
11. Selänniemi 1996, 184.
12. Hapuli 2003, 82–84.
13. Varpio 1997, 212.
14. Varpio 1997, 9.
15. Jokinen & Veijola 1990, 45.
16. Kyrönseppä 2004, 91–92.
17. Tynkkynen 2003, 23.
18. Tynkkynen 2003, 87.
19. Tynkkynen 2003, 208–209.
20. Sepänmaa 1998, 19.
21. Kinnunen 1993, 206.
22. Hapuli 2003, 145.
23. Compare with Selänniemi 1996, 173.
24. Piela 1993, 238–239.
25. Kinnunen 1993, 208.
26. Tynkkynen 2003, 19.
27. Selänniemi 1996, 221.
28. Varpio 1997, 212.
29. Varpio 1997, 212.
30. Selänniemi 1996, 25–26.
31. Vakkuri 1997, 93.
32. Selänniemi 1996, 176.
33. Vakkuri 1997, 42.

34. Varpio 1997, 213–214; See also Hapuli 2003, 24.
35. Hapuli 2003, 21.
36. Kyrönseppä 2004, 201.
37. Compare with Selänniemi 1996, 203.
38. Vakkuri 1997, 31.
39. Vakkuri 1997, 64.
40. Tynkkynen 2003, 255.
41. Nyytäjä 2002, 94.
42. Nyytäjä 2002, 94.
43. Vakkuri 1997, 260.
44. Kyrönseppä 2004, 214.

BIBLIOGRAPHY

Hapuli, Ritva 2003. *Ulkomailla. Maailmansotien välinen maailma suomalaisnaisten silmin.* Suomalaisen Kirjallisuuden Seuran Toimituksia 911. Helsinki: Suomalaisen Kirjallisuuden Seura.

Jokinen, Eeva & Veijola, Soile 1990. *Oman elämänsä turistit.* Alkoholipoliittinen tutkimuslaitos. Helsinki: Valtion painatuskeskus.

Karisto, Antti 2000. Suomalaiselämää Espanjassa. Helsinki: Suomalaisen Kirjallisuuden Seura.

Kinnunen, Eeva-Liisa 1993. Läskiä kantapäissä. Huumori naisten omaelämäkerroissa. Piela, Ulla (ed.), *Aikanaisia. Kirjoituksia naisten omaelämäkerroista.* Tietolipas 137. Helsinki: Suomalaisen Kirjallisuuden Seura, 188–212.

Kyrönseppä, Kari 2004 (2002). *Provencen syleilyssä.* Helsinki: Otava.

Nyytäjä, Outi 2002. Maailman laidalla. Kertomuksia Bretagnesta. Helsinki: Tammi.

Piela, Ulla 1993. Arjen unelmat. Piela, Ulla (eds), *Aikanaisia. Kirjoituksia naisten omaelämäkerroista.* Tietolipas 137. Helsinki: Suomalaisen Kirjallisuuden Seura, 235–255.

Selänniemi, Tom 1996. Matka ikuiseen kesään. Kulttuuriantropologinen näkökulma suomalaisten etelänmatkailuun. Suomalaisen Kirjallisuuden Seuran toimituksia 649. Helsinki: Suomalaisen Kirjallisuuden Seura.

Sepänmaa, Yrjö 1998. Matkan estetiikkaa. Matka koettuna ja kokemus teoksena. Hakkarainen, Marja-Leena & Koistinen, Tero (eds), *Matkakirja. Artikkeleita kirjallisista matkoista mieleen ja maailmaan.* Joensuun yliopisto: Kirjallisuuden ja kulttuurin tutkimuksia n:o 9. Joensuu, 13–34.

Tynkkynen, Merja 2003. *Valkoinen sohva Rivieralla.* Helsinki: Kustannusosakeyhtiö Nemo.

Vakkuri, Aaro 1997. *Kylä Provencen taivaalla.* Helsinki: WSOY.

Varpio, Yrjö 1997. *Matkalla moderniin Suomeen. 1800-luvun suomalainen matkakirjallisuus.* Suomalaisen Kirjallisuuden Seuran Toimituksia 681. Helsinki: Suomalaisen Kirjallisuuden Seura.

KATRI TANNI

Perspectives on Australian Multiculturalism

Go West – Life is peaceful there
Go West – In the open air
Go West – Where the skies are blue
Go West – This is what we're gonna do

(…)

Together – We will love the beach
Together – We will learn and teach
Together – Change our pace of life
Together – We will work and strive[1]

These lyrics by the popular group Village People in the late 1970s perfectly fit the history of Finnish immigration to Australia after the Second World War. The expectations and experiences of the Finnish emigrants under the Southern Cross[2] has, to a considerable extent, been affected, even shaped, by the natural wonders of Australia, such as the blue skies, the sunshine, and beaches. Finns who decided to seek a new life in Australia did so under the impression, at least that they were, initially, going to a Western country, despite the fact that they were traveling geographically to the East. Australia was, and still is, widely considered as a Western country due to the fact that British colonials transmitted "Britishness" and, thus, Western traditions to Australia from the eighteen century onwards. Despite Australia's strong British cultural heritage, however, the country has been transformed into a colorful mixture of people of different nationalities since the Second World War.

Aim of the Paper and Methodology

This setting offers a fascinating field for research and raises several important issues. Traditionally the transformation of Australia into a multicultural nation has been covered from a macrohistory point of view, but this article approaches and evaluates Australian multiculturalism at the microhistorical level. Specifically, living in multicultural Australia is evaluated from the point of view of Finnish-born women who have experienced the changes in Australian society since the Second World War. Women were selected as a reference group, as it has been suggested by, for example, Olavi Koivukangas that Finnish women have adjusted to Australia better than men, and, because there are indications that women in particular have established contacts with people from other cultures.[3]

Life experiences, level of adjustment, and identity of the Finns living in Australian multicultural society is an untapped field of study.[4] This article aims to offer an insight into these issues by concentrating on everyday experiences of Finnish-born women in Australia, their relations both with other Finns and with people from other cultures living in Australia. These contacts are considered from three perspectives, since, in terms of cultural exchange, three levels of interaction can be identified as taking place in countries which have high levels of immigrants. Two Australian social scientists, M. L. Kovacs and A. J. Cropley, who have studied migrant assimilation, argue that immigration can be viewed as a process "in which two highly organized value systems come into contact, the one represented by the immigrant, the other by the receiving society,"[5] but I would argue that especially in the case of Australia, a third level of cultural interaction must be taken into account as immigrants interact with each other. In addition to this approach, the individual histories of Finnish-born women in Australia are placed in the context of the population history of Australia and its transformation into a multicultural society.

Due to the presumption that Finnish women in Australia have more contacts with people from other cultures than Finnish men, a research questionnaire was distributed to first generation Finnish-born women in Australia who attended a Finnish Women's day in Canberra on 22 October 2005.[6] The questionnaire had two aims. Firstly, it was designed to reveal the national identity of these women, their attachment to both Finland and Australia, and their images and perceptions of these countries having lived several decades in Australia. The second aim of the questionnaire was to identify the level of interaction between Finnish women and other Finns and people from other cultures in Australia. These two research questions hypothesize that Finnish-born women in Australia have kept a tight hold on their Finnish cultural background and that they have formed lively contacts with each other. Based on the population history of Australia with its biased connotation of being a "White British Outpost in the Pacific", it was assumed that first generation Finnish women in Australia did not have intensive contacts with non-Europeans.

For the purpose of this article, sixty-five Finnish-born women who settled in Australia after the Second World War were questioned. The majority of them, 88 per cent, migrated to Australia during the period of high migration in 1958–1973.[7] The average age of these women on arrival was 27, which means that the majority of them were adults, whereas 20 per cent of those questioned arrived in Australia when they were less than 18 years old. At the time the questionnaire was distributed, these Finnish-born women were approaching the age of retirement; their average age was 62. During their life

65

in Australia, slightly over half of these women had been housewives or had
worked in casual jobs, such as dressmaking or cleaning, whereas only twenty-
three per cent did clerical or public service work. Thus, from the Australian
point of view, these women were not widely an answer to Australia's need
for laborers, as the Australian government was particularly interested in
attracting European migrants to replace Australians in workforce who were
moving into the white-collar sector.[8] Against this background and due to
the nature of this sample group, careful generalizations can be made on the
basis of the answers provided by these Finnish women about their everyday
life experiences in multicultural Australia. It has to be pointed out that, for
the purpose of this article, this group of sixty-five Finnish-born women is
evaluated as an entity and no cross comparisons between each women are
attempted.

Finns and Emigration to Australia in the Twentieth Century

On the eve of the Second World War, in which Australia participated as a
member of the British Commonwealth, there were only seven million people
living in Australia. The shortage of people in Australia was particularly
striking as they inhabited a continent double the size of continental Europe.[9]
Another striking characteristic of the Australian population at that time was
that it was essentially of European descent.[10] This European, particularly
British, character of Australia was affirmed at the inauguration of the
Australian Federation in 1901. The White Australia Policy, which has been
a racially restrictive guideline for Australian population policy since the late
nineteenth Century prohibiting immigration of non-Europeans, was taken
as a guideline for building the Australian nation, and its effect was seen in
the composition of the Australian population. Indeed, the White Australia
Policy, although not set down in law, effectively prevented non-European
coming to Australia. In practice, it was the task of the immigration authorities
to check and affirm that successful applicants to Australia were at least
75 per cent of European descent. However, for Finns and other Northern-
Europeans Australia's racially biased immigration policy did not present
any obstacles. According to an Australian population historian James Jupp,
even in the nineteenth century when administrators adhered to a racially
rigid population policy, Nordic people were warmly welcomed due to their
cultural and physical similarities with the British.[11]

The preference given to Northern-Europeans continued after the Second
World War when Australian officials became truly aware of the lack of
population on their continent. The Second World War reached Australian
shores in the forms of attacks by the Japanese and the fact was that Australia
was only saved by the intervention of the US. As a result, Australian
politicians started to plan a postwar immigration program which would, in the
future, ensure steady population growth and, thus, a better ability to defend
the country. The first Minister for Immigration, the Labor Party's Arthur
Calwell gave his ministerial statement on immigration in the Australian
Federal Parliament in August 1945. He declared that Australia would start to

seek "new healthy citizens who are determined to become good Australians by adoption".[12] These new healthy citizens, who were supposed to assimilate smoothly into Australian society, initially meant Western-European and Nordic people. In order to entice these people to migrate to Australia on a large scale, the Australian government offered assisted passages, that is, free trips to Australia from 1954 onwards to people from the US, Sweden, Switzerland, Norway, Denmark, and Finland.[13] Apart from the number of immigrants, another factor to which immigration officials paid particular attention was the gender structure, or balance, of the immigrants. Women in particular were warmly welcomed to balance the male prominence in Australia and, thus, assure the natural renewal of the population. A shortage of women in Australia before the Second World War can be seen, for instance, even in the case of the Finns. According to Koivukangas, there were already 1,158 Finnish men in Australia in 1947 but only 215 women.[14]

The decision of the Australian government to entice more newcomers was well received by the Finns. In comparison with Scandinavians, the Finns responded better to the warm Australian invitation. It seems that conditions in Finland after the War were indeed prompting Finns to move to Western countries, especially to Sweden, the US, Canada, and Australia. The end of the 1950s and the end of the 1960s were particularly high periods of Finnish immigration to Australia. Statistics reveal that 1958–1959 and 1959–1960 saw high levels of immigration from Finland to Australia: in 1956–1958, 679 Finns arrived in Australia on a long-term and permanent basis, whilst in 1959–1960 a staggering 4,467 Finns arrived on Australia's shores.[15] Transformation of Finnish society from agricultural to industrial society and Australian government's appealing recruitment programs were factors contributing to the escalation of immigration to Australia. After a more subdued phase in the early 1960s, another peak in immigration occurred in the late 1960s when several hundred Finns arrived per year.[16] However, these were the last peak years in terms of recruited European migrants to Australia. Changes in the international situation in terms of migration patterns, and changes made by the Australian government severely reduced migration flows in the early 1970s. For example, the newly-elected Labor Party government terminated the assisted passage schemes in 1972, which effectively meant that Australian immigration in the future was to be regulated and administered according to new criteria. Up to this point, and, thus, during the main Finnish migration period, from 1959 to 1973, a total of 11,772 Finns arrived in Australia with the intention of settling permanently in the country.[17]

Identity of Finnish Women in Multicultural Australia

What kind of experiences and what sort of lives have Finnish women had in Australia that was gradually turning into a truly multicultural society? Have they established a close and tight ethnic group or have they assimilated into Australian society? James Jupp argues that the large numbers of Nordic migrants who leave Australia to return to their homeland indicates that they experience considerable difficulties in settling permanently in Australia.

However, a similar pattern can also be found among the British, Dutch, and German immigrants to Australia.[18] It must be pointed out that there are many other factors apart from cultural differences and different lifestyles that affect on the decision to return to one's home country, such as relatives or improved economic conditions.

As for Finns who have settled in Australia, it is interesting to ask about their recollections of Finland and their views about their current identity; whether they feel Finnish, Australian, or consider themselves as expatriate Finns. The Director of the University of Adelaide's Centre for Intercultural Studies and Multicultural Education, Jerzy Smolicz, has defined national identification as "the individual's self description in national or ethnic terms", which, he argues, includes both "the subjective sense of identifying with a particular group, as well as the objective indicators of membership, such as ancestry, language or birthplace".[19] Supporting this theory, Koivukangas argues that the preservation of Finnish identity among Finns in Australia, as in the whole of the southern hemisphere, has depended on their resorting to Finnish culture.[20] Indeed, "Finnishness" has been maintained ever since the early days of Finnish immigration to Australia through strong communal links provided by Finnish societies, Finnish relatives, and Finnish religious organizations, such as the Lutheran church and the Pentecostal church.[21]

Within this theoretical framework, the sample group of sixty-five Finnish-born women were asked whether they define themselves as Finns, Australians, or expatriates. Interestingly, more than half of them, 58 per cent, identified themselves solely as Finnish and 23 per cent identified themselves as expatriates, which also suggests that they have preserved a sense of Finnishness. In addition, nine per cent selected a mixture of the given categories, that is, they chose all, or selected two, of the different options. Surprisingly, only seven per cent described themselves as Australians. This signals a strong adherence to Finnishness and to their Finnish identity. These results are especially significant bearing in mind that the majority of these Finnish women left Finland over thirty years ago. It would appear that in defining themselves as Finns, hereby preserving their Finnish national identity, they have a significant resource, as a group, which, however, might affect their relations with other ethnic groups in Australia.

Jerzy Smolicz, D. Hudson and M. Seacombe argue that ethnic identity provides an indispensable bond which holds human groups together.[22] Based on this definition, it seems that the national identity of Finnish women in Australia is particularly strong and well maintained. This can be verified by the fact that almost 70 per cent of the respondents said that they met other Finns several times a week, whilst 24 per cent met other Finns approximately once a week. Does this intense connection among Finnish women signal that they have not adjusted to multicultural Australia, or that the Finns as a group are in some sense separate from Australian society? Not necessarily, since according to a theory concerning national identity developed by a Polish sociologist and specialist in the sociology of culture, Antonina Kloskowska, an individual can have several national identifications. Kloskowska argues that it is possible to develop both single and dual national identities, and an individual can, for instance, effectively have a bivalent national identity, which means that he or she is competent in two cultures.[23] In the case of these Finnish women and their adherence to Finnish identity, more factors need to be discussed to find out whether they are competent in both Finnish and Australian cultures, and in addition, how intense relations they establish with other migrants in Australia.

Contacts Between Finns and Other Cultures in Australia

As mentioned above, Finnish women in Australia seem to retain a tight hold on their Finnish heritage and this creates an interesting background to the level of interaction they have with people from other cultures in Australia. Thus, when asked with which ethnic group or nationality they had the most frequent contact, except other Finns, 66 per cent selected "Australians". This category is problematic in that defining "Australian" is difficult due to the cultural mix of Australian society, and, therefore, too far-reaching conclusions cannot be drawn. However, the rest of the answers can offer an insight into the relations between Finns and people from other cultures. It is surprising that only ten per cent of these women said they had regular contacts with Scandinavians and nine per cent said they had most contacts with people from some other part of the world, such as Asia or Southern-Europe (these examples were given in the questionnaire). As this last category encompasses a massive geographical and culturally colorful area and yet only a minuscule number of those questioned selected it, one might come to the conclusion that Finnish women do not interact much with Southern European or Asian people, for instance. Regarding their contacts with Asians, one explanation might be that these Finns established contact networks during the first years of their residence in Australia in the 1960s and early 1970s, when there were not a great number of Asians or non-Europeans living in Australia.

Another question designed to reveal the cultural interaction of Finnish women in Australia with "others" asked them to describe which cultures, other than Finnish, they have been most effectively influenced by. A substantial proportion, two-thirds said they had been mostly influenced by Australian culture. Only seven per cent mentioned Asia, whereas a European country was the answer in 12 per cent of the cases. Furthermore, Nordic countries were mentioned by only three per cent of respondents. As with the question about contacts with other people, the answer "Australian" does not reveal much since, as indicated earlier, the concept "Australian" can contain a great variety of cultures. Having said this, one must keep in mind, though, that it is common to consider that Australian culture still signifies British cultural traditions. However, one can conclude, based on the frequency of the references to Australian culture, that Finnish women in Australia have experienced the richness of Australian multiculturalism which offers a variety of cultures from which individuals are able to select or absorb several cultural influences. Therefore, it might be the case that Finns absorb influences from Asian cultures, for example, without actually noticing or paying too much attention to it, but this suggestion cannot be convincingly verified here.

Finnishness and Finnish traditions in Australia are maintained by keeping contacts with other Finns. Here, Finnish-born women, who gathered in Canberra to meet other Finnish women in October 2005, enjoy Finnish-style coffee and buns. Photo: Ritva Nuorala.

The Goal of Assimilation in Australia and the Preservation of Western Traditions

Australian governments from the Second World War until the mid-1960s specifically made the assimilation of immigrants as a national goal. The intention was that new migrants would give up their old national identities, that is, smoothly alienate themselves from their old traditions, and adapt to "the Australian way of life". According to an Australian scholar, John Murphy, Australian officials encouraged the assimilation process for new immigrants by planning, selecting, and imposing immigration quotas and, in addition, by keeping an eye on what the economy could handle and what public opinion regarded as acceptable.[24] Officials attempted to define and introduce Australians as fun- and sport-loving, natural people who were committed to a "fair deal" for all. However, this image of Australians and therefore model for new immigrants to emulate was developed within British cultural boundaries. Researchers of immigration and multiculturalism, Stephen Castles, Bill Cope, Mary Kalantzis and Michael Morrissey, argue that the doctrine of assimilation did much to "reinforce both the sense of homogeneity and the sense of superiority of the Anglophone population".[25]

From the late 1970s onwards, minority cultures within Australia were acknowledged as a national asset and given a chance to flourish. The first initiatives in this direction were made by the Minister for Immigration, Al Grassby, in 1973, when he offered a new image for Australia as "a united family of the nation and a mosaic of cultures".[26] In the process, the goal of assimilation was replaced by a policy of integrating immigrants in the 1970s, and the Fraser Government in particular introduced significant initiatives to review programmes and services for immigrants after their arrival and to make recommendations for their improvement. As a result, cultural differences were regarded in a new light. For example, in 1977, the Fraser Government proclaimed that "every person should be able to maintain his or her culture without prejudice or disadvantage and should be encouraged to understand and embrace other cultures".[27] A similar liberal atmosphere affected Australian relations with Asian countries. The main cause for problematic relations between Australia and Asian countries until the early 1970s was the maintenance of the White Australia policy.[28] The effect of the White Australia policy, although Australian officials denied its very existence, was particularly well revealed by population censuses. For example, according to the census of 1961, less than one per cent of the Australian population had been born outside Australia or Europe.[29]

It seems that the White Australia policy also determined, to the considerable extent, the way of life of Finnish women in Australia as they had maintained a tight hold on their "Western" traditions and contacts. When asked which culture or geographical area they considered the most unfamiliar, most of the women, 26 per cent, answered Asia. Africa was the answer in 17 per cent of the questionnaires and the Middle-East was chosen by 8 per cent of the women. In addition, 20 per cent answered that Asia, Africa, and the Middle-East taken together were the most foreign cultures. These results support the hypothesis that although Asian cultures are now well represented in Australia so much so that, from the 1980s onwards, there have been even claims of an "Asianisation of Australia", migrants who came to Australia before the country eased its racially-biased immigration restrictions still consider non-European cultures as foreign.[30]

As pointed out earlier, the difference with non-European cultures does not mean that the immigrants who arrived between 1945 and 1972 have not accepted non-Europeans. Two scholars of Australian immigration policy and its restrictions, Lakisiri Jayasuriya and Kee Pookong argue that, due to the establishment of the immigration recruitment program from the late 1940s onwards, Australia has been transformed from a parochial monocultural society to a cosmopolitan, polyethnic society, "characterized by a marked degree of diversity and pluralism in all areas of social life".[31] During the years of massive European immigration to Australia, it was other European migrants with whom Finns formed the closest relation because of their cultural proximity. It can be argued that the Finns in Australia first learnt to live with other Europeans, a phase which essentially taught them to accept new and different cultures. Thus, it must be pointed out that there are significant cultural differences between Europeans as well. One Finnish woman recalled how, in the late 1960s, after being in Australia only a couple of months, she was astonished and confused when an Italian female colleague at work approached her kissing her on both cheeks. Because neither she nor the Italian spoke English, this Finnish woman had no idea why the Italian woman was kissing her in this way. She recalls further how this conduct was something new and unfamiliar to her as people in Finland at that time were not used to even seeing emotional expressions in public.[32]

Despite certain cultural differences, it seems that Finnish women have had positive experiences in Australia which implies their smooth reception of Australia's multicultural character. The majority of these women had positive perceptions and comments concerning both Finland and Australia. This sample group of 65 Finnish women was asked to describe briefly the best characteristics of Finland and Australia. Interestingly, the most striking feature of these answers was that in both cases, nature and people were mentioned most often as being the most valuable qualities of these two countries. It is no surprise that their image and recollections of Finland were somewhat romanticized. Thus, altogether 52 per cent mentioned subjects relating to nature, such as light summer nights, unpolluted nature, greenness, and the clear difference between four seasons. Slightly over one-third mentioned that relatives and friends in Finland were the most valuable factors for them. Moreover, the trustworthy nature of the Finnish national character was warmly remembered by 12 per cent of respondents, and childhood memories were cherished by 11 per cent of the women. Only two out of the total 65 questionnaires reflected some alienation from Finland. One woman, who arrived in Australia in 1960 and who rarely visited Finland, wrote that she had no idea what the best characteristics of Finland were.[33] Similarly, one woman, who had arrived in 1971, admitted that on her last visit to Finland she had felt as if she was in a foreign country.[34]

Just as Finland was seen mostly in a positive light with several non-material values being mentioned, so too in Australia's case, climate and natural wonders were often mentioned (43 per cent), or family and relatives who were also in Australia (14 per cent). However, clearly, the most frequently referred appealing attribute in Australia was its free atmosphere, generally known as "the Australian way of life". This characteristic was mentioned in 48 per cent of the questionnaires, and in addition, nine per cent mentioned Australian multiculturalism as Australia's most valuable asset. It is clear that for these women, as for Finns generally, nature and climate are both highly valued. However, even more striking is the fact that these answers about the characteristics most appreciated by these Finnish women clearly demonstrate the success of Australia's transformation into a multicultural society and the integration of immigrants into the free and easy-going Australian way of life.

The success of Australia's transformation is also borne out by other case studies. Based on his case study of higher degree students and their personal memoirs on multiculturalism in Australia, Smolicz suggests that the Australian multicultural agenda has succeeded, which, he argues, indicates that a stable and cohesive multicultural nation can be established.[35] This is also supported by the fact that during the course of its history, Australia has only once, on December 2005 in Sydney southern suburbs, experienced severe racial riots between ethnically different minority groups.

A Japanese-born student came to buy Finnish "pulla" from a Finnish stand during a multicultural week in Canberra, in February 2004. This is just one indicator that different traditions are alive and mix smoothly in Australia.
Photo: Katri Tanni.

Conclusion

Even though this case study of Finnish women in Australia reveals the maintenance of a strong Finnish heritage and identity, it does not downplay the fact that Australia is seen as a good place to live with many positive features. This supports Kloskowska's theory on bivalent national identity and its realization among Finnish women in Australia as they seem to be competent in both cultures, and in addition, adapt well into Australian multicultural society. Especially since the late 1970s, Finnishness, as other minority cultures, has been given a place to be part of, and a role in forming a multicultural Australian nation. This article has shown that Finnish women in Australia have had a fervent desire to cherish and practice their culture, for instance, through having strong contacts with other Finns.

Conclusions concerning the intensity of contacts with non-European people or the absorbing of influences from non-European cultures is more complicated to draw. Nevertheless, the answers of this sample group demonstrate that there is not much interaction between Finns and non-Europeans peoples, even though Australia nowadays offers particularly good opportunities for such interaction. Two possible explanations can be given for the lack of contacts with, or references to, the "East". One is that Finnish women have defined themselves strongly as representatives of a Western cultural heritage, and live in a society with strong British roots. At the time of their arrival, in the 1950s and 1960s, Australian society was indeed culturally a duplicate of Britain, and it was the purpose of Australian governments to strengthen newcomers' Western values. Another explanation is that Australian multiculturalism has truly succeeded in reducing the differences between cultures. This can be seen in this study, for example, by the large number of references given to "the Australian way of life", the free and open atmosphere in Australia, and its multicultural character. In short, according to the lyrics of Village People in their hit Go West, it seems that through the experiences of these Finnish women, the Australian multicultural quest has been successful. Therefore, it can be concluded that from the perspective of these Finnish women, life has been peaceful in Australia's open air.

NOTES

1. A song by Village people, Go West 1979.
2. Australia is generally referred to as being "under the Southern Cross", which is a constellation in the shape of a cross used to determine the direction of the South Pole when traveling in the southern hemisphere.
3. Koivukangas 1986, 283–284.
4. Koivukangas 1975, 1986, 1998; Korkiasaari 1989.
5. Kovacs & Cropley 1975, 18.
6. Questionnaires handed out at the Finnish Women's Day in Canberra, arranged by the Finnish Lutheran Church on 22 October 2005.
7. The major arrival years for these women reflect peak years in Finnish immigration as a whole, since 10 of those questioned arrived in Australia in 1960, 8 arrived in 1968, 13 in 1969 and 10 arrived in Australia in 1970.
8. Castles & Cope & Kalantzis & Morrissey 1988, 39.
9. http://www.ga.gov.au/education/facts/dimensions/compare.htm, (Accessed on October 26, 2005.)
10. Markus 1994, 151.
11. Jupp 1999, 28.
12. Calwell 1945, 4911–4915.
13. Australia concluded the first Assisted Passage agreement with Great-Britain in 1947, followed by similar agreements with Italy and the Netherlands in 1952. Lack & Templeton 1989, 218.
14. Koivukangas 1986, 277.
15. Department of Immigration, 1961, Australian Immigration. Quarterly Statistical Bulletin, Vol. 2, No.1, Table 4.

16. Department of Immigration, 1968, Australian Immigration. Quarterly Statistical Summary,. Vol. 3, No. 8. Table 11.
17. Department of Immigration 1973, Australian Immigration. Quarterly Statistical Summary, Vol. 3, No. 27. Table 11.
18. Jupp 1999, 38.
19. Smolicz 1999, 55.
20. Koivukangas 1999, 208.
21. Koivukangas 1986, 297–298.
22. Smolicz & Hudson & Seacombe 1998, 319.
23. Kloskowska 1993, 5–6.
24. Murphy 1993, 137.
25. Castles & Cope & Kalantzis & Morrissey 1988, 45.
26. Lack & Templeton 1995, 218, 219.
27. The Galbally Report 1978, 3–5.
28. Goldsworthy 2001, 6–8.
29. Official year book of the Commonwealth of Australia 1965, 278.
30. Jayasuriya & Pookong 1999, 1–2.
31. Jayasuriya & Pookong 1999, 10.
32. Questionnaire no. 2.
33. Questionnaire no. 15.
34. Questionnaire no. 22.
35. Smolicz 1999, 56.

SOURCES

Printed Sources

Commonwealth Parliamentary Debates 1945. Australian Government Publishing Services, Vol. 184, Canberra.
Department Of Immigration 1961. Australian immigration. Quarterly Statistical Bulletin, Vol. 2, No. 1, November 1961.
Department Of Immigration 1968. Australian Immigration. Quarterly Statistical Summary, Vol. 3, No. 8, June 1968.
Department Of Immigration 1973. Australian Immigration. Quarterly Statistical Summary, Vol. 3, No. 27, March 1973.
The Galbally Report 1978. Australian Government Publishing Services, Canberra.
Official Year Book Of The Commonwealth Of Australia 1965. Commonwealth bureau of census and statistics, No. 51, Canberra.

Interviews

Questionnaires delivered for Finnish-born women in the Finnish Women's Day in Canberra. Arranged by the Finnish Lutheran Church in Canberra, on October 22, 2005.

Internet sources

Australian Government, Geoscience Australia, Australia's size compared. Http://www.
ga.gov.au/education/facts/dimensions/compare.htm.

BIBLIOGRAPHY

Castles, Stephen & Cope, Bill & Kalantzis, Mary & Morrissey, Michael 1988. *Mistaken
Identity. Multiculturalism and the Demise of Nationalism in Australia,* Sydney:
Pluto Press.

Goldsworthy, David 2001. *Facing North: A Century of Australian Engagement with Asia,*
Volume 1, Melbourne: Melbourne University Press.

Jayasuriya, Lakisiri & Pookong, Kee 1999. *The Asianisation of Australia? Some Facts
about the myths.* Melbourne: Melbourne University Press.

Jupp, James 1999. Seeking whiteness: the recruitment of Nordic immigrants to Oceania.
Scandinavian and European Migration to Australia and New Zealand. Olavi Koivukangas
(ed.), *Migration Studies C 13,* Vammala: Institute of Migration, 28–41.

Kloskowska, Antonina 1993. National Identification and the transgression of National
Boundaries: The Steps towards Universalisation. *Dialogue and Humanism 4,* Warsaw:
Warsaw University, 5–17.

Koivukangas, Olavi 1975. *Suomalainen siirtolaisuus Australiaan toisen maailmansodan
jälkeen,* Kokkola: Siirtolaisuustutkimuksia.

—— 1986. *Sea, Gold and Sugarcane. Attraction versus Distance. Finns in Australia
1851–1947,* Migration Studies C 8, Turku: Institute of Migration.

—— 1998. *Kaukomaiden kaipuu. Suomalaiset Afrikassa, Australiassa, Uudessa-Seelannissa
ja Latinalaisessa Amerikassa.* Suomalaisen siirtolaisuuden historia 4, Jyväskylä.

—— 1999. Finns in the southern hemisphere – a comparative approach. *Scandinavian
and European migration to Australia and New Zealand,* Olavi Koivukangas (ed.),
Migration Studies C 13, Vammala: Institute of Migration, 185–214.

Korkiasaari, Jouni 1989. *Suomalaiset maailmalla. Suomen siirtolaisuus ja ulkosuomalaiset
entisajoista tähän päivään,* Turku: Siirtolaisuusinstituutti.

Kovacs, M. L. & Cropley, A. J. 1975. *Immigrants and Society: Alienation and Assimilation,*
Sydney: McGraw-Hill Book Company.

Lack, John & Templeton, Jacqueline 1989. *Sources of Australian Immigration History. Volume
1: 1901–1945.* Melbourne: University of Melbourne Publications and Printing Services.

—— 1995. *Bold Experiment. A Documentary History of Australian Immigration since
1945.* Oxford: Oxford University Press.

Markus, Andrew 1994. *Australian race relations 1788–1993,* Sydney: Allen & Unwin.

Murphy, Brian 1993. *The Other Australia. Experiences of Migration,* Cambridge:
Cambridge University Press.

Smolicz, Jerzy 1999. National identity and cultural valence in an ethnical pluralist setting:
the case of Australia. *Scandinavian and European Migration to Australia and New
Zealand.* Olavi Koivukangas (ed.), Migration Studies C 13, Vammala: Institute of
Migration, 55–69.

Smolicz, J. J. & Hudson, D. M. & Seacombe, M. J. 1998. Border Crossing in 'Multicultural
Australia': A Study of Cultural Valence. *Journal of Multilingual and Multicultural
Development,* Vol. 19, No. 4, St Francis Xavier University, Canada 318–336.

The Second Generation

The Second Conflict

HANNA SNELLMAN

Going to School in a Diaspora

Within a decade, from 1960 to 1970, the Finnish population in Sweden more than doubled. In 1960, there were 100,000 people living in Sweden who had been born in Finland and were also Finnish citizens. In 1970, the figure was more than 200,000 and in 1980 the figure was 250,000. However, if we add to the figure people who had not been born in Finland but had Finnish by background, the figure is even bigger. In 1980, in Sweden, there were approximately 131,000 Finnish children under the age of 18 who belong to the second generation. The second generation is defined as persons whose parents, or at least one parent, were born in Finland. At the turn of the millennium of Sweden's population of nine million there were about half a million Finns of whom almost half belonged to the second generation.[1]

Finnish immigrants in Sweden have not usually been conceptualized as a diaspora. Traditionally, the concept has applied primarily to Jews, Armenians, and Greeks. However, lately it has been applied to emigrants, refugees, expatriates and labor migrants.[2] These migrant populations have maintained (to some degree) emotional and social ties with their original homeland.[3] The new, broader definition of the concept regards any dispersion of a people as a diaspora, any segment of a people living outside the homeland for whatever reason and for however short or long a time.[4] In short, a diaspora is simply about not being in one's homeland.[5] However, it has been argued that the definition is so broad that the concept is losing its strength. The universalization of a diaspora, paradoxically, means the disappearance of a diaspora, argues Rogers Brubaker.[6]

Several scholars have sketched out the core elements that make up a diaspora.[7] According to Rogers Brubaker, they are dispersion, homeland orientation and boundary-maintenance. Finns in Sweden have crossed state borders thus fulfilling the criterion of dispersion. They have maintained a collective memory or myth of their homeland, and for a long time members of the first generation cherished the idea of returning "home" thus fulfilling the criterion of homeland orientation. Because Finland and Sweden are neighboring countries, forming a transnational community, even before the arrival of e-mail and cheap flights, has not been difficult, so fulfilling Brubaker's third criterion of a boundary-maintenance. To what extent

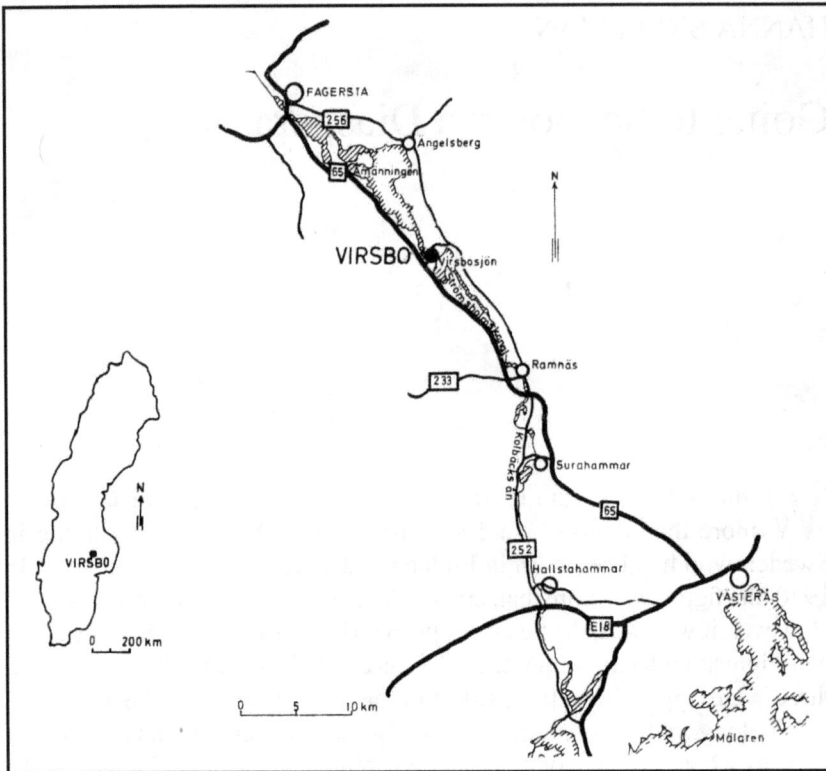

The map of Virsbo area.

and in what form, boundaries are maintained by a second and following generations in the future is a question of some relevance for the existence of a diaspora.[8]

The editors of the book *Diaspora, Identity and Religion* (2004) suggest that "ethnographic close-up studies of [diaspora] experiences are needed to provide a testing ground for theoretical concepts and generalizations". There is a special interest in how diasporic identities are formed over time.[9] This article is an attempt to discuss the Finnish diaspora in Sweden at the beginning of the 1970s, a time when the majority of Finns had only recently migrated to Sweden.

Gathering Data

In the early 1970s, the National Museum of Cultural History (in Swedish *Nordiska museet*), the Department of Ethnology at the University of Jyväskylä, Finland, and the Department of Geography at the University of Umeå, Sweden, launched a research project "Migration Finland–Sweden" dealing with migration from Finland to Sweden after World War Two. Since the 1960s, ethnologists have been interested in contemporary events, not just history.[10] Thus the research project was a reflection of certain changes within ethnology as a discipline. And not only that, it was also a reflection of changes in Swedish society, as well. In 1975, Sweden introduced a new immigration policy, based on integration, not assimilation as earlier.[11] Everyone who lives in Sweden should have the same rights, responsibilities, and opportunities regardless of their ethnic and cultural background. Society should be based on diversity, and differences should be respected as long as the basic democratic values of society are respected.[12]

As a result of the project, there are about 60 binders of material at the Archives of the National Museum of Cultural History in Stockholm. Some research reports have been written based on that material, but there is a lot yet to be written.[13] The material consists mainly of interviews made in Sweden, Virsbo in the Bay of Mälaren area, and Upplands Väsby near Stockholm, as well as interviews conducted in Finland with people who had migrated to Sweden but returned to Finland, or who were from areas where emigration had been typical. Both Finns with Finnish and Finns with Swedish as their mother tongue were interviewed. In addition, field-work notes, photographs, brochures, and protocols of the meetings can be found in the binders.

One of the binders is full of school essays written in 1975 in Virsbo and Upplands Väsby. The essays were written by pupils of different ages and from different backgrounds. Unfortunately, it is not known how the teachers were tutored by the researchers, nor how the teachers instructed the pupils. All the essays were written in Swedish. Not all the pupils were of Finnish descent. Some had Swedish parents, and some had foreign, that is, non-Swedish backgrounds other than Finnish. Some of the essays, especially the ones written by pupils with Swedish as their mother tongue, have fictional themes. The Finnish children had obviously written biographical essays regardless of the actual title of the essay. One gets the impression that writing the essays had not been an unpleasant task for the children. In my opinion, the material is exceptional: it gives us a chance to examine how children experienced the diaspora, both good and bad.[14]

In this article, I will analyze the school essays written by Finnish pupils in Virsbo and Upplands Väsby in order to shed light on the experiences of Finnish immigrant children in 1975, the same year Sweden adopted its new immigration policy.[15]

Restricting the Subject

Because the source material for this article comes from a school setting, a short history of school policy is needed. Only a few Finnish speaking children migrated to Sweden in the 1950s. Parents did not demand instruction in Finnish for them, nor did teachers usually try to arrange it. During the 1960s, a policy of assimilation was in force where the aim was to Swedenize Finnish speaking children as soon as possible, regardless of the child's or parents' wishes. In the 1970s, new goals were set, and the aim was to

An apartment building in Virsbo in 2006. Photo: Hanna Snellman.

arrange instruction in Finnish and teach children to be bi-lingual. In 1975, at the time when the material was collected, Finnish speaking children had – in principle, though not always in practice – the opportunity to receive education in Finnish for 1–2 hours per week or join a mixed class where half of the pupils spoke Swedish as their mother tongue and the other half spoke some other language. Some lessons were taught in Finnish. This was all in line with the integration policy's statement that "immigrant children should have the right to maintain and develop their cultural and linguistic identity in public schools".[16]

From the middle of the1980s, teaching in Finnish was reduced dramatically because of belt-tightening. Parents fiercely protested the new policy. For example, there were even school strikes in Upplands Väsby in 1987. As the flow of Finnish immigration to Sweden stopped at the beginning of the 1970s, there are even fewer Finnish speaking children in Sweden today. Parents' efforts have been crucial in arranging education for them. Schools have become the subject of ethnopolitical debate. From the1990s onwards, some Finnish Swedish schools were founded. Of the nine Finnish Swedish schools in Sweden in 1999, one was in Upplands Väsby.[17]

According to Anette Rosengren, one of the researchers in the "Migration – Finland Sweden" project, Virsbo and Upplands Väsby were chosen for the research because of their typicality. In 1970, Virsbo had circa 2,000 inhabitants of whom 28 per cent were of Finnish descent. A quarter of them spoke Swedish as their first language. The company Wirsbo Bruk had been the employer of the majority of residents for decades. The other important employer was Nordanöverken.[18]

During my fieldwork in Västerås in 2005 I also visited Virsbo. It was easy enough to find the apartment houses some distance away from the center of town, typical homes of Finnish immigrants in every Swedish industrial town. When a geographer Lars-Erik Borgegård wrote his research report from Virsbo, he pointed out that the majority of the inhabitants of Virsbo, 58 per cent of the Swedish and 25 per cent of the Finnish citizens, lived in small houses. The majority of Finns were gathered in two districts with apartment houses built in the 1950s and 1960s.[19]

A description of Upplands Väsby is available in the archives of the Department of Ethnology, at the University of Helsinki. A Finnish ethnology student worked in the local hospital in the winter of 1969–1970 and interviewed three Finnish immigrants. She described Uppland Väsby as follows:

> The community was about 30 km South-West of Stockholm. I heard it is exceptionally Finnish, but I do not know what percentage of the population is Finnish speaking. Upplands Väsby is a lot like all the small communities on the Stockholm–Uppsala railroad. They live in the shadow of Stockholm and get their vitality from there. Traffic heads to Stockholm, not Uppsala, and a lot of people work in Stockholm. The town center of Upplands Väsby is small, even though the community in itself is large in area. Offices, a couple of shopping centers, several banks, and an 'all in one' restaurant-movie theater-pub-dancing hall are in the center.[20]

Upplands Väsby truly is a Finnish community even today. In 1990 it was ranked the sixth biggest Finnish commune in Sweden after Haparanda, Övertorneå, Surahammar, Fagersta and Skinnskatteberg in terms of the number of people born in Finland. Almost ten percent of the commune's population was born in Finland.[21]

In the following, I let the children tell their story. For my analysis, I selected all the essays written by Finnish pupils which did not seem to be fictional in content, but biographical. Altogether, there were fifteen such essays. The pupils did not necessarily say they were Finnish but their names reveal their origins. I have translated the essays from Swedish to English. The citations are transcribed in full. If part of the citation has been left out, it has been marked with – –.

My analysis proceeds in four phases. First, the selection of the essays and determining their Finnish authorship, second, my translation of the essays into English, third, a consideration of how the empirical material is structured, and fourth, my conclusions.

When I Migrated to Sweden

Only one Finnish pupil, 14-year-old Taina[22] had chosen to write her school essay under the title "When I migrated to Sweden".[23] Her narrative is a typical migration story as far as the contents are concerned. However, her essay is exceptionally long and descriptive. She described her move from Evijärvi, in Northern Finland, to Surahammar (near Virsbo), in Sweden in a way that brings home the experiences of these immigrant children. There is hardly any other source material which would do it as well:

> The name of my home village in Finland is Evijärvi. We lived in the country. There was only a store in the village. Therefore, if you wanted to buy clothes, for example, you had to travel further away to a "church village", if you translate the name from Finnish. There was a department store, a bank, a pharmacy, etc. It was some kilometers away. My father owned a garage there. We were seven children. Mother was a housewife and she was at home with us when father was at work. He worked from morning until evening. Sunday was the only day of rest for him.
>
> It was one Sunday when mother said, "what would you say if we moved to Sweden". We were sitting and watching TV. She started explaining that we would have a much better life in Sweden. Perhaps we would have our own house, and in any case father would have a better job. He would travel beforehand in order to find work and an apartment for us. So the day came when father was supposed to travel. He stayed a month, but visited us as well. The first time he came home he said that he had found work in Virsbo, but was living in Surahammar. When he was supposed to go back, my little sister refused to say goodbye, because she was so sad he was leaving again. Then finally the day came when father was back at home to take us to Sweden. In a way it was fun to be able to come to a new country and go to a new school and make new friends, but that is not how it was. My smallest brother was not even a year old when we moved, and I had started third grade [9 years old, H.S]. It was sad to leave my friends and the place where we had lived. I had never traveled in a boat before. It was exciting. We ran around on the boat.
>
> At the harbor there was a car that took us to Surahammar. It was a concrete house we lived in. Then one had to wait for the worst. It was school. We went with father and another man who could speak Swedish. The director was really nice. We would start school the next day. Those first days we were with a teacher who taught us Swedish. When I went to my future class room with the teacher for the first time I was really nervous. She knocked on the door. My real teacher opened the door. She said that I was welcome. Everyone in the class room stared at me, and I blushed.
>
> There was only one girl in the class who was Finnish. There was no-one who I could be with during breaks, and I was totally alone. When I walked home, boys from my class shouted at me "Finnish devil" [finnjävel in Swedish] and spat at me. I did not want to go to school. It was painful to go there. They just mocked or stared at me. The teacher wanted to help me and she talked to me, but I did not understand what she said. One time I was with the Finnish girl from my class. She was

The Finnish class is having a Christmas party in a Swedish school. The picture was taken in 1977 in Västerås. Photo: Maija Parviainen.

so nice to me. We lived half a year in Surahammar. We moved to Virsbo when our house was ready. I hoped it would be better in Virsbo.

There are several Finnish pupils in my class. I had a friend straight away. Now I have no problems. I have a friend who I can rely on and have no problems with the language. Both mother and father are working. We will have lived five years in Sweden, soon.[24]

Four children who wrote essays with the title "About moving to another country"[25] had same kind of experiences even though they were not as verbose as Taina: they did not have friends to play with and they were lonely. The biggest problem was the language. At that time, there were no lessons in Finnish, and the children had to cope without language skills. "It was not nice to move to Sweden, because I could not speak or understand Swedish. I had no play mates", wrote one girl called Tarja, from Virsbo.[26] Her friend, called Arja, also wrote about the lack of friends:

When I moved to Sweden [spelt Svärje instead of Sverige in the original text] I could not speak Swedish and I did not have anyone to play with, but then I got many playmates and I played with them every day. When I moved to Ramnäs I wanted to stay [in the community where she had first lived in Sweden] because I had it cool with my playmates, but I could not and I cried, but the next day we moved to Ramnäs and there I got even more playmates and one of them is Tarja. She was my best playmate and I started playing again and I got even more playmates. When we traveled to Finland, I wanted Tarja to come with us, but she could not, and when we left I gave her a present and I got a present from her.[27]

Esa wrote that it was nice to live in Sweden, but it would be nicer to live in Finland, because there he would have more friends. However, he assumed that those who had been born in Sweden and had moved back to Finland would rather live in Sweden. Leena wrote that it was nice to move to another country for the first time, but that it was a little lonely when one did not have any friends. Perhaps she was referring to the fact that it was common for labor migrants to move from one place to another in search of work – and the children had to follow regardless of their hopes.

Being a Finn in Sweden

Of the essay title choices the title "About being a Finn in Sweden"[28] was the most popular one. Six pupils had chosen to write an essay with under that title. A 14-year-old girl called Ulla from Virsboskolan, in all probability a Swede, had interviewed a Finnish friend called Eeva for her school assignment.

> My name is Eeva. I have lived in Sweden for four years now. First my father moved here and found a job and an apartment. At first we lived in a place which was more or less a barracks. We lived there for two and a half years. At first everyone called me *finnjävel* and other awful names. It made me terribly sad. Now I don't have any problems. At first I did not dare to take my friends home. It was so crowded and dirty. But after a while I brought some friends to my home and they seemed to understand that we had not been given anything better. When we came to Sweden I started fifth grade, because I could only speak a few words of Swedish. Now I am in the ninth grade and have no difficulties with the Swedish language. I could not move back to Kemi. Now we live in a place called Karlskrona.[29]

In her own essay, Eeva describes the everyday life of Finnish immigrants: How fathers went to Sweden first with mothers and children following later to live in homes which were not exactly houses but flimsy barracks.[30] One of the typical features of these first generation immigrants' narratives is descriptions of summer holidays spent in Finland. Fifteen-year-old Timo from Virsbo is waiting for the summer holiday to begin:

> When I moved here I started first grade. It was awful at first. One was totally silent. Now I think there is no big difference between us. When I lived in Finland there was a lot of snow in winter and the summers were warm. But here in Sweden there is hardly any snow in winter. I can speak Swedish quite well, but sometimes it is a problem. One lives here day by day and waits for the summer holiday.[31]

Both writers touch upon a topic which is seldom spoken aloud by the first generation, that is difficulties and even bullying at school. A 14-year-old girl called Pirjo from Rundby school, Upplands Väsby, also wrote about bullying:

> It is awful that they call us *finnjävlar*. It is almost the same in Sweden as it is in Finland, although the language is very difficult. – –. But they mock us in Finland, too. It is good to be able to speak Finnish if your parents are Finnish, and that is why it is important that they have organized Finnish lessons for us. And it is good to live in Sweden, because if one is a Finn, one lives close to Finland. We have learnt so much Swedish that we know Finnish less and do not want to move back to Finland. And we have almost forgotten Finnish. The salaries are better in Sweden than in Finland.[32]

Aune, most likely from the same class, also mentions that Finnish children were bullied when they visited Finland as well:

> It is bad that they are called *finnjävlar*. There are some in Finland who mock us for being Swedes. It is good that there are lessons in Finnish at school, but when there is group work, it would be nice to be with the others. It is nice to be an immigrant in Sweden and not some other country because you don't have to travel so far to be able to meet your relatives in Finland. People have better salaries here in Sweden compared to salaries in Finland. One would like to move back, but we already have learnt Swedish and almost forgotten Finnish.[33]

Aune had a hard time deciding whether she is writing about herself or about other Finnish children, not including herself. First she says that Finnish children in general were mocked, and in the next sentence she refers to Finnish children as "us". 15-year-old Pia from Ramnäs school in Upplands Väsby wrote about similar themes:

> I have never had problems in Sweden because I come from Finland. But I think there will be problems when one is looking for a job, or something like that, in the future. My parents have tried to buy a house for years but the bank will not give them a loan. It is because we are Finns. There are not so many Finns who become engineers in Sweden, for example. That is because Finns in fact never become real Swedes. By real Swedes I mean people who can be called Swedes, not half Finns, etc. Even if a Finn has lived in Sweden for many years he is never called a Swede.[34]

It is hard to believe another boy's, Nico's, optimism:

> It is not so cool for all Finns in Sweden. I am a Finn myself, but it is not so bad. I have almost never heard something humiliating, for example, 'finnjävel' or 'go back to Finland'. So it is not so bad.[35]

87

The school of Virsbo in 2006. Photo: Hanna Snellman.

One boy, 13-year-old Kari, from Rundby skolan in Upplands Väsby, compared Finland and Sweden:

> I think it is better to live in Finland. However, things are quite well organized for Finns in Sweden. There is sometimes fighting and the older children tend to harass us sometimes. When I am in Finland on holidays, I often find good friends. I think they think about children's well-being more in Finland than in Sweden. In Finland one can do sports, etc, more.[36]

My Life

Three pupils had chosen the biographical title "My life".[37] A fourteen-year-old Anne from Virsbo summarized her life story as follows:

> I was born in Rovaniemi, in Finland in 1961. I went to school for one year in Rovaniemi. One day my mother and father had the idea that we would move to Sweden, because they had such poor salaries in Finland. My mother worked as a hairdresser and my father worked in a bar. Father moved a couple of months earlier and I followed with

mother and my little sister. I was seven years old and my sister was three years old. We moved to Åliden in Ramnäs. Now, I have gone to school here for almost seven years, and I get along well.[38]

Ilona, who was fifteen years old, had moved to Sweden with her six siblings and her parents. For Ilona being a twin had been very important:

I was born in 1960 as the seventh child in the family. My twin sister was born fifteen minutes earlier. The fact that we looked alike was no big deal. Newborns all look the same. I have been called Pia many times even though my name is Ilona.

It is fun to be a twin. One always has a friend to be with. It is an advantage when you do homework. We do homework together. That way we learn better. One side effect of being a twin is that one never has to be alone. You get so dependent on one another, uncertain of yourself. For example, when you buy clothes you have to have the other's opinion. Even though there are two of us, we are individuals.

I am very happy, because I have a twin-sister. In elementary school, some kids who had flunked their class, kept mocking us. Why, I do not know. Perhaps I (we) could not fight properly. Or perhaps it was because we lived a little further away and I didn't have the chance to play with my classmates after school. Besides, I was Finnish. My friends' provocations have followed me throughout my school years, but I have tolerated it because there are two of us.[39]

15-year-old Sanna from the same school in Virsbo described her life in terms of learning Swedish:

I was born in Finland and I have gone to a Finnish school. I was nine years old when we moved to Sweden, first to Surhammar and later to Virsbo.

When I first came to Sweden, I could not speak a word of Swedish. I had the chance to study Swedish for the first two months. There were about fifteen other children. After that we could start school for real. There was a Finnish girl in the class who was an interpreter for me. I studied Swedish a couple of hours a week, as well. It was so difficult. I almost didn't understand a thing. It took about one and a half years before I could speak Swedish well enough to manage.

Then we moved to Virsbo. We have lived five years here now, and I like it. I would never want to move back to Finland even though I sometime miss it there. In the beginning they called me a "Finn" among other things, but not anymore.[40]

An Experiment in Cultural Analysis

According to two Swedish ethnology professors, Billy Ehn and Orvar Löfgren, there are a lot of myths about how scientific research is done. In textbooks, the process is usually described as well planned and systematic, all the way from presenting the research questions to the final report. However, the process is seldom as smooth as it seems. On the contrary, there is often a chaotic history behind the facade. Ehn and Löfgren emphasize flexibility. The characteristics of a good scholar include openness, curiosity, and the ability to change one's plans. Cultural analysis regards this chaos in the research process as a powerful resource. Following periods of frustration and dead ends – a series of depressing November Monday mornings when nothing gets done – one can get inspiration and actually move forward with one's research. For stimulation and inspiration, Ehn and Löfgren have listed five ways to engage in cultural analysis: (1) applying perspective, (2) contrasting, (3) dramatizing, (4) experimenting, and (5) applying patience.[41]

I will re-read the school essays and see how Ehn's and Löfgren's check-list on cultural analysis helps me with my concluding analysis. When one starts doing research one has to ask questions, formulate research problems, and most importantly, choose a perspective from which to approach the study. In choosing a perspective one has to rule out, question, and intellectualize. Even though human beings are quite predictable – usually we want to improve our circumstances, be loved, have self-respect, and have control over our lives – nothing should be taken for granted. Ehn and Löfgren urge us to see alternative patterns, change between different ways of thinking (use the eagle's and the mole's perspective), conceptualize with metaphors, find synonyms, treat everything as symbols, compare and use one's own experiences in the course of one's research analysis.[42]

What metaphors and key symbols can be found in these school essays and how can they deepen the analysis? Could calling Finnish children "Finnish devils" be more than mocking? What is the role of silence in immigrant settings? What is loneliness for a child? How about the physical journey, the boat trip between Finland and Sweden? Why do children write about their parents' salaries and dreams about their future home?

First of all, Swedish children must have heard the term "finnjävel" from their parents or other adults. It is most unlikely that children of that age had read it in newspapers, which also used the term frequently in the 1970s. Why would an adult use such a term when talking about a neighbor or fellow worker? After all, the majority of Finns were hardworking, ordinary people although those with social problems received more attention in the press. According to surveys, Finns were considered either too lazy or too hard-working by their Swedish neighbors. The lazy ones were thought to live on Swedish social security. The "problem" with the hard-working ones was that they worked too hard in contract jobs, and therefore, helped lower the salaries of the others.[43] Echoes of parents' frustration is heard in their children's bullying.

Almost all the children mentioned their friends, playing, and the language (or rather the lack of it) in their essays. That triangle acts as a metaphor for adjusting to new cultural surroundings. It is surprising that even in such Finnish dominated communities as Virsbo and Upplands Väsby a child was a social outcast at the beginning. It is most likely that it was not only the language which was the problem even though the children wrote about language and silence. Perhaps, it was also the way one acts, a sort of choreography of a Swedish school. In the process of learning a new language, the children also learned to act the right way – and were accepted by friends, and had someone to play with. They didn't have to be silent anymore.[44]

An apartment building made of concrete is often understood as a symbol of a gloomy living environment whereas a privately-owned house is perceived as just the opposite. This is also how Taina presented her housing history in Sweden. One of the reasons her parents moved to Sweden was to have a privately-owned house. At first, they had to live in an apartment building made of concrete, but eventually they got a house of their own. Pia criticizes Sweden for the fact that her parents were not given a bank loan to buy a house, which she says was because they were Finnish. Her dream of having a house had not come true because of Swedes. A crowded and messy home symbolizes poverty for Eeva.

Home can be a metaphor for many things. However, one has to be careful in jumping to conclusions. A home in an apartment block in a suburb might symbolize warmth and running water. A house in the Finnish countryside did not necessarily have modern conveniences. For most, emigration meant eventually a better standard of living – at least in a material sense.[45]

The boat trip to Sweden can also be interpreted as a metaphor. It symbolizes fun, and it also symbolizes the trip from Finland to Sweden, the actual act of migrating. For those who did not drive to Finland via Northern Sweden, the boat symbolizes summer vacations, opportunities to meet Finnish relatives – and perhaps another kind of bullying, this time about being a Swede. The boat embodies the diaspora.

Several children rather surprisingly mention salaries in their essays. A salary is hardly an everyday life experience for a child. However, better salaries were the main reason for migrating, in the first place, for many adults, and children knew that. Perhaps, parents had comforted their children with the promise of better living standards. One of the striking things in the essays is the fact that almost every story was a success story. They mention how at first life had been miserable, but that it was not like that anymore. Partly it is a question of attitude, a wish to be happy; you are happy if you say you are happy. Probably, it was also partly a question of the teacher's presence in the school setting. Even though the essays were not graded, perhaps even not read by the teachers, the pupils knew that the teachers had access to the material.

Ehn and Löfgren urge us to think in alternative ways in order to see things differently. They argue that everything can be described in many different ways, and that way to break usual habits is to give well-known things new names. Finding a perspective is a linguistic process. They believe that exchanging usual concepts for unusual ones leads to new thoughts or new lines of enquiry.[46] The empirical material and the analysis of the material in this article has involved playing with the Finnish, Swedish, and English language. The children have written the essays in Swedish, a language which was not their first language, at least not the language they first learned. I read the essays in Swedish, and translated them into Finnish – with the help of a dictionary – and wrote the analysis in English, again with the help of a dictionary. I was forced to rename things which had an effect on my analysis. I agree with Ehn and Löfgren in their statement that a dictionary is full of opportunities for analysis.[47]

For example, Swedish words "*längta efter*" can be translated either as one is missing something or one is waiting impatiently or longing for something. Therefore, when 15-year-old Timo writes about Finland and summer holidays one is not sure whether he means that he misses Finland even after living in Sweden for seven years, or whether he is simply looking forward to the summer holiday, as children usually do, or whether he is looking forward to the holidays because they are in Finland.[48]

Ehn and Löfgren mention using one's own experiences as part of the process of finding a perspective. We have all been to school, experienced the first day at school, and written school essays. Many of us – myself included – have children of school age and school still figures in our everyday lives, even today. It's an arena where we are all experts. Therefore, it is easy for us to relate to the experiences of Finnish children writing school essays and use our own experiences as tools for analysis.[49]

I belong to a generation where children especially in rural areas were not necessarily in kindergarten before going to school, but at home. Therefore, as children, my generation did not necessarily have the experience of being in, or mixing with, a large group of children, which is the norm when we go to school. For me, one of the shocks of going to school was the large number of people. I clearly remember the anguish I experienced on the first day at school. I was not alone in my feelings. Many of my schoolmates were crying when their parents left them in the class-room. If I had not understood the language the teacher and the other pupils were speaking, it would have been intolerable. This is how it has been for Finnish children in Swedish class-rooms. I was born the same year and less than a hundred kilometers from the town where Anne was born. Reading her school essay tested my imagination: "What if" is a productive question in cultural analysis – how might my life have turned out?

One way of doing cultural analysis is to use your imagination, playfulness, and even fiction in the process.[50] If we, in our imagination, build a scene where we put a Finnish child in a Swedish speaking school, we can actually feel in our spines the feelings the child is going through. School-time experiences and especially those of bullying follow us throughout our lives. For many Finnish children in Sweden, the diaspora experience has been like balancing on a high wire in a circus with one end in Finland and the other in Sweden, the home and the homeland.

NOTES

1. Korkiasaari 2000, 164–166.
2. Hoerder 2002, 7, 35.
3. Brubaker 2005, 2.
4. Diaspora 2002, 2.
5. Ackermann 2004, 162.

6. Brubaker 2005, 3.
7. For example, Andreas Accermann lists the following qualifications for a diaspora:
   (1) Dispersal from an original homeland or 'centre', often traumatically, to two or more foreign or 'peripheral' regions: alternatively, the departure from a homeland in search of work or in pursuit of trade;
   (2) A strong (ethnic) group consciousness together with a collective memory and myth about the homeland and the desire to eventually return;
   (3) empathy for, and solidarity with, co-ethnic members in other countries of settlement. Ackermann 2004, 162.
8. Brubaker 2005, 4–7.
9. Kokot & Tölölyan & Alfonso 2004, 1.
10. See Kritisk etnologi 2001, 7.
11. Ahrne & Roman & Franzén 2000, 150.
12. See www.integrationsverket.se.
13. E.g. Rosengren 1975; Arnstberg 1975; Velure 1975; Borgegård 1978; Tyrfelt 1975.
14. Migrationen Finland–Sverige, Upplands Väsby, Virsbo, skoluppsatser. Binder 40.
15. This article is a part of my ongoing study on the integration of Finnish immigrants in Sweden financed by the Academy of Finland (decision number 211152).
16. See Korkiasaari 2000, 262, 273; Kangassalo 2003.
17. Korkiasaari 2000, 282, 289.
18. Rosengren 1975, 4; Borgegård 1978, 11.
19. Borgegård 1978, 125.
20. University of Helsinki, Department of Ethnology. Karhunen 1970.
21. Reinans 1996, 77.
22. All the names have been changed.
23. In Swedish, *"När jag flyttade till Sverige"*.
24. In Swedish, "Evijärvi heter den platsen där vi bodde i Finland. Vi bodde på landet. Det fanns bara en affär, men om man skulle köpa t ex kläder var man tvungen att åka till 'kyrkbyn', om man översätter det finska ordet. Där finns alla varuhus, bank, apotek osv. Dit var det några kilometer. Pappa ägde en bilverkstad där. Vi är sju ungar i familjen. Mamma var hemmafru och tog hand om oss när pappa jobbade. Från morgon till kväll jobbade han. Söndag var den enda vilodag han hade.
Det var en söndag så mamma sa det. Vi satt och tittade på TV.
– vad skulle ni säga om vi flyttade till Sverige? Frågade hon. Hon började förklara att vi skulle få det mycket bättre där. Kanske skulle vi ha eget hus, men att pappa skulle få bättre jobb var bra. Pappa skulle åka i förväg till han hade fått jobb och lägenhet för oss att bo i. Så kom den dan pappa skulle åka. Han stannade en månad, men kom och hälsade på. Första gången när han kom hem sa han att han hade fått jobb i Virsbo men bodde i Surahammar. När han skulle åka tillbaka ville inte min lilla syster säga hejdå, för hon var så ledsen när pappa skulle åka igen. Så kom äntligen den dan då pappa kom hem för att hämta oss. På ett sätt var det kul att få komma till ett nytt land och ny skola med nya kamrater, men så blev det inte. Min minsta bror var inte ett år när vi flyttade och jag hade börjat trean. Det var ledsamt att lämna kamraterna och den platsen där jag bott. Jag hade aldrig förut åkt med båt förut. Det var spännande. Vi sprang omkring i båten.
I hamnen här i Sverige väntade en bil som vi skulle åka med till Surahammar. Det var ett betonghus vi skulle bo i. Sen skulle man vänta på det värsta. Det var skolan.

93

Vi gick med pappa och en annan gubbe som kunde svenska. Rektorn var jätte bussig. Nästa dag skulle vi börja skolan. Dom första dagarna gick vi hos en fröken och läste svenska. När jag första gången gick med fröken till den klass som jag skulle gå i, var jag jätte nervös. Hon knackade på dörren. Min riktiga fröken öppnade. Hon sa, att jag var välkommen. Alla i klassen glodde på mig och jag blev alldeles röd i ansiktet. Det fanns bara en flicka i klassen som var finsk. Jag hade ingen att vara med på rasterna och var jämt ensam. När jag skulle gå hem skrek killarna i min klass "finnjävel" och spottade efter mig. Jag ville inte gå till skolan. Det en pina för mig att gå dit. Dom bara retade eller glodde på mig. Fröken ville hjälpa mig och pratade med mig, men jag fattade ju inte vad hon sa. En gång var jag med den finska flickan i min klass. Hon var jättesnäll mot mig. Ett halvår bodde vi i Surahammar. Till Virsbo flyttade vi när vår villa blev klar. Jag hoppades att det skulle gå bättre här i Virsbo.

Det finns flera finska elever i min klass. Jag fick en kompis direkt. Nu har jag inga problem. Har en kompis som jag kan lita på och inga svårigheter med språket. Både mama och pappa jobbar. Nu har vi bott snart fem år i Sverige."

25. In Swedish, "Att flytta till ett annat land".

26. In Swedish, "När jag flytta till Svärje då var det inte så kul. För jag kunde inte svenska Och inte förstå. Jag hade inga lekkamrater. När jag jik i en skola var man skule lära svenska. Och då kunde jag svenska. Och förstå och då kunde jag leka med. De andra som var svenska. Och kunde gå i svensk skola."

27. In Swedish, "När Jag flyttade till Svärje då kunde jag inte svenska och jag hade ingen lek kam rat men sen fik jag monga lek kam rater och jag lekte med de varje dag men nar jag skule fluta till rämnäs då ville jag stanna kvar där för jag hade så kul med mina lek kamrater men det fik jag inte då börja jag gråta men nästa dag åkte vi till rämnäs och då fik jag enu mera lek kamrater och en heter [...]. Hon var min bästa lek kamrat och jag började lek igen då fik jag enu mera lek kamrater när vi skule åka till finland vile jag att [...] skule följa mä oss till Finland fast det fik hon int och när vi åkte fikk [...] en presen från mej och jag fik från hene."

28. In Swedish, "Att vara finsk i Sverige."

29. In Swedish, "Jag heter [...]i och är finsk. Men sedan fyra år tillbaka bor jag i Sverige. Först flyttade pappa hit och skaffade jobb och bostad. Vi bodde först i nogåt som liknade en barack. Där bodde vi 2 ½ år. I början kallade alla mig finnjävel och en del andra tråkiga ord. Det gjorde mig hemskt ledsen. Nu är det inga problem. I början vågade jag inte ta hem mina kamrater. Vi hade ju så fult och stökigt. Men efter ett tag tog jag hem en del av mina vänner, och alla visade sig förstå att vi inte fick något bättre. När vi om hit började jag i 5:an, eftersom jag kunde några få ord av svenska språket. Nu går jag i 9:an, och har inga språksvårigheter. Jag skulle inte kunna flytta tillbaka till Kemi. Vi bor nu på en plats som heter Karlskrona."

30. See Snellman 2003, 127–133.

31. In Swedish, "När jag flyttade hit skulle jag börja i 1:an. Det var rätt taskigt i början. Man satt alldeles tyst. Nu tycker jag att det inte är någon större skillnad på oss. När jag bodde i Finland så var det jätte mycket snö på vintrarna och somrarna var varma. Men här i Sverige såfinns det knappast någon snö alls på vintern. Jag kan prata svenska rätt bra, men det är problem ibland. Man går här dag för dag och längtar till sommarlovet."

32. In Swedish, "Det är tråkigt för att dem retar oss för finnjävlar. Det är nästan likadant i Finland som är i Sverige och språken skiljer väl bara ock kostar lite mer här och mer i Finland. Men en del retar oss i Finland också. Det är bra att kunna finska om

föräldrarna är finska och därför är det bra att dom har ordnat finska skoltimmar. Och det är bra att man bor i Sverige för om man är finsk då har man så nära till Finland. Vi har lärt oss så mycket svenska och kan mindre finska då vill man inte flytta tillbaka. Och vi har nästan glömt bort finskan. Det är bättre löner här i Sverige än i Finland."

33. In Swedish, "Det är tråkigt för att dom retas för finnjävlar. Det finns några i Finland som retar oss för svenskar. Det är bra att det finns finska timmar i skolan men när det är grupparbete i skolan skulle man villa vara i klassen. Det är bra att vara invandrare här i Sverige än i ett annat land för man behöver inte åka så långt bort om man ska till sina släktingar som bor i Finland. Man får högre lön här i Sverige än i Finland. Man skulle vilja flytta tillbaka men vi har redan lärt oss svenska och nästan glömt bort finskan."

34. In Swedish, "Jag har aldrig haft problem i Sverige för att jag kommer från Finland. Men jag tror att problemen dyker upp när man ska ha jobb eller något liknande i framtiden.

Mina föräldrar har försökt i många år att skaffa en villa, men banken vill inte låna ut pengar. Det beror väl på att vi är finnar.

Det är inte många finnar som blir t ex ingenjörer i Sverige. För finnar lär sig nog aldrig att bli riktiga svenskar. Med riktiga svenskar menar jag att folk verkligen kallar en för svensk i stället för halvfinne m.m. Hur många år en finne än har bott i Sverige så blir han nog aldrig kallad för svensk."

35. In Swedish, "Det är nog inte så kul för alla finländare i Sverige. Jag är finne själv men det är inte så farligt. Jag har nästan aldrig hört något nedsättande, t ex finnjävel eller stick till Finland med dig. Så det är inte så farligt med den saken."

36. In Swedish, "Jag tyker det är bätre att bo i finland. Men det är ganska bra årdnat för finskar i Sverige. Dett brukar ju bli brått ibland och dom äldre brukar ju retas. Då när jag är i finland på semestern får jag åfta bra kamrater. Jag tror dom tänker på barnen i finland mer ä i Sverje. I finland kan man träna sport och sont mer."

37. In Swedish, "Mitt liv".

38. In Swedish, "Jag föddes 1961 i Rovaniemi i Finland. Jag gick ett år i skolan i Finland. Sen fick mamma och pappa för sig en dag att vi skulle till Sverige, för de hade så dåliga löner hemma i Finland. Mamma jobbade som hår-frisörska och pappa jobbade på en bar. Pappa flyttade till Sverige några månader före, sen åkte mamma, jag och min lille syster. Jag var sju år och min lilla syster var tre. Vi flyttade till Åliden i Ramnäs. Nu har jag gått här i skolan nästan sju år och jag trivs bra."

39. In Swedish, "Den x juli 1960 föddes jag som nummer sju i en barnaskara. En kvart tidigare hade min tvillingsyster kommit till världen. Att vi var lika då, är väl inte så konstigt. Nyfödda ser ju ganska lika ut. Men fortfarande tar folk fel på oss. Jag har ofta heta [...] fastän jag egenligen heter [...].

Visst är det roligt att vara tvilling. Man har alltid någon kompis att vara med. Vid läxläsning är det en fördel. Vi brukar förhöra varandra. På det viset lär man sig bättre. Det kan ha sina nackdelar, att aldrig vara ensam. Man blir väldigt beroende av varandra, osäker på sig själv. Vid t ex klädköp måste man först höra den andras åsikt. Fastän vi är två, är vi som en individ.

Jag är då verkligen tacksam att min syster funnits. För på lågstadiet fanns det några översittare som hackade på oss. Vad det berodde på vet jag inte riktigt. Kanske jag (vi) inte kunnat riva i ordentligt. Eller beror det på att min familj bott lite avsides, och därför har jag inte haft möjligheter att umgås med mina klasskamrater på fritiden.

Dessuttom är jag finländare.

Kamraternas retningar har följt mig hela skoltiden, men jag har stått ut bara för att jag är två."

40. In Swedish, "Jag är född i Finland Och jag har gått i en finsk skola. Jag var tio år när vi flyttade till Sverige. Först bodde vi i Surhammar, sen flyttade vi till Virsbo. Först när vi kom till Sura kunde inte jag ett ord svenska. Vi fick gå och läsa svenska i två monader. Det fanns ca 15 st. andra finska barn där. Sen fick vi börja den riktiga skolan. Det fanns en finsk tjej i min klass som fick vara tolk åt mig. Fortfarande gick jag och läste svenska några timmar varje dag. Det var jättesvårt. Jag fattade nästan inget alls.

Det gick ca 1 ½ år innan jag kunde så mycket svenska å jag klarade mig.

Sen flyttade vi till Virsbo. Vi har bott fem år i Sverige nu och jag trivs jättebra. Jag skulle aldrig vilja flytta tillbaks till Finland. Fast ibland längtar jag dit. I början retade dem mig för "finne" m.m. Men det gör dom inte mer."

41. In Swedish, perspektivering, kontrastering, dramatisering, experimenterande and väntan. Ehn & Löfgren 2004, 151–152.

42. Ehn & Löfgren 2004, 153–156.

43. Snellman 2005, 120–122.

44. The silence of Finnish immigrants and children in particular has been noticed in earlier research. See Lainio 1996, 312; Sjögren 1991, 11; Toukomaa 1973, 4.

45. Snellman 2005, 161.

46. Ehn & Löfgren 2004, 155.

47. Ehn & Löfgren 2005, 155–156.

48. Marja Ågren pointed out these different meanings of längta efter when she commented on the manuscript of this article. I want to thank her and Lotta Weckström for their valuable comments on this article.

49. See Being there 2003, 48–49.

50. Ehn & Löfgren 2005, 161, 165–166.

SOURCES

Archives of the National Museum of Cultural History, Stockholm
Migrationen Finland–Sverige, Upplands Väsby, Virsbo, skoluppsatser. Binder 40.

University of Helsinki, Department of Ethnology
Karhunen, Eva-Lisa 1970: Ruotsinsuomalaisten kontakteista Upplands Väsbyssä
    N:o 139.

BIBLIOGRAPHY

Ackermann, Andreas 2004. A double minority. Notes on the emerging Yezidi diaspora. *Diaspora, Identity and Religion. New directions in theory and research*. Waltraud Kokot, Khachig Tölölyan & Carolyn Alfonso (eds). Routledge: London & New York, 156–169.

Ahrne, Göran & Roman, Christine & Franzén, Mats 2000. *Det sociala landskapet. En sociologisk beskrivning av Sverige från 50-tal till 90-tal*. Bokförlaget Korpen: Göteborg. (2. Tryckningen).

Arnstberg, Karl-Olov 1975. *Om användbarheten av begreppen sociala nätverk, nisch och karriär i förklaringen av migrationsbeslut.* Forskningsprojektet Migrationen mellan Finland och Sverige efter andra världskriget. Forskningsrapport 2. Nordiska museet: Stockholm.

Being There. New Perspectives on Phenomenology and the Analysis of Culture 2003. Frykman, Jonas & Gilje Nils (eds.) Nordic Academic Press: Lund.

Bordegård, Lars-Erik 1978. *Finländares och svenskars lenadsvillkor. En fallstudie fron Virsbo samhälle i Västmanlands län.* Forskningsprojektet Migrationen Finland-Sverige. Forskningsrapport 4. Nordiska museet: Stockholm.

Brubaker, Rogers 2005. The diaspora diaspora. *Ethnic and Racial Studies.* Vol. 28 No. 1 January 2005, 1–19.

Diaspora 2002. *A Journal of Transnational Studies.* Vol. 11. Number 1.

Diaspora, Identity and Religion. New directions in theory and research. 2004. Kokot, Waltraud & Tölölyan, Khachig & Alfonso, Carolin (eds) Routledge: London & New York.

Ehn, Billy & Löfgren, Orvar 2004. *Kulturanalyser.* Gleerups: Malmö. (2. Tryckningen).

Hoerder, Dirk 2002. The German-Language Diasporas: A Survey, Critique, and Interpretation. *Diaspora. A Journal of Transnational Studies.* Vol. 11, Number 1, 7–43.

Kangassalo, Raija 2003. Finska språkets ställning i den svenka grundskolan: en tillbakablick på de senaste decennierna. Raija Kangassalo & Ingmarie Mellenius (EDS), *Låt mig ha kvar mitt språk. Antakaa minun pitää minun kieleni.* Umeå: Umeå universitet.

Korkiasaari, Jouni 2000. Suomalaiset Ruotsissa 1940-luvulta 2000-luvulle. *Suomalaiset Ruotsissa. Suomalaisen siirtolaisuuden historia 3.* Jouni Korkiasaari & Kari Tarkiainen (eds). Siirtolaisuusinstituutti: Turku.

Kritisk etnologi 2001. Artiklar till Åke Daun. Blehr, Barbro (ed.) Prisma: Stockholm.

Lainio, Jarmo 1996. Finskans ställning i Sverige och dess betydelse för sverigefinnarna. *Finnarnas historia i Sverige 3.* Jarmo Lainio (ed.). SHS & NM: Helsingfors.

Reinans, Sven Alur 1996. Den finländska befolkningen I Sverige – en statistisk-demografisk beskrivning. *Finnarnas historia i Sverige 3.* Jarmo Lainio (ed). SHS & NM: Helsingfors.

Rosengren, Annette 1975. *Memma och kalakukko. Rapport om mathållning hos finländarna i Virsbo.* Forskningsprojektet Migrationen mellan Finland och Sverige efter andra världskriget. Forskningsrapport 1. Nordiska museet: Stockholm.

Sjögren, Annick 1991. Introduction. *Ungdom och tradition. En etnologisk syn på mångkulturell uppväxt.* Annick Sjögren (ed.). Invandrarminnesarkivet: Stockholm.

Snellman, Hanna 2003. *Sallan suurin kylä – Göteborg. Tutkimus Ruotsin lappilaisista.* Suomalaisen Kirjallisuuden Seuran Toimituksia 927. Suomalaisen Kirjallisuuden Seura & Ruotsinsuomalaisten Arkisto: Helsinki & Tukholma.

Snellman, Hanna 2005. *The Road Taken. Narratives from Lapland.* Kustannus Puntsi: Inari.

Toukomaa, Pertti 1973. *Korutonta kertomaa. Suomalaisperheet ruotsalaisessa teollisuusyhdyskunnassa.* Tampereen Yliopiston sosiologian ja sosiaalipsykologian laitosten tutkimuksia 1. Tampereen yliopisto: Tampere.

Tyrfelt, Annika 1975. *Aldrig blir den bruden jungfru mer, aldrig bär hon krona... Rapport om finländska invandrares högtidsseder i Virsbo.* Forskningsprojektet Migrationen mellan Finland och Sverige efter andra världskriget. Forskningsrapport. Nordiska museet: Stockholm.

Velure, Magne 1975. *Kniv, sprit och sisu. En preliminary rapport om stereotypisering av finnar i Sverige.* Forskningsprojektet Migrationen mellan Finland och Sverige efter andra världskriget. Forskningsrapport 3. Nordiska museet: Stockholm.

MARJA ÅGREN

"Hello, my name is Pirkko and I am…"

Gothenburg, May 2000: I am doing an interview with Pirkko, as part of my work on a thesis in ethnology on identifications among individuals born in Gothenburg whose parents migrated from northern Finland to Sweden in the 1960s.[1]

During the interview, Pirkko talks for rather a long time about her job as a stewardess on a huge cruiser travelling around the world. She even shows me pictures of herself and other members of the crew, and of some of the places the ship has visited. (She carries these pictures in her handbag in case someone wants to see them – friends or family that she meets during her short stay in Gothenburg). I am wondering, as the minutes pass on this subject, if I will ever find anything in this part of our conversation of relevance for my study, for the understanding of young adults in Gothenburg with a Finnish background. Nevertheless, the episode has lingered in the back of my mind ever since. Something was being said there too, I keep thinking, something of relevance.

Webs around the World… (Being Connected)

The reason why Pirkko works on a cruise ship is to finance her studies at a university in the USA. At the time of the interview, she had one year left before taking her exam as an art director. The practice and business of commercials, including the opportunity to sketch and draw, is her passion, and ever since her early twenties (she was 31 at the time of the interview) she has been searching for a way to realise her dream of working with art in some form. She wishes that someone had explained to her earlier that there was a chance to receive a loan from the Swedish government to study abroad, but she is glad that she finally found out anyway. However, soon after starting at the American university they doubled their yearly fee, and Pirkko had to start working during the summer. Normally the students' courses include a summer semester, so for Pirkko the course has taken more than one extra year so far, but that doesn't worry her. She is determined to finish her studies and be able to start work in the occupation she loves, and she says that the mix of work and studies suits her since she is a person that quickly tires of one occupation. After a season at sea she longs to get back to school, and vice versa. During the university semesters she spends more or less all her time studying, including weekends, she says.

Change of scene: I spend January 2002 on vacation in Australia. During my holiday I visit the island of Tasmania. The morning I am leaving Tasmania and its capital, Hobart, I notice that a huge cruise ship has arrived in the harbour during the previous night. The name of the ship is the same as the name of the ship Pirkko had told me that she used to work on. She said that she normally only works during the summer, and this is in January, but I cannot help thinking that maybe, possibly, we are both in Hobart at the same time. And even if that is not the case, just the sight of the big ship reminds me of my meeting with Pirkko one and a half years earlier, and makes me wonder what she is doing now, if she has finished her studies, and where she is. It establishes a worldwide connection between Gothenburg, where we met each other, the city in the US where she was studying, the little town of Hobart where I am located now – and Salla, the community in Northern Finland where Pirkko's parents are from, which is also part of my study. I leave Tasmania with the pleasant feeling of somehow being connected.

In this article, I use Pirkko's experiences as the basis for a discussion about the different social positions available to individuals born in Sweden with parents from northern Finland. During the work for my doctoral thesis in ethnology, I have interviewed eight women and six men who were born in Gothenburg between 1967 and 1978, whose parents migrated from Finnish Lapland in the 1960s.[2] The interviewees have told me stories from their lives – stories about childhood and school years, growing up, education, interests in life, choice of occupation, starting a family of one's own, etc. The discussions have for the most part revolved around questions of whether they consider themselves to be Swedes or Finns or something else, and what follows from that. We have also in different ways been talking about the consequences of making such (national, ethnic, and other) categorisations.

Being Swedish?

Pirkko was born in Gothenburg but her parents moved twice during her childhood, so between the age of five and ten she lived in two smaller towns in the south of Sweden. After moving back to Gothenburg, Pirkko grew up in Gårdsten, a suburb northeast of the city center. Her parents had industrial jobs; her mother works at Volvo, but her father died when Pirkko was in her twenties. She also has a brother. Pirkko moved away from home when she was sixteen. At upper secondary school (*gymnasiet*) she followed a program in the humanities, and after that (after a few months work at Volvo, and a shorter stay in a city in southern Europe, working as an au pair) she got a job in the service staff with a ferry company in Gothenburg. She worked for the company for several years, even though she made other plans and did other things on the side. Then, in her mid twenties, she began her studies in the USA to become an art director.

"Roots" in northern Finland. Photo: Marja Ågren.

Pirkko is a Swedish citizen, like most of the people I have interviewed. Two of the interviewees are Swedish citizens by birth (because one of their parents had already changed from Finnish to Swedish citizenship by the time they were born); the others were Finnish citizens by birth. However, at the time of the interviews, eleven of the fourteen were Swedish citizens. The reasons they give for having chosen Swedish citizenship are mostly practical. Five of the six men wanted to avoid military service in Finland, and being a Swedish citizen has made it easier for the interviewees to get different types of student loans, and has sometimes facilitated travelling. In order to vote in the Swedish governmental election (*riksdagsval*) one has to be a Swedish citizen, and that is also a reason why some have changed their citizenship. As one person put it: "To vote is not only a right, it is an obligation. You must take responsibility for the society where you live."

So Pirkko was born in Sweden and has Swedish citizenship, and when someone in the USA asks her where she is from, she always says that she is Swedish. However, in Sweden she cannot say that she is Swedish, she says. This has something to do with her name, which gives her away. Both her given name and her surname sound Finnish, so Pirkko says that when she is introduced to people in Sweden they immediately ask her where her parents are from, and then when she says Finland, they immediately draw the conclusion: "So you are Finnish." And apparently Pirkko sees no way of arguing against that, even though she was born and raised in Sweden, has gone to Swedish schools, speaks Swedish better than Finnish and has Swedish citizenship. "I just cannot say Hello, my name is Pirkko and I am Swedish", she says.[3]

Today it is a well-established belief among social scientists that nations are to be seen as the results of political will and actions transmitted over time into a common and shared experience of something natural. Benedict Anderson (1993) has revealed many of the mechanisms that have made (and make) nation states what they are today, and many other thinkers and writers have examined how the ideas and concepts of nations and nationality – by different means, with different purposes, and by different agents – are upheld.[4] This means, for example, that "the Swedish nation" is considered by most people to be a very stable, fixed, and defined entity, with clear borders, one true history and composed of Swedes – people who are easily defined as "Swedish". However, the definition can be tricky. Does living in Sweden make you Swedish? Having a Swedish passport? Do you have to be born in Sweden to be Swedish? Or is it your parents that have to have been born there? Or their parents…?

These questions are part of the reason why Pirkko feels she cannot say "Hi, my name is Pirkko and I am Swedish."[5] And, of the persons I have interviewed, she is not the only one who mentions experiences like this. There are stories of being excluded, or of being treated (slightly) different than "Swedes with Swedish parents". Some interviewees were mocked in school, they have all met stereotypical perceptions of what Finns are supposed to be like, and, in other ways, they have been placed in categories defined beforehand, categorisations that they themselves might not have chosen in the same situation if they had been in a position to decide.

Being Finnish?

Nevertheless, all the interviewees consider themselves to be Swedish, in one way or another. This is usually expressed as a result of being born in Sweden, living in Sweden, and having Swedish citizenship. Since the choice of citizenship was usually made when the interviewees were in their late teens, it would appear that the decision to become a Swedish citizen was primarily their own, and connected with a step into adulthood. A few even mention that their parents disliked their decision. The decision to apply for Swedish citizenship can be seen symbolically as a choice between Finland and Sweden, where the individual concerned has decided that she or he belong to Sweden.

That is, however, to simplify a complex reality. The question of belonging has a multitude of dimensions. One aspect of this, related to the discussion above, is that the fact of having Swedish citizenship, and, thus, formally belonging to Swedish society, does not automatically mean that one is perceived as being Swedish. Furthermore, as already mentioned, in many cases the reasons given by the interviewees for choosing Swedish citizenship were practical rather than emotional. The woman who talked about the obligation to vote did not change her citizenship until she was in her late twenties, and she says that the decision was not easy to make, despite her wish to use the opportunity that citizenship offered her to influence society. She felt strongly that her Finnish citizenship was her own personal link to

Manifestation of "Finns in Sweden" in a shopping mall in Gothenburg. Photo: Marja Ågren.

Finland and to her Finnish background, quite apart from her family ties. Another woman who, at the time of the interview, had not applied for Swedish citizenship also talked about the emotional importance of Finnish citizenship, especially when she was in her teens. Now, she says, "I know that I feel Finnish anyway, even if I became an American one day."

The interviewees all appreciate the connection they have with Finland, even though the extent to which it manifests itself in their lives today varies. As Pirkko puts it: "My bonds to Finland are actually not that strong, but somehow you have been brought up with it, that Finland is the best!" They all spent their childhood summer holidays in northern Finland, but today there are only four or five who still go there regularly. "Finland" for the interviewees in most cases means "northern Finland", that is, the areas where their families are from. As the older generation disappears, the bonds with Finland, in most cases, grow weaker. Finland as a nation is not so interesting, and only one or two of the interviewees would consider living there.

But there are also other aspects to their relationship with their Finnish background. There are other expressions of what could be called their ethnicity, or "Finnishness" in their lives. Ethnicity is a term that is not easily defined and can lead to oversimplified interpretations. In line with many researchers that deal with the subject of ethnicity today, I choose to see it as something that an individual *does*, not something she/he *has*. Ethnicity is also used, reproduced, and manifested in relation to others.[6] Some of the interviewees use expressions such as "I have Finnish blood", or "my roots are Finnish" to describe how they "are Finnish". These metaphors for some

103

biological attachment to a place or country, which suggest the biological links between generations, are not uncommon, but they can be problematic. They are examples of the type of reasoning used when people claim that one's family has to have been born in a country for generations in order for you to belong. For people in Sweden with Finnish parents such metaphors can be a way to express that they belong to something else apart from Swedish society, and the proof of that belonging is in their blood, and as such impossible for anyone to question. However, as soon as "blood" and "roots" become factors in sorting people into different categories, judgments about "the right to belong" become very complicated. They can even provide fuel for racism and other ideologies based on such principles of categorisation.[7] Another way the interviewees articulate what their "Finnishness" means, is by saying that it is something they have "inside". In this way, it is something extra in their lives, but it is not attached to them, nor is it stable or fixed. It is rather as if they are carrying their personal history books around with them, books that are constantly in the process of change, or under revision. In this way, their Finnish background becomes something they can choose to use and shape; an extra asset in their lives, along with all the other aspects that make up their personal histories.[8]

When reflecting on the customs or traditions she remembers from her childhood, which she would consider Finnish, Pirkko says:

> It was the time we spent in Finland every summer. And then of course mum made some Finnish food, but I really don't know what Finnish food is either... (...) What ever it was, it was just something that came from home; a way of being, values and of course the language. Language can mean a lot... But it is really hard to say. Since I have not been brought up in a Swedish family I can't really say what the difference would be. It is difficult to compare, to say that this is typical of Finns, and this is typical for Swedes. And then it is mixed, it is all mixed.

She also points out that her parents are from northern Finland, and that some of their customs or practices were due to the rural way of life, rather than something national. Other interviewees also mention – when asked what they consider to be Finnish in their lives – things or customs that are just there, in larger or smaller proportions. They may be pointed out in an interview situation, but do not require constant reflection.[9] Mostly it is habits in relation to food, or regular sauna baths, that are mentioned.[10] Another significant factor is the use of the Finnish language. All of the interviewees speak and understand Finnish, but there is a large variation in the extent to which they use it, and how comfortable they are using it. For some the language has a specific emotional value, for others it is just an extra language they know (which of course is considered an asset). All of them communicate in Finnish with their parents, and flexibility seems to be the key word when it comes to shifting between Swedish and Finnish. Pirkko hardly ever speaks Finnish today, apart from with her mother, and even then it is mixed with many Swedish words. She is a little sad that she does not have a better mastery of the language and she even says that she would be slightly ashamed if she had to talk Finnish to her relatives in Finland today. On the other hand – if she had time to study languages she would rather learn Spanish, she says.

Being Swedish-Finnish?

Another experience that eleven of the interviewees share is that of going to separate Finnish-speaking school classes (for three, six, or nine of their school years).[11] These people were in general pleased with their school years, and thought that it gave them a good opportunity to keep the Finnish language alive. The interviewees who had no, or little, experience of Finnish-speaking school classes seem to be content with that, as well. They mentioned that they were glad not to have been separated in the same manner, since sooner or later you would still have to join the Swedish-speaking context. None of the interviewees would like to let their own children (the children they have or those they might have in the future) go to Finnish-speaking classes. Pirkko even calls it "madness", and claims that there should not be any separate school classes, for any language. By contrast, the prevailing opinion among the interviewees is that the Swedish language is the most important when you live in Sweden, and then there ought to be good opportunities to learn your own native language, as well.

Many of the interviewees' parents have been, and still are, involved in Swedish-Finnish societies. These societies also organise activities (like sports, dancing, singing, and playing instruments) for children, as well as parties and celebrations of various annual events.[12] Pirkko says that her mother still spends lots of time with people from her Finnish-speaking network. She has not mastered the Swedish language very well, or English, so she has never visited Pirkko in the USA. "She doesn't even dare to take her car in to town because she is afraid that she wouldn't find her way out!" Pirkko says, laughing. "You live in Gårdsten, and you drive to the Volvofactory and then you work there and then you drive back and then you go to the local center. That's how it is."

A researcher in ethnology, Mirjaliisa Lukkarinen Kvist, who is working on a thesis about a particular Swedish-Finnish community, says in an article that there has been an increase in Swedish-Finnish activity in recent years.[13] Today the Finnish language has the status of a national minority language in Sweden, and there is a variety of political activity among the Swedish-Finnish minority network.[14] My interviewees have different opinions about the organised efforts of the Swedish-Finnish network. They of course acknowledge the hard work their parents have done in Sweden, and the will to be seen and respected for that. The need to have certain civil services available in the Finnish language, especially for elderly people, is also understood by some of them, but most of them do not think that minority groups are the best way to go. Some of them really have no opinion on the matter and do not seem to care. Others express an interest in working on these kinds of issues on a professional basis, but with the whole society, not just the interests of the Swedish-Finnish group. None of the interviewees defined themselves as Swedish-Finnish when talking to me.[15]

Being in Relation to Others

The position of people in Sweden who were born in (or with parents born in) Finland, whether organised as Swedish-Finns or not, has changed over the years, as several of the interviewees mentioned. The situation has changed from the time when most of the Finns arrived – and were considered strangers by many Swedes, had to face lots of prejudices, and mostly kept to themselves – to today when these people seldom are seen as "different", and perhaps not even noticed that much (as group members), at all. However, the positions, and the borders that mark them, are never simple; they are constantly shifting, and cross through different categorisations and locations.

When Pirkko, for instance, talks about the things that sometimes made her feel different, or uneasy in relation to other people, when she was young, it is her position on the geographical and social map of Gothenburg in the 1980s that she refers to. She lived in a flat in a suburb dominated by concrete houses several stories high, in a low-status area, which did not attract people on higher incomes who could choose where to live. She went to an upper secondary school in the city center where most of the other students came from other parts of town, many from high-status areas inhabited generally by people with relatively high incomes. For Pirkko, her time at this school was tough, and she felt that she was not regarded as equal to the other students, neither by the classmates, nor by the teachers. "They looked upon us as different; suburbia-kids, immigrants", she says. Being regarded as an immigrant is always negative, she claims. But she is also aware that the attitudes of others depended on their earlier experiences with, or knowledge about, (in this case) Finns. For instance, if someone she met looked upon Finns as working class people with no money, that view would also be attached to her.[16]

Being in-between?

The term "immigrant" (*invandrare*) is very common in Sweden, and the meaning of the term has changed from the purely etymological one of someone who has immigrated, to signifying a whole complex of – more or less problematical – circumstances.[17] The interviewees do not look upon themselves as immigrants, and they state that people of Finnish extraction in Sweden today are rarely seen as immigrants. "Immigrants" are in many people's eyes people who have come from further away, with more foreign looks, names, and languages.[18] As long as the idea of the nation as a body with a core of "Swedishness", where people are measured on a scale in accordance with their degree of "integration", continues to prevail in so many people's thoughts and in so many social structures, the mechanisms of exclusion based on extraction will continue to work.

From this point of view, any change in the position of people of Finnish extraction in Sweden can be seen partly as the result of the arrival of new groups of immigrants in Sweden. (Other explanations include the heterogenisation of the group over time, changes in other structures in Swedish society, and/or changes in the relationship between the Finnish and Swedish nations.) The Swedish-Finnish group can be perceived as positioned in-between "the Swedes" and other groups of people with other extractions. On the "scale of exclusion" the Swedish-Finns are no longer in the most exposed position. One effect of this shift might be an increased hostility towards groups or individuals of other extractions, who might threaten the "safer" position now occupied by Swedish-Finns. Another possible effect might be a sense of "disappearing", or becoming "too integrated" and thus loosing the specificity of the group.

The interviewees have different opinions on this issue. One interviewee said that she hated foreigners; others talked about the obligation of immigrants to adapt, as well as the inability of the system in Sweden when it comes to meeting and handling the requests of asylum seekers; others underlined the complexity of these questions, and expressed the view that the bottom line is that we are all humans and equal. Pirkko speaks about friends, with good education but foreign names, from other parts of the world, who have not been able to get jobs, and she talks about the frustration and hopelessness that they feel, and that she sometimes shares. "How do you change people's mentality?" she asks.

The interviewees' opinions are not specifically Finnish; rather they reflect the spectrum of public opinion in Sweden today. However, these individuals have personal experiences of the process of becoming a member of Swedish society. Even if they are, in one sense, members by birth, they have found themselves, and can still find themselves, in many situations where their non-Swedish extraction plays a role. Yet they have lived in Sweden all their lives, and been able to follow the changes over the years, so they could, in some sense, be considered experts on these questions.[19] On the other hand, when looking at this issue from the point of view that we are all human – then we are all experts and we should all be concerned about structural segregation and discrimination. There are deep problems in Swedish society (and others) today, and it is not enough to state that we are all human beings and should be treated equally. It is necessary to work with these injustices on many levels, structural as well as individual. Many researchers suggest, for instance, that new forms of residence rights should be worked out, which would give people the right to vote and access other civil rights, even though they might not fulfil the criteria for citizenship. This is a step in the right direction in a process where the whole concept of nation-states and national (as well as ethnic or religious) identities ought (according to these researchers) to be re-thought and re-organized.[20]

Just Being...

On a smaller scale, the personal experiences of individuals in Sweden of Finnish extraction, such as Pirkko's, are important, and can reveal what people think about these issues today. What is important in people's lives, what choices do they make, in which ways do family, history, and traditions play a part in their lives? The interviewees resist simple categorisations. They are not Finnish *or* Swedish, they are both, and as such they are much more than their national or ethnic identity might suggest. As one man put it: "I am different because I am who I am, not because I am from Finland." A common expression says that the children of immigrants "belong in two worlds". Rather, I think, the interviewees live in one world – but that world is a complex one. One of the results of my study is that questions like these are not easily answered, and should not be. If they were easy to answer the world would be less complex, more uniform, and standardized, in other words, less human.

Pirkko does not have a lot to do with Finland today, and she might find herself living in the USA or elsewhere in the world once she has taken her degree. She feels most at home in Gothenburg, but this also depends on where her friends live, and whether she would someday, somewhere meet a partner to settle down with. Salman Rushdie has suggested in an essay that our stories will be the traces we leave after us in the world.[21] Pirkko's stories about her life, even the smallest detail like the experience of working on a cruise ship, have left traces in me. Now her story can continue to leave traces, following a trajectory of its own, as it has been written down in this article.

NOTES

1. Pirkko is not the interviewee's real name.
2. The material for the thesis also consists of two interviews of the same kind with two men born in the 1980s as well as information gathered at more informal meetings with different representatives of the group of Finns in Gothenburg, and on visits to northern Finland. There is also a large amount of media material, including articles about Finland and Finns in the local newspaper (*Göteborgs-Posten*), systematically collected over a three year period, recordings of a TV program by, and for, Finns in Sweden, a few radio recordings on the subject, information brochures, commercial leaflets, and photos. I have also read fiction literature from Finland, and on the subject of migration, and some extracts from different novels are used in the thesis (Ågren 2006). My study is part of a project lead by ethnologist Hanna Snellman, called "Gothenburg – the largest village of the Salla parish". This project also includes an historian, Marianne Junila, and is part of the research program *Interaction across the Gulf of Bothnia*.
3. This statement made by Pirkko is based on her own experience, and I can hardly question it. Yet it made me think of my own name, and my own national identification, and in which ways they are comparable to Pirkko's. She and I are the same age, we were both born and raised in Gothenburg, we speak Swedish, and are Swedish citizens. I also have a given name that sounds Finnish and is actually more common in Finland than in Sweden. However, I have never had any problem saying "Hello, my name is Marja and I am Swedish". My parents and grandparents were (as far as I know) all born in Sweden – is that then what makes the difference?
4. Anderson 1993. For an overview and discussion of the subject, see, for instance, Brnic 2002, 15–30.

5. See Azar 2001.
6. See, for instance, Baumann 1999; Eriksen 2004.
7. See, for instance, Eriksen 1996.
8. See Österlund-Pötzsch 2003.
9. See Hall 1999; Eriksen 2004.
10. It might be noted that "Swedishness" in this sense, things that the interviewees do and say that they consider to be Swedish, has not been addressed in the same way in the interviews. This has a lot to do with my unreflected identification with being Swedish, and my understanding of what that implies. I took the interviewees "Swedishness" for granted, which had the effect that I did not ask them very much about how their "Swedishness" takes form – apart from formal citizenship. There must be situations (for instance, when they are abroad) when the interviewees are asked, or wish, to express what Sweden means to them, in a similar way. In other words, "being Swedish" was the norm when the interviews were done, and "being Finnish" was what had to be explained. This can also be related to questions raised by researcher Lotta Weckström (2003) concerning the significance of the interviewers perceived nationality or ethnicity (and the language used) when doing interviews on those same topics.
11. For more on the development of Finnish-speaking school classes in Sweden in the 1970s and 1980s, see, for example, Lainio & Wande 1996; Peura & Skutnabb-Kangas (eds) 1994 and Rodrigo Blomqvist 2002.
12. See Tarkiainen 1996; Snellman 2005.
13. Lukkarinen Kvist 2005.
14. See web page: www.rskl.se For more on language issues, see Josephsson 2004, 41–143 and on minority politics in general, see, for instance, Benhabib 2003.
15. Which does not mean that they could not do that in another context. Compare with the articles of Lukkarinen Kvist and Weckström in this book.
16. For more on segregation in Sweden, see Andersson Roger 1999.
17. See, for instance, de los Reyes et al. 2002; Tigervall 2005, 19–22.
18. See, for instance, Lange 1995.
19. See Andersson Åsa 2003; Sernhede 2001.
20. See, for instance, Eriksen 2004, 119; Benhabib 2003, 227–237; Baumann 1999, 141.
21. Rushdie 2004, 364.

SOURCES

Interviews

Fourteen interviews, conducted between 2000 and 2003, 1–3 hours long, transcribed into 330 pages and kept by the author.

BIBLIOGRAPHY

Anderson, Benedict 1993. *Den föreställda gemenskapen: reflektioner kring nationalismens ursprung och spridning*. Göteborg: Daidalos.

Andersson, Roger 1999. Segregationens Sverige. *Invandrarskap och medborgarskap. Demokratiutredningens skrift nr 13.* Stockholm: SOU 1999:8.

Andersson, Åsa 2003. *Inte samma lika: identifikationer hos tonårsflickor i en multietnisk stadsdel.* Stockholm/Stehag: Symposion.

Azar, Michael 2001. Den äkta svenskheten och begärets dunkla objekt. *Identitetens omvandlingar. Black metal, magdans och hemlöshet.* Ove Sernhede & Thomas Johansson (eds). Göteborg: Daidalos.

Baumann, Gerd 1999. *The multicultural riddle. Rethinking National, Ethnic and Religious Identities.* New York/London: Routledge.

Benhabib, Seyla 2004. *Jämlikhet och mångfald. Demokrati och medborgarskap i en global tidsålder.* Göteborg: Daidalos.

Brnic, Anita 2002. *Speaking of Nationality. On Narratives of National Belonging and the "Immigrant".* Göteborg: Department of Sociology, Göteborg University.

De Los Reyes, Paulina, Molina, Irene & Mulinari, Diana (eds) 2002. *Maktens (o)lika förklädnader. Kön, klass & etnicitet i det postkoloniala Sverige.* Stockholm: Atlas.

Eriksen, Thomas Hylland 1996. *Historia, myt och identitet.* Värnamo: Bonnier Alba Essä.

Eriksen, Thomas Hylland 2004. *Rötter och fötter. Identitet i en föränderlig tid.* Nora: Nya Doxa.

Hall, Stuart 1999. Kulturell identitet och diaspora. *Globaliseringens kulturer. Den postkoloniala paradoxen, rasismen och det mångkulturella samhället.* Catharina Eriksson, Maria Eriksson Baaz & Håkan Thörn (eds) Nora: Nya Doxa.

Josephson, Olle 2004. *Ju. Ifrågasatta självklarheter om svenskan, engelskan och alla andra språk i Sverige.* Stockholm: Svenska språknämnden och Norstedts Ordbok.

Lainio, Jarmo & Wande, Erling 1996. Finskan i utbildningsväsendet och sverigefinnarnas utbildning i Sverige. *Finnarnas historia i Sverige 3. Tiden efter 1945.* Jarmo Lainio (ed.). Helsingfors och Stockholm: Finska historiska samfundet och Nordiska museet.

Lange, Anders 1995. *Den svårfångade opinionen: förhållningssätt till invandring och invandrare.* Stockholm: Centrum för invandringsforskning (CEIFO).

Lukkarinen Kvist, Mirjaliisa 2005. Hemtrevligt band. *Bruket av kultur. Hur kultur används och görs socialt verksamt.* Magnus Öhlander (ed.) Lund: Studentlitteratur.

Peura, Markku & Skutnabb-Kangas, Tove (eds) 1994. *Man kan vara tvåländare också... Sverigefinnarnas väg från tystnad till kamp.* Stockholm: Sverigefinländarnas arkiv.

Rodrigo Blomqvist, Paula 2002. *Från assimilation till separation. Den finska invandrargruppens krav på finskspråkig skolundervisning.* Förvaltningshögskolans rapport nr. 47 Göteborg: Förvaltningshögskolan.

Rushdie, Salman 2004. *Överskrid denna gräns. Essäer och artiklar 1992–2002.* Albert Bonniers förlag.

Sernhede, Ove 2001. Förortens krigare. Hip hop och utanförskap i Det Nya Sverige. *Identitetens omvandlingar. Black metal, magdans och hemlöshet.* Ove Sernhede & Thomas Johansson (eds). Göteborg: Daidalos.

Snellman, Hanna 2005. *The Road Taken – Narratives from Lapland.* Inari: Kustannus Puntsi.

Tarkiainen, Kari 1996. Sverigefinska infrastrukturer. *Finnarnas historia i Sverige 3. Tiden efter 1945.* Jarmo Lainio (ed.). Helsingfors och Stockholm: Finska historiska samfundet och Nordiska museet.

Tigervall, Carina 2005. *Folkhemsk film – med "invandraren" i rollen som den sympatiske Andre*. Umeå: Sociologiska institutionen, Umeå Universitet.

Weckström, Lotta L. 2003. *The Invisible Opponent. Argumentative Discourse About Feelings of National Belonging, Finnishness and Immigration of Second Generation Finns in Sweden*. Amsterdam: Department for Speech Communication, Rhetoric and the Study of Argumentation, University of Amsterdam.

Ågren, Marja 2006. *"Är du finsk, eller...?" En etnologisk studie om att växa upp och leva med finsk bakgrund i Sverige*. Göteborg: Arkipelag.

Österlund-Pötzsch, Susanne 2003. *American Plus. Etnisk identitet hos finlandssvenska ättlingar i Nordamerika*. Helsingfors: Svenska litteratursällskapet i Finland.

LOTTA WECKSTRÖM

Symbiosis of Language and Identity?

S cene one: We begin by going back in time to a village in the rural
northwest of Finland, in the early 1960s. The memories of World War II
are slowly fading, the payments to Russia are completed, and a new era of an
unexpected unemployment is about to begin. Unemployment rates hit record
levels no one could have dreamed of causing a rapidly growing movement
from the rural areas southwards towards the capital city, and industrial cities.
The cities, however, cannot provide all new comers with jobs and housing.
For many the point has come where they decide to try their luck elsewhere
and immigrate to Sweden.[1]

Scene two: The early 1970s, a middle sized town on the bay of Mälaren,
central Sweden, whose wealth comes from mining and other heavy industries.
The local industry recruits actively through advertisements in Finnish
newspapers, and even sends "head hunters" to persuade Finns to join the
growing troops of factory workers in Sweden. Newcomers find housing
and employment easily with help of Finns who have already established
themselves. Most adults, women and men, work hard, many in three shifts
manufacturing cars, refrigerators, or working for the mining industry.[2]
Lacking Swedish skills does not matter in the factories: it is too loud to chat
anyway. Finns have a reputation of being hard-working, silent people who
have heavy drinking habits and like to keep to themselves.[3] The years go
by, families grow, property is bought and children go to school. Some of the
families merge with the Swedish way of life, the Swedish way of thinking
and talking, whilst others continue their "Finnish" life in the new country.

Scene three: Thirty years later in the same middle sized town on the Bay
of Mälaren, the year 2004. A second generation Finn sits with a Finnish
researcher over a cup of coffee; she is being interviewed for a PhD dissertation
about second generation Finns and their language identity in Sweden. The
researcher presses the play button of her minidisk and starts asking questions.
The narrator answers, sometimes asking a question or two herself. During the
long weeks of fieldwork the mini discs are filled with dozens of recorded hours
and notebooks are written full of observations of Finnish life in Sweden.

As always, there are several potential stories to tell about such interviews,
this article, however, is about how the narrators argued for their standpoints
and defended their arguments when the interview touched topics that

turned out to be controversial, one of these topics was language. I call this way of arguing the phenomenon of *dialogical monologues*. By dialogical monologues I refer to an arguing pattern that resembles a sophisticated rhetorical move: to acknowledge and to refute counter arguments in order to make one's initial standpoint look superior, and, therefore, the only right possibility.[4] In these sequences the narrators play two roles, for and against their opinion, and present the roles of a proponent and an opponent. It is interesting to note that these sequences no verbal criticism from my side, whatsoever, took place when narrators adopted the roles of antagonist and protagonist and started to negotiate about their opinions. In this article, I will, firstly, illustrate this phenomenon with some examples originating from sequences in which we talked about the meaning of the Finnish language and its significance for the narrators' Finnish identity and, secondly, I will suggest possible explanations for why language issues heated up the interviews causing dialogical monologues.

This article is based on interviews I have gathered as part of my ongoing PhD project about second generation[5] Finnish immigrants in Sweden.[6] The interviews were gathered with thirty-five second generation narrators in the area of Mälaren bay in Central Sweden during four fieldwork periods between the spring of 2002 and the autumn of 2005. All of the narrators were born between 1970 and 1976 and have at least one parent who is a Finnish speaking Finn who came to Sweden as a part of the large waves of migration of the 1960s and 1970s. Most importantly, the narrators identified with the concept of "Finnishness" in Sweden to such a degree that they became active participants in this research. To gather the interview material, I used a technique involving a double set of interviews, one of which was a semi-structured thematic interview, whilst the other was devoted to feedback conversations. This means that I met most of the narrators for a recorded interview at least twice. The interviews were conducted in Swedish or Finnish, according to the narrators wish.

The core interest of the research project and, consequently, the interviews, is to shed light on the impact, meaning, and possible consequences of having a Finnish background and, especially a knowledge of the Finnish language for the second generation narrators' everyday lives. Is Finnishness present in the lives of the second generations? What does it take to be a Finn in Sweden? Is the Finnish language important for Finnishness? The theme of minority languages in Sweden is highly important as in 2000 the country ratified EU regulations to protect and promote its' five national minority languages, including Finnish. In 2005, an extensive research report about the position of Finnish by the Swedish Ministry of Justice was published, in which it appears that the position of Finnish has not changed for the good since 2000, rather the opposite.[7]

Negations

When the narrators discussed Finnishness in the interviews, it was hard for many of them to define what Finnish identity in Sweden consisted of, or what meanings, consequences, or values it had in the narrator's life. Interestingly, I was given many reasons why Finns do not stand out: there is no visible difference between Swedes and Finns, from which others could tell straight away to which group, or category, of society one could belong. Many narrators also considered Swedish and Finnish traditions, religion, and culture as "almost the same", which is, of course, true to some extent if one compares them with non-Scandinavian cultures. When the narrators started to find fragments of something that could in their view contribute to a Finnish identity, language was always paraded as the first. Language was without exception mentioned in connection with Finnish identity, although its importance was sometimes negated. In the following, rather long example (1a)[8] a female narrator explains why it is not important to speak Finnish to be an upright Finn. She considered herself to be a "good Finn" although speaking Finnish was not a part of her daily life and she chose to have the interview in Swedish. The segment also serves to illuminate the criticism of the symbiosis between a minority identity and the respective minority language. All examples in this article are my own translations of the original quotations, that is Finnish or Swedish, the originals can be found at the end of the article.

Example 1a

L: Do you think that one can be a Finn or a Finnish
immigrant without mastering the language?

R: Yes. Absolutely. I have friends who are Finns with out speaking the language. They feel Finnish to me anyway; they have it in their blood. They function in Finnish, they think Finnish. The are down right Finns. Much depends on the language but I have also met the people who do not speak Finnish and I see that there still is something more to that. See, she is a girl friend of mine and she is special, she is like me, a bit crazy. I think every thing is like glued together, every thing floats together and it never became in particular a Finnish or a Swedish way of thinking. If people ask whether I think in Swedish or Finnish of course I reply "in Swedish" but maybe I do think in Finnish I do not know. I think in Finnish, maybe not in particular the WORDS as such but I have the mentality and do Finnish things, think different. And yes, I am a Finnish citizen.

L: Are you a Finn?

R: Yes, yes, 110 per cent.

L: 110 per cent?

R: Yes always. And there is always this little debategoing on. Some of my Swedish friends cannot understand why I call myself a Finn. They reckon that because I was born here I am a Swede. They do not understand how I can call myself a Finn. But I can't agree with that. I feel myself, it depends, but every human being knows where one's roots come from. If a Turk lives here for 30 years he will never be a Swede in Swedish terms, but me with my blue eyes and pale skin, I should, in their eyes, feel like a Swede, because I look like one.

L: But you don't feel like a Swede?

R: No! I would never want to be a Swede! (Laughter)

L: Why?

R: No, I really like Finns better. They are honest, straight forward, they
are bit special. You love them or you hate them. That is the way it is.
I lived in Rinkeby before and there are many foreigners living there and
they liked Finns better than Swedes. Finns are so straight and
honest they said, they said what they felt and that's it. It
was like good that way.

Woman born 1976, interviewed 6/2002

This narrator is clearly a proponent of the non-essential character of language in the formation of a minority's identity. Her standpoint, the main claim, which is supported by arguments, of this sequence could be formulated as follows: "It is not essential to master Finnish in order to be a Finn." To back up this standpoint, she acknowledges the fact, that language can make a great contribution to one's minority identity, but, more importantly, there are other features that are more significant: having a Finnish mentality, thinking in Finnish ways, and being a Finnish citizen. She does not refute, per se, the importance of a minority's language, but through the acknowledgement, and then by advancing other, more important aspects she shows how insignificant the language issue is in her opinion. This move can be seen as a negation of the importance of language. To reinforce her standpoint she refers to her Finnish girl friend who does not speak Finnish but is, in her opinion, a downright Finn and "a bit crazy", apparently in a positive, Finnish way. She suggests that parts of both, Finnishness and Swedishness, are glued together forming a pact that cannot be separated.

The narrator uses the technique of introducing counter arguments and then refuting in order to defend her own definition of Finnish identity, which does not include the Finnish language. When she speaks about her Swedish friends who cannot understand or approve of her preference for Finnishness, she presents the two sides of the dispute: on the one hand, the arguments against calling herself a Finn because of the facts they mention (she was born in Sweden and looks like a Swede), and on the other hand, her deep feelings of having roots in Finland and experiencing herself as a Finn. She continues by giving the example of a Turkish immigrant. According to the respondent, a Turk in Sweden will never be considered a proper Swede. In this statement, she points out that the argument used by her Swedish friends' of being born in Sweden always equals Swedishness is wrong because it only works for blond and blue-eyed people. Although she strongly underlines the insignificance of language for her ethnic identity, she came back to the value of knowing Finnish later in the interview. After the sequence in the example she continued describing bilingualism as a gift, although she did not make use of Finnish for instance, in the interview, or in her daily life. She said that she tries to make an effort to speak Finnish with her mother or with a girlfriend so they have a secret language in the subway. Like many other narrators she spoke about having received two languages for free, and, in principle, she appreciates that. For her, this appreciation does not necessarily require an active use of Finnish; it is more about the access to the parental background, partly, through language.

115

To Acknowledge and To Refute

The argumentation technique the narrator used in example (1a) has the dynamic of acknowledging and refuting counter-arguments and works like a game. In this situation, the narrator takes both the proponent's and the opponent's role, and shows both sides of the coin (or many different sides of the topic in question) by presenting arguments in favor, as well as against the issue that she or he is discussing. If we imagine a proponent and an opponent of any given topic standing facing one another, the arguments could be visualized as little balls the contestants are throwing, receiving, and passing back again. In my interviews the narrators did not face a flesh and blood opponent, but passed the imaginary ball of argument between their own hands.

In the next example (1b) a narrator, a man in his thirties and a father to two young children, defends his standpoint that a command of Finnish does not create the core of a Finn by using the same technique of first, acknowledging, and then, refuting counter arguments to his initial standpoint. He chose to have the interview in Finnish and did not seem to have any trouble speaking the language, such as searching for expressions, worlds, or phrases, yet he, rather surprisingly estimated his Finnish skills were "not too good". He was not the only narrator who spoke fluent Finnish and considered language to play less significant role in the minority identity of Finns in Sweden.

> Example 1b
> L: What about the language then? Is it important?
> B: Mmhm... knowledge of Finnish cannot be the most essential thing
>   in being a Finn. There are for instance also Swedish speaking
>   Finns in Finland and they are Finns just as much as Finnish-
>   speaking Finns are. I think that people who are so fussed about the
>   language have not considered other features of Finnishness, at
>   all. It really isn't necessary to speak the language in order to be
>   a Finn.No, I do not think so. Sure it could be nice if my child would
>   speak a couple of words of Finnish, but it doesn't make him more
>   or less a Finn if he does or not. But it would be nice if he could talk
>   to my parents in Finnish. But they speak Swedish anyway. My
>   parents I mean. So they will be talking to each other anyway. That
>   is, I reckon more important than what language is spoken or how
>   well it is spoken. And they seem to have a good time together. And
>   all this talk about the generations drifting apart and loosing contact
>   with their roots. The roots are there and the children will get Finnish
>   habits anyway. Some habits.
> L: ...yes...
> Man born 1973, interviewed 4/2002

Let us begin by taking a brief look at the structure of the argumentation of this sequence and the moves the narrator makes in presenting his argument. He begins his argument by presenting his standpoint, his view, namely, "One does not have to speak Finnish in order to be a Finn." To support his argument he uses the method of introducing a counter argument, and then attacking it in order to show the soundness and the superiority of his standpoint. We can see structurally the argumentation proceeding in the following way:

Standpoint	One does not have to speak Finnish in order to be a Finn
Argument 1	The knowledge of Finnish cannot be the most essential thing in being a Finn (This cannot be the case, because...)
Argument 2	There are for instance also Swedish speaking Finns in Finland, and they are Finns just like the Finnish speaking are
Argument 3	There are also other significant features about Finnishness
Counter Argument 1	I think that people who are so fussed about the language have not considered other features of Finnishness at all
Counter Argument 2	Sure it would be nice if my child would speak a couple of words of Finnish, but it doesn't make him more or less a Finn if he does or not. But it would be nice if he could talk to my parents in Finnish.
Refuting Counter Argument 2	But they speak Swedish anyway. So they will be talking to each other anyway. That is, I reckon more important than what language is spoken or how well it is spoken.
Counter Argument 3	And all this talk about the generations drifting apart and loosing contact with their roots
Refuting Counter Argument 3	The roots are there and the children will get Finnish habits anyway (therefore the counter argument is nonsense)

In this case the narrator tries (and, in my opinion, succeeds) in refuting counter arguments to his standpoint by advancing more arguments in favor of his standpoint. His proceeds by mentioning that it could, of course, be an advantage and even beneficial in some situations to have a knowledge of both languages, Finnish and Swedish. By mentioning this fact he shows his awareness of general attitudes concerning bilingualism, yet does not completely subscribe to them. By acknowledging, and then refuting, the argument that language is the most essential aspect of a minority's identity, he makes his initial standpoint even stronger.

117

Affirmations

While some narrators assigned a minor role to language in the manifestation of Finnishness and their own Finnish identity, most argued strongly that there was a fundamental connection between a minority's language and its respective identity.[9] First of all, they defended the opinion that if a person did not speak Finnish, she or he could not really be considered as a Finn. Secondly, they strongly pleaded for the significance of the language, not only for the individual but also for the whole minority. These narrators found Finnish to carry both functional and emotional values. Knowledge of Finnish had a functional value in the practical sense of being able to communicate with relatives in Finland, and, through this contact, not only to share but also to live out, and reproduce Finnishness. Its emotional value was based on an objective feeling, for example, of feeling comfortable with the language and with Finnish speaking peers, or the view that it was an obligation to pass Finnish on to the next generation.

In the following example (2a) the narrator is talking about her child's knowledge of Finnish, and stresses that the connection with Finnish relatives is reasons enough for the child to keep on investing in the language.

> Example 2a
> L: Do you think it is important that he speaks Finnish?
> H: Yes, very important. We have lot of family in Finland so he
>   understands and also speaks [Finnish][10]. And, we have like other
>   friends as well and their children speak Finnish. Like...
> L: Everybody says that it would be nice...
> H: Mmmm. If we take, like, T and F, they also could have taught
>   their girls Finnish like P and me myself have done. Like, T is,
>   she is a bit different, that is the thing, she is like Swedish, but F,
>   he is a Finn.
> L: So you think that there is a difference between being Finnish and
>   being Swedish?
> H: Yes. But it is a bit different like with my siblings. My sister can
>   speak Finnish well, although she is Swedish. It has always been
>   our thing. But her children can't [speak] Finnish neither do the
>   children of my brother. Because they have, like, a Swedish
>   spouse, it is more difficult, like, to talk some other language. But
>   they should speak Finnish although it is difficult at times, other
>   wise it will disappear.
> Woman born 1975, interviewed 6/2002

The narrator is acknowledging problems connected to keeping up with two languages in the family and gives an example of something as close as her own siblings. Although it is not a counter argument as such, it is more of a counter example, a piece of evidence of what happens to people who do not share her understanding of the nature of ethnic identity and neglect passing the language on to their spouses and children. This sequence is also a typical answer that includes explanations to reinforce the narrator's opinion about a problematic issue under discussion.

In the following example (example 2b) a narrator is presenting counter examples which, in fact, appear as counter arguments as well:

> Example 2b
> L: Is it that Finnishness is the same as the Finnish language? Or does it contain some other things? What is it, like, what is Finnishness?
> A: I think that it is the language, or culture, or well, it is the language that is in the center. I know someone from my old class in the Finnish school here close by who married a Swede and doesn't speak Finnish anymore. Her children can't speak Finnish, they don't even understand Finnish. I don't know if you can really forget a language but you surely can stop talking it, like this one girl has. So it just disappears, like after her there will be no one and then there will be no continuation of Finnishness, because how could her children ever just start talking Finnish if they never even heard it? So in my opinion Finnishness ends right there. Sure there are people feeling Finnish but not speaking Finnish, and I guess it is their good right, but I would like to know what Finnishness then is for them if not language?
> Woman 1976, interviewed 6/2002

For this narrator, Finnishness is strongly dependent on language. She explains the essential importance of the language by giving it an almost a physical form, the well-being and survival of which depends on constant efforts. She refers to an acquaintance, who started a family with a Swedish-speaking partner and decided not to speak Finnish any more. The narrator describes the situation and argues that the acquaintance had put an end to Finnishness:

> So it [the language, and consequently Finnishness] just disappears. Like after her there will be no one and then there will be no continuation of Finnishness, because how could her children ever just start talking Finnish if they never even heard it? So in my opinion Finnishness ends right there.

This example shows how destructive the decision, not to talk Finnish to the children, was for the language and to Finnishness, and therefore, does not need to be refuted, because it is evident, in this context that her choice was lethal to Finnish identity. The refutation follows in the form of a rhetorical question "Sure there are people feeling Finnish but not speaking Finnish, and I guess it is their good right, but I would like to know what Finnishness then is for them if not language?" This remark is the counter argument that has already been refuted in the example the narrator gave at the beginning of her argumentation.

119

Why Do Narrators Argue about Language?

When one starts to take an interest in Finns living in Sweden, be it the modern migration, the first, or second generation, or the Forest Finns, the *Metsäsuomalaiset*, who lived in complete isolation in the large forests in the Northern parts of Sweden keeping their form of Finnish free form influence for centuries,[11] language always stands out as a core issue. Therefore it was not such a big surprise that narrators in my data set also quickly established a connection between Finnishness and the Finnish language. But why did the language identity combination trigger them to start a dialogical monologue? There are many alternative answers to this question, depending on the angle one approaches this issue. One fruitful analysis would be to discuss the role of the interviewer[12] in the dialogical monologues. For this article, however, I have chosen to look for explanations in the migratory history of Finns in Sweden and the idea of the symbiosis of language and identity, which is a crucial political issue for the Finnish minority in Sweden.

Language is considered to be one of the strongest features in separating one group from another and a fundamental component in the creation of identities.[13] This is a fact that cannot have gone unnoticed by anyone who has followed the discussion about Finns in Sweden, or is a member of any immigrant or ethnic minority in Sweden. The Finnish language in Sweden has been gaining political weight since the 1980s. Two decades ago the silent Finnish minority started to raise its voice and to demand, for example, education in Finnish for their children and organized school strikes.[14] To rise against the Swedish status quo had been quite unthinkable before. Finns had rather taken the path of assimilation but in the early 1980s they were ready to play an active roll in the society. The best-known school strike took place in the Stockholm suburb of Rinkeby, in 1984 and lasted two months, receiving plenty of media attention. As an effect of the strike, Finnish speaking primary and secondary education was secured for the following ten years. In the 1990s Finnish "free schools"[15] were established, some of them are still operating and enjoy considerable social prestige. Finnish language is, thus, a recognized part of primary education in Sweden.

The latest evidence of the politicization of the Finnish language and the group considering themselves "Finns" in Sweden is a report by the Swedish Ministry of Justice criticizing the state for not acting according to the minority directives it had ratified in 1999. The Swedish Parliament (*Riksdagen*) recognized five national minorities: the Sami, the Finnish Swedes, the Tornedalers, the Roma, and the Jews. By ratifying the European Charter for Regional or Minority Languages and the Framework Conventions for the protection of National Minorities, Sweden has undertaken a national commitment to protect its national minorities and support their cultures and languages. Thus, on paper, the Finns are a national ethnic minority in Sweden and one of the rights of a national minority is to receive financial assistance from the state, including health care, child care and schooling, in order to preserve and promote its languages.[16]

Many narrators who in principle were in favor of speaking Finnish with the next generation expressed their frustration with trying to live up to the expectations to succeed in raising bilingual children. The Swedish practice of keeping minority languages out side the public sphere, when, for example, it advised the parents of the 1980s not to encourage their children to speak Finnish, and to push it deep into the private sphere of the home can be clearly heard in the interviews.[17] The narrators' opinions of who was responsible for taking care of minority languages also highlighted the practices of Swedish decision makers. Although it is the responsibility of the state to make sure Finnish schooling is available for those who want it, all the narrators who spoke about the third generation considered it to be the responsibility of the home to keep the language alive.

What about those members of a minority who do not consider language that essential? Is there room for them to live out their ethnic selves? The notion of the essential nature and importance of language for a minority was argued both for and against in the interviews, as can been seen from the examples. When I asked the narrators to tell me what Finnishness meant in Sweden there was usually a long silence. The narrators found it difficult to identify anything apart from language that would make Finns different from Swedes. When a narrator denied that the Finnish language was important for Finnish identity, this might be read as a counter act to the discursive belief in the essential importance of language for ethnic identity. When the narrator's opinion conflicted with the generally accepted "truth", the status quo of the surrounding society, the dialogical monologues started. The narrators performed two sides of the dispute, acting as both proponent and opponent of the topic, and demonstrated the superiority of her or his opinion by refuting opposing arguments.

We can understand the dialogical monologues of the narrators who perceived themselves as Finns but did not consider language very important as acts of creating free spaces, in which different forms of ethnic identities could unfold. These narrators described their Finnish identity as being based on a strong feeling of having roots in Finland, feeling connected to other Finns, maybe preferring the company of Finns to that of Swedes or members of other ethnic groups. Yet they communicated often in Swedish.[18]

The public image of Finns in Sweden has changed dramatically since the times of the big migration waves[19] and the realities of the first and second generation are often very different.[20] Many of the first generation narrators I spoke to during the fieldwork periods stressed their differences from Swedes, whereas the second generation had more problems in finding differences between themselves and their Swedish friends. I see the dialogical monologues also as dialogues between generations and the different expectations, anticipations, and realities of the two groups. The Finns in Sweden are slowly changing from seeing themselves and being seen by others as immigrants to seeing themselves and being treated by others as an ethnic minority.

Simply Rhetoric?

The tactic of first acknowledging and then refuting counter arguments in the process of arguing can, of course, also be seen as serving a mainly rhetorical purpose. Example (1b) is an illuminating example of this rhetorical use of the tactic of acknowledging and the refuting of counter arguments. When the narrator does not add new contents to the argumentation, but rather recycles what has already been said in different words, the usage of the technique can be seen as serving mainly a rhetorical purpose. Snoeck Henkemans, a Dutch argumentation analyst, notes, that the acknowledging of counter arguments, whether the speaker attacks them or not, always has rhetorical effects: her or his audience would, generally speaking, perceive the person as an objective and honest person. Acknowledging and refuting counter arguments also indicates that the speaker is very sure about her or his arguments since she or he voluntarily mentions a counter arguments to her or his own standpoint.[21] When narrators introduced counter arguments to their initial standpoints in this way, I considered the use of this tactic to be a reaction to anticipated criticism. The narrators were anticipating what they assumed would be the reaction of their opponents, their audience, or their counter parts. To react to something before one's opponent even raises it, reveals that one is sensitive to the issue inherent in the topic, and, of course, the conversation might take. A narrator of my interviews who wants to underline the insignificance of the Finnish language certainly knows that there are plenty of people who do not share this view and who have strong opinions to the contrary. The narrator might even know that a majority thinks that her or his position is wrong. If we think of this dynamic from a rhetorical point of view, this move shows that the speaker is aware of other opinions, has considered the different ways of approaching the issue being discussed, but has solid grounds for thinking that she or he is right. Some narrators even phrased themselves clearly indicating the pro and contra arguments as follows: "of course I know there are others saying X and Y, but in my opinion Z is the only way because..." or, as in example (1a), the narrator said "of course language is important, but..."

Concluding Thoughts

In this article I have discussed with the help of some examples the phenomenon of dialogical monologues which is frequently found in the interview data I have collected with second generation Finnish immigrants in Sweden. I have also attempted to explain why language related topics led the narrators to start a dialogical monologue. In these sequences, the narrators started to argue by acknowledging and refuting counter arguments, as if they were arguing with someone. Regardless of the particular opinion they themselves held, many narrators used this rhetorical technique in formulating their arguments, and defended their opinions about the status of Finnish language in their lives, as part of their Finnish identity and discussed its significance for Finnish identity in Sweden. In this process they presented arguments in favor and against their opinion and by acknowledging and refuting these counter arguments they worked their way towards finding the stronger and, thus, superior opinion.

To argue in this manner simulates an "ordinary argument" between two participants, but in these sequences the narrators themselves took both roles and presented all the arguments for and against themselves. The interesting thing about these arguing sequences is that no verbal criticism, whatsoever, took place when the narrators started to present the pros and cons of their standpoints and attached to the arguments that followed.

I have analyzed that the dialogical monologues could, on the one hand, be triggered by the discourse about Swedish-Finns, about how they ought to live their lives, and how immigrants, generally speaking, are seen and treated in Swedish society. The generally accepted idea of the significance of the Finnish language for the Finnish minority was an even more controversial subject, which the narrators felt an even greater need to argue about. Those narrators who felt that their opinion was not generally accepted used dialogical monologues to prove that their opinions were superior. For those narrators who were convinced of the essential importance of language for minority groups, the same technique proved to be a useful tool in arguing for their view. For both viewpoints the issue of language led to dialogical monologues. On the other hand, dialogical monologues can be understood as dialogues between generations and be the torch carriers for new ways of living out a Finnish ethnic identity. The experiences of their parents' generation of Sweden, starting with the physical journey of migration, and getting to know their new country, right up to the decision to stay for good is more often than not very different from the experiences of their children's generation. I also see dialogical monologues as signposts for changing identities. When something new is about to be born, some storms can be expected.

NOTES

1. See, for example, Lainio 1996; Snellman 2003.
2. In the 1960s approximate two-thirds of Finnish immigrants in Sweden found employment in heavy industry, Korkiasaari & Tarkiainen 2000, 174. For Finns on the Swedish labor market, see also Nelhans 1973, 110–116.
3. Trankell 1974, 175–187.
4. See Snoeck Henkemans 1997, 132. For implicit criticism and reactions, see van Eemeren & Grootendorst & Snoeck Henkemans 2002, 5, 28–29.
5. In this article, I will, for the sake of clarity, use the term second generation immigrant when referring to the narrators. Some of them would not subscribe to this definition, but would, rather, call themselves Swedes, Finns, or Finnish Swedes. It is disputable whether the term "second generation" is an appropriate concept in the first place, but it is not the purpose of this article to discuss problematic definitions and concepts.
6. A large number of Swedish speaking Finns emigrated to Sweden too, but I focus only on Finnish speaking Finns because my interest is in language and the meaning of a minority language to a minority group. Moreover the problems the Finnish immigrants had in the beginning were strongly connected to language.
7. SOU 2005:40.
8. To protect the narrators' privacy I refer to them with a random capital letter. The letter "L" stands for myself.
9. Linguistic research considers language as one of the most essential features of minority identity and vital for its existence, see Heller 1999; Skutnabb-Kangas 1986.

123

10. Additions inside brackets are done by myself for clarification.
11. See Huovinen 1986; Korkiasaari & Tarkiainen 2001.
12. See van't Land, 2000.
13. Lainio 1996; SOU 2005:40.
14. Jaakkola 1989; Pelkonen & Vuonokari 1993; Skutnabb-Kangas 1986; Lainio 1996; Korkiasaari & Tarkiainen 2001.
15. A direct translation of the Swedsih word *fri skola*, literally free school, describing a privately owned school operating in Sweden.
16. SOU 2005:40,17.
17. See, for example, Arnstberg 2005, and for the private sphere vs. the public sphere in Sweden Cantomeris 2004.
18. See also Österlund-Pötzsch 2003.
19. Cantomeris 2004,78.
20. Ågren 2002; Weckström SOU 2005:40, 447–492.
21. Snoeck Henkemans 1997, 131–143.

Original quotations:

Example 1a

L: Vad tycker du, är det okej att kalla sej Finne eller finsk invandrare om man inte behärskar finska språket?

R: Joo-o, det tycker jag nog, absolut. Jag har kompisar som är finnar utan att prata finska. Dom känns finska till mej, dom har det i blodet. Dom funktionerar på något sätt på finska, dom tänker finskt. Dom är nog upprätta finnar! Det ät ju sant att mycket beror nog på språket men jag har verkligen träffat så många människor som inte pratar finska men jag ser att där är det ändå, finskheten. Jag har en tjej kompis, hon är mycket speciell, hon är som jag, så där lite crazy. Jag tror att allting flyter ihop och limmas vid varan, det blir aldrig så där riktigt finskt eller svenskt. Om folk frågar om jag tänker på finska eller på svenska, så då svarar jag nog, svenska. Men kanske tänker jag finskt, kanske inte PÅ finska men på något sätt finskt. Ja, jag tänker inte kanske ord på finska men det är nog ett annat sätt att tänka på saker, jag har finsk mentalitet och gör finska saker. Och jag är ju också finsk medborgare.

L : Är du finsk?

R: Jaa jaa mensan, 110 per cent.

L: 110 per cent?

R: Joo, alltid. Och det är lite diskussion, en del av mina svenska kompisar dom kan inte förstå att jag kallar mej själv finsk. Jag är svensk därför att jag är född här, tycker dom. Men jag håller inte med, jag känner mej, det beror på, varje människa känner sej var ens rötter kommer ifrån. Som utlänningar även om en turk har bott här i trettio år han kommer aldrig att bli svensk i svensk jargong men bara att jag är ljus och har blåa ögon så då tänker dom aha, ...

L: Men du känner dej inte svensk?

R: Nej, jag skulle aldrig villa vara svensk! (Skratt)

L: Varför?

R: Nää, jag gillar faktiskt finnar bättre i regel. Dom är raka, ärliga, dom är lite, speciella: Antingen älskar man dom eller hatar dom. Så är det. Men dom flesta, jag bodde ju i Rinkeby förut, och där bor ju mycke' utlänningar och dom tyckte

bättre om finnar än svenskar. Finnarna var så raka och ärliga dom sade vad de tyckte och that's it. Och det var liksom bra.
Woman 1976, 6/2002

Example 1b

L: No entäs sitten kieli, onko se tärkeetä?

B: No se suomen kielen taito ei voi olla se tärkein osa suomalaisuutta. Onhan niitä suomalaisiakin jotka puhuu vaan ruotsia, ja ne ovat ihan yhtä suomalaisia kuin ne suomenkielisetkin. Musta sitä paitsi tuntuu, että ne jotka on niin kiihtyneitä tuosta suomen kielestä eivät ole ajatelleet muita aspekteja ollenkaan. Se ei oikeesti ole tärkeetä se kielen puhuminen, ei se suomalaisuus siihen kato. En usko, en. Oishan se varmaankin kiva jos noi lapset puhuis suomea, mutta ei se tee siitä sen suomalaisempia tai vähemmän suomalaisempia. Että puhuuko vai ei. Mutta oishan se kiva jos mun vanhemmille, suomea. Mutta nekin puhuu ruotsia. Vanhemmat siis. Joten ne puhuu toisilleen kuitenkin. Ja niillä oikeesti näyttää olevan ihan kivaa yhessä. Ja kaikki tää puhe näistä sukupolven menee erilleen ja juuret unohtuu. Ne juuret on kumminki siellä ja ne lapset oppii suomalaisia tapoja kuitenki. Jotain tapoja.

L: ...niin...
Man, 1973, 4/2002

Example 2a

L: Onko se sun mielestä ihan tärkeetä et hän osaa suomee?

H: On hirveen tärkeetä. Meillä on niin paljon sukulaisia Suomessa, että se osaa, että se ymmärtää ja osaa puhua ite. Ja niinkö meillähän on muut kaverit, jossa se on käynyt, nii niitten lapset osaa niiko Suomessa. Niinkö..

L: Kaikki kyl sanoo, että ois tosi kiva et n osais, mut

H: Mm. Sanotaan T ja F, nehän vois yhtä hyvin opettaa niitten tytöille suomea, niin kuin P ja minä ollaan tehty. Et T on, se on varmaan se mikä on vähän se ei-ii niinkö...Se on ruotsalainen. Mmm. Mut F on suomalainen sitte.

L: Elikkö sun mielestä siinä on ihan selkee ero, et onko ruotsalainen vai suomalainen?

H: On. No, mut jos on, se on vähän eri juttu niinko mun veljellä ja mun siskolla. Mun sisko osaa suomea ihan hyvin vaikka se on ruotsalainen, se on ollu niinko meiän tapa aina. Mutta sen lapset ei osaa, eikä mun veljen. Kun nehän on niinko ruotsalainen mies, se on vähän vaikeempaa, että niinko puhua muuta. Mutta kyl niitten pitäis vaikka se onki vaikeeta, muute se kyl hävii.
Woman 1975, 6/2002

Example 2b

L: Et onks suomalaisuus sama kun se suomen kielen osaaminen, vai liittykö siihen jotain muita juttuja. Mikä se on se suomalaisuus?

A: Kyl mä luulen et se kieli on, tai kulttuuri, kyl se kieli siinä niinku keskellä on, mun mielestä se liittyy siihen. Niinku mä tiiän semmosiakin jotka tota mun kanssa samaa luokkaa käytiin semmoset suomalaiset, ruotsalaisen kanssa naimisiin, sen lapset ei osaa suomee, ne ei ymmärrä suomee, mä luulen et hänkään ei tota, tota, hän ymmärtää suomee. Hän ei puhu suomee ollenkaan. Emmä tiiä voiko kieltä sillee unohtaa, mut kuitenki voi lopettaa puhumasta. Se on niinku se vaan sit häviää pois. Et kun hän ei oo niinku alkanu lapsilleenkaan sitte puhumaan suomea, niin eihän ne tiiä ja

125

tunne sitä sitte. Että hänen jälkeen ei tuu enää sitten, et suomalaisuus ei jatku sitten. Joo tietty on ihmisiä jotka ei puhu silleen ja silti tuntee ittensä suomalaisiks, mutta kysynpähän vaan että mitä se suomalaisuus sitte niille on jossei se oo se kieli. Woman 1974, 6/2002

SOURCES

Interview data collected by Lotta Weckström. Author's private collection. Collected 2002–2005 in Western Sweden with Finnish immigrants second generation.

BIBLIOGRAPHY

Arnstberg, Karl Olof 2005. *Typiskt Svenskt. 8 essäer om det nutida Sverige.* Carlssons.

Cantomeris, Christian 2004. *Det Ohyggliga Arvet. Sverige och Främlingen genom tiderna.* Ordfront.

Van Eemeren, Frans & Grootendorst, Rob & Snoeck Henkemans, Anne Francisca 2002. *Argumentation. Analysis, Evaluation and Presentation.* Lawrence Erlbaum Associates, Publishers Mahwah: New Jersey & London.

Heller, Monica 1999. *Linguistic Minorities and Modernity: A Sociolinguistic Ethnography.* Real Language Series. Longman: London & New York.

Huovinen, Sulo 1986. *Finland i det Svenska riket.* Kulturfonden för Sverige och Finland. Norstedts.

Jaakkola, Madgaleena 1989. *Skolstrejken i Rinkeby/ Rinkebyn koululakko.* Stockholms universitet, CEIFO, Skriftserie Nr 3.

Korkiasaari, Jouni & Tarkiainen, Kari 2000: *Suomalaiset Ruotsissa. Suomalaisen siirtolaisuuden historia 3.* Siirtolaisuusinstituutti. Gummeruksen kirjapaino.

Lainio, Jarmo & Leppänen, Annaliina 2005: *Sverigefinnars tankar om finskans möjligheter och rättigheter i Stockholm och Mälardalen – En intervjustudie.* SOU 2005:40, Rätten till mitt språk, Förstärkt minoritetsskydd. Delbetänkande från Utredningen om finska och sydsamiska språken, 493–681.

Lainio, Jarmo (ed.)1996. *Finnarnas historia i Sverige 3. Tiden efter 1945.* Finska Historiska Samfundet & Nordiska Museet: Helsingfros & Stockholm.

Van't Land, Hendrikje 2000. *Similar Questions, Different Meanings. Differences in the meaning of constructs for Dutch and Moroccan respondents: effects of ethnicity of the interviewer and language of the interview among first and second generation Moroccan respondents.* Proefschrift Vrije Universiteit Amsterdam.

Nelhans, Joachim 1973. *Utlänningen på arbetsmarknaden.* De rättsliga förutsättningarna för utlännings tillträde till den svenska arbetsmarknaden. Stuideliteratur, Lund.

Pelkonen, Juhamatti & Vuonokari, Erkki (eds) 1993. *Luokan kynnyksen yli. Ruotsinsuomalaiset kirjoittavat kouluhistoriaa.* Ruotsinsuomalaisten arkisto/ Sverigefinnarnas arkiv, Stockholm. Gummeruksen Kirjapaino Jyväskylä.

Skutnabb-Kangas, Tove 1986. *Minoritet, språk och rasism.* Liber.

Snellman, Hanna 2003. *Sallan suurin kylä – Göteborg.* Helsinki: Suomalaisen Kirjallisuuden Seura.

Snoeck Henkemans & Anne Francisca 1997. *Analysing Complex Argumentation. The construction of multiple and coordinatively compound argumentation in a critical discussion.* SicSat. Second edition.

Trankell, Arne 1974. *Svenskarnas fördomar mot invandrare.* Invandrarutredningens huvudbetänkande, bilagadelen. SOU 1974:70.

Weckström, Lotta 2005. *Unga Sverigefinnarnas tankar om finsk identitet i Sverige.* SOU 2005:40. Rätten till mitt språk. Förstärkt minoritetsskydd. Betänkande från utredningen om finska och sydsamiska språken, Statens offentliga utredningar, 447–492.

Ågren, Marja 2002. Vad sägs om finskhet? Stereotypa skildringar av finnar i Sverige. *Entnisk komplexitet. Nordiga länder kulturvetenskapliga perspektiv.* Magnus Berg & Riina Reinfelt & Line Alice Ytrehus (eds) Göteborg: Etnologiska föreningen i Västsverige, 122–142.

Österlund-Pötzsch, Susanne 2003. *American Plus. Etnisk identitet hos finlandssvenska ättlingar i Nordamerika.* Helsingfors: Svenska litteratursällskapet i Finland.

127

MIRJALIISA LUKKARINEN KVIST

Helping Us Remember

Migration from Finland to Sweden increased after the Second World War. The migrants who came to Sweden in the 1950s–1960s and early 1970s are today entering, or have already entered, retirement. In my doctoral thesis I have focused on a group of people born and raised in Finland who are now approaching retirement. The interviewees in my study originate from Haapajärvi in Northern Ostrobothnia (Pohjois-Pohjanmaa). Like many other places after the Second World War, Haapajärvi was affected by structural changes, on its way to becoming a modern, industrialized society. Many people from Haapajärvi migrated to Mälardalen (the Bay of Mälaren area), to places like Eskilstuna and Surahammar.

The Haapajärvinens

People from Haapajärvi, or Haapajärviset[1], living in Sweden have had their own Local Heritage Society (*kotiseutuseura*) for 35 years. It is called "Mälardalenin Haapajärvi-seura". About 40 people with connections to Haapajärvi gathered in October 1970 in Eskilstuna to investigate the interest and commitment among the haapajärviset to start a Local Heritage Society. As it turned out, there was great interest in the idea. To maintain contacts with Haapajärvi, to keep alive the commitment to the local heritage among the haapajärviset, and to preserve the culture and traditions of Haapajärvi have been the aim of the society since its founding. The society also wants to create opportunities for immigrants in Sweden with connections to Haapajärvi to stay in touch with each other. The Mälardalenin Haapajärvi-seura is still active today, mainly in Eskilstuna, and has around 100 members.

The Mälardalenin Haapajärvi-seura is a phenomenon connected to migration in a global world. The society operates in Sweden whilst at the same time being part of a Local Heritage Society in Haapajärvi, in Finland. As the members residing in Sweden engage in preserving the culture and traditions of Haapajärvi, they also exhibit a multilocal engagement by taking part in other important social issues that are often related to the Finnish group of immigrants in Mälardalen or in Swedish society as a whole. The members of the Mälardalenin Haapajärvi-seura can be seen as living in "a polygamous place"[2] as their lives and the activity of their society involve (at least) two places and countries.

As stated in the article by Hanna Snellman in this anthology, the term and concept of a diaspora has seldom been used by researchers in analysing Finns in Sweden even though a diaspora today has a broader definition than before. I suggest that the concept of a diaspora can be a useful analytic tool in discussing migration movements from Finland to Sweden in order to explore the connections, relationships, and sense of belonging of individuals and groups of people. People living in a diaspora tend to uphold a collective memory.[3] They maintain a shared vision, or myth, of a common origin, its physical place and history. This article focuses on how a group of immigrants from Finland uphold a collective memory in a diaspora. The article is based on observations and interviews conducted for my doctoral thesis.[4]

The fieldwork was conducted between the autumn of 2002 and the autumn of 2004 and consisted of participating observations and interviews. During the fieldwork, I took part in various activities organized by the Mälardalenin Haapajärvi-seura and I interviewed fourteen members of the society. The people interviewed in Mälardalen have been living in Sweden for decades. Thus, they have a long experience of, as well as a long perspective on, life as immigrants. I also interviewed six people in Haapajärvi who all have a connection to the Mälardalenin Haapajärvi-seura.

The interviews focused on the individuals' childhood and life in Haapajärvi, the migration to Sweden and their life there, but also on relationships with other people and places, then and now. The interviews touched on the present as well as plans for the future. At the time of the interviews, all of the people interviewed planned to remain in Sweden and to spend their old age there. I was interested in their explanations of why they remained in Sweden, how they identify themselves, and how they describe their relationships with their place of origin and their present place of residence. The descriptions of how the people interviewed look at and identify themselves with their place of origin and their current place of residence is the main focus of the interviews.

They Were Young at the Time

The interviewees were young when they moved to Sweden. Our age impacts powerfully on how we see ourselves and how other people see us. In all societies, there are life phases that are socially defined and related to norms, expectations, rights, and responsibilities.[5] At the time of their migration, many of the interviewees were between adolescence and adulthood, a transition in life when they were expected to find a job, earn their living, and start a family of their own.[6] The question of migration was raised in this phase of their lives. There was a certain tradition of migration in the locality. Many people had moved to other countries, mainly to Sweden, or to other localities in Finland. Many people also chose to remain in Haapajärvi although they – for some period, shorter or longer – worked outside Haapajärvi. To migrate was, in other words, a common and normal strategy for young people on their way to becoming independent adults. The decision to migrate can be seen as a reaction to social conditions at the time with unemployment, harsh work conditions, low wages, and bad housing, even if a sense of adventurousness and a curiosity about life outside Haapajärvi were also part of the decision.

The interviewees were part of a network of relatives and neighbors connecting Haapajärvi with several localities in Sweden. At the time of their migration they knew someone, or several people, living in Sweden. These were the people that enticed and encouraged them to move to Sweden. Due to this network, they were able to adjust themselves quickly upon their arrival in Sweden.[7] Life in Sweden started to roll on, day by day. Only two of the people interviewed intended at that time to stay in Sweden permanently whereas the others had no such plans. They had an open mind about their stay in Sweden. For many years, even decades, they thought or dreamt about returning to Haapajärvi or some other locality in Finland. Everyday life came in between the dreams of returning. Work gave them stability and an income. The children started school. The dream of returning stayed with many of them for a long time; they just postponed it to a more distant future.[8] As time went by they came to the realisation that the dream of returning had died, to return was no longer a realistic option.

The haapajärviset were linked to each other through neighbourhood, kinship, and friendship forged already in Haapajärvi. These links were important and active in their migration. The networks that the haapajärviset in Mälardalen had already established were activated when some enthusiasts started to ask about the interest in a Local Heritage Society. The social relations already established in Haapajärvi therefore continued to be important in Sweden. One can find a similar phenomenon in other groups of Finns in Sweden. An inventory of friendships shows that many childhood and adolescent friendships were preserved in Sweden. Kinship relations were upheld as well.[9] The shared experience of migration seems to facilitate contacts with other people in the same situation. Experiences as immigrants, belonging to the same ethnic group, and a common native language seem to bring people together. Migration did not break the network of kinship and friendships among the haapajärviset in the diaspora. Due to the Mälardalenin Haapajärvi-seura and its members, old ties between Mälardalen and Haapajärvi were preserved.[10] At the same time new ties were created in the form of cultural exchanges and reciprocal visits.

The interviewees had not been engaged in the local heritage movement, but some of them were active in other associations in Haapajärvi. Breaking away from the home community and moving to a new environment were probably the main ingredients in their decision to become involved in the Local Heritage Society. This would suggest that the identity of an individual was constructed in interaction, and in a dialectic relationship, with other people.[11] A new environment challenges one's identities in a way that can lead one to reflect on one's own sense of belonging. These reflective thoughts can be triggered by ordinary everyday conversations. In Sweden one could be asked "Are you going home to Finland during your vacation?" The relatives and former neighbors in Finland could comment "The Swedes are here for a vacation." These seemingly shallow and ordinary statements raise the question of national, ethnic, and local identifications. People living outside their country of origin develop an ethnic consciousness over time.[12] In a similar way, a local identification with Haapajärvi was created among the interviewees as they were now at a distance from Haapajärvi. Perhaps the haapajärviset were able to see Haapajärvi in a different way because they were far away? The consciousness of Haapajärvi as a home community came at the same time as the people became aware of other places, of other new home communities. The image of the home community left behind appears in a new light when it is looked upon from a distance.

As the haapajärviset in Mälardalen in the 1970s founded the Local Heritage Society, they copied other societies from the Finnish countryside. The inspiration for organizing an association came from the ideas and experiences they had carried with them to Sweden, gathered into a collective memory. In the 1970s, the haapajärviset would often dance to the rhythms and tunes of their own orchestra. The association would organize celebrations for holidays, they would travel and make small trips in and outside Sweden. In winter, ice fishing was organized and in summer they would go camping together.

Today all of this is mainly history and memories. The Mälardalenin Haapajärvi-seura is still active even if the focus of its activities has changed as have expressions of commitment to the Local Heritage Society. The change is a reflection of several factors. The members have aged and there are not many young people entering the society such as the children or grandchildren of the migrants from Haapajärvi or more recent immigrants. Time spent in Sweden is probably also a factor. The members have different needs today compared to the early days when the association provided them with an important safety network and a place to meet each other.

The common background in Haapajärvi continues to be a central part of their being together, and socialisation with other haapajärviset is so appreciated that the association carries on. During the time I was conducting my fieldwork the association offered classes in English, cooking, and the history of Haapajärvi. They also continue to organize cultural activities and trips. The society today is more like an association for the retired since the average age among the active members is rather high. It is the middle aged and elderly members that study the history of Haapajärvi and conduct the documentation of the society. In other words, it is they who are involved in the active construction of the collective memory of the group. It is also they who arrange cultural exchange events between Haapajärvi and Mälardalen, preserve the culture and traditions of Haapajärvi, as well as maintain a place for meetings for the haapajärviset in Mälardalen. Next, I will discuss how the haapajärviset in the diaspora construct their collective memory through the documentation of their association.

"It is Important to Know One's Own Roots"

The Mälardalenin Haapajärvi-seura is in itself a tangible reminder to its members of their common background. The members actively work in order not to forget their origins and to construct and uphold their collective memory as a group. The collective memory is important for the identity and unity of the group and it also contributes to the definition of the group in relation to other groups, thereby contributing to the definition of others. It forms a platform for understanding and communication for the members and plays a central role in the group's understanding of itself. The memory functions as boundaries against others. The collective memory contains specific occasions, people, and places that are memorable for the group. This memory forms the basis of their social identity. But, the memory of a group is as equally selective as the memory of an individual. The memory is constantly reconstructed in order to fit current circumstances. Today always seems to be a logical continuation of yesterday.[13]

Those that participated in the history study circle play a central role in the construction of the group's collective memory. At the last meeting in the spring of 2003 the leader of the study circle made a comment about the work waiting for them in the coming autumn. Several chapters in the history book of Haapajärvi still remained to be read, and the documentation of the haapajärviset was not yet complete. All the participants were interested in continuing the history study circle in the autumn. The leader, as had several members earlier, commented that it is important to know one's roots and that it is easier and nicer to explore that together in a group. Individual members have, on several occasions, declared that they would never study the history of Haapajärvi on their own, but that studying it in a group is very rewarding. At one time, the leader stressed the importance of not having any gaps in their knowledge of the history of Haapajärvi.

To reminisce, to talk about people, places, and events in the past are the things that are most appreciated by the participants in the history study circle. On one occasion as the group was reading a passage on the history of Haapajärvi, Lassi, one of the interviewees, said that he would not have remembered the events and people by himself, he had forgotten about them, but it all came back to him in readings and discussions with the group. "This circle makes you remember", as he said. Another member agreed saying "It is true! You can rewind the film here."

On several occasions, the participants of the history study circle stressed the importance and value of studying one's background and roots. Roots is often used as a metaphor in interviews, a strong and widely used metaphor. It implies that people are linked to a specific place and its traditions by birth and heritage. This connection seems to take an almost metaphysical form. Identification with these roots is connected to a specific place.[14]

In the history study circle they read about the history of Haapajärvi. It is the history of individuals, events, and buildings that other people have chosen to represent the history of Haapajärvi. The participants of the study circle complete this history with their own memories about other persons, events, and so on. This takes place in a continuous interaction between the text and the personal narratives. In a study of orally narrated local history, the researcher Anne Bergman describes narratives of the past as a mosaic of different topics and themes. In these narratives one can find the narrators' personal memories, thoughts, and observations about the local community together with information found in books and archives and conclusions drawn from discussions with academic scholars. According to Bergman, the history of a home community can be regarded as a lifestory narrative as the Self is constantly present in the historical account. Events in the home community are linked together with the narrators' own lives.[15] This also happens in the history circle of Mälardalenin Haapajärvi-seura as the individual members' lives are related to and linked together with, broader processes of social change. The participants discuss the effects of historical events on society as a whole as well as on their own personal lives.[16]

The participants of the history study circle construct and uphold a collective memory that contains people who lived long ago, and events, and places that were important in the past. But the collective memory also includes people of today, current events, and important places in Haapajärvi as well as in Mälardalen. Stuart Hall discusses a diasporic identity constructed by both "where you come from" and "where you are now". The identity of an individual is formed by several places and multiple histories. The diasporic identity is continuously constructed and reconstructed by imaginary homelands and home communities. These lands and communities are created through images, narratives, and fantasies as well as the actual places where people currently reside. Hall sees the construction of identity as an ongoing process that varies over time and space.[17] Through the documentating of the haapajärviset in the diaspora, the members of the history study circle are also actively writing their own history in Mälardalen, the place where they are now. At the same time, the documentation is constantly related to Haapajärvi, their place of origin. Their documentation becomes an ongoing narrative of places they have been to and where they now are. It also becomes a narrative about how individuals position themselves in relation to these places.[18]

To Do a Memory Puzzle

At the time I was conducting my fieldwork the Mälardalenin Haapajärvi-seura was in a new and exciting phase in the construction of a collective memory. The association had, at the time, been active for over 30 years. Members, mainly those studying the local history of Haapajärvi, had actively and purposefully started to document and gather the memories and experiences of members and other haapajärviset in a questionnaire that was sent to all the haapajärviset they knew about. The questionnaire contained 18 questions about how long they had been in Sweden, the purpose of their stay, how often they visited Finland and Haapajärvi and which newspapers they read, etc. There was also a question asking where they felt they belonged and where they felt most at home. The respondents were given space to write down their thoughts about their lives as immigrants. There were also questions about their children and grandchildren in terms of citizenship, mother language, visits to Finland, and whether they regard themselves as Swedes, Finns or Finns in Sweden. Three hundred and thirty-two questionnaires were sent all over Sweden. Two hundred and nine people answered.[19] What explains this rather large response? People probably regard questions about identity as very important. It may well be that they make a deliberate choice to take part in this recording of history.

I find the questionnaire as a phenomenon and its meaning to the association and its members very interesting. The participants have simply tried to remember all the people that migrated from Haapajärvi to Sweden. They remember relatives, neighbors, and friends of neighbors. "Were there not several young boys that travelled to Sweden from that farm in the neighboring village?" asks one and an other remembers the family name and yet another their first names. One piece at a time they fill in the puzzle until they have finally mapped out whole villages. Images of farms and villages emptied of people were thrown into focus during their discussions. In the summertime, cars with Swedish registration plates were visible on the village roads. On many farms one could even see several Swedish registered cars at the same time. The villages were lively. With the end of the holiday season the village became quiet. Young men and women followed those returning to work in Sweden, and Swedish society and workplaces were populated by those who had emigrated. The silent countryside after the Second World War is a common theme in Finnish films and novels. This kind of narrative is also common among immigrants from Finland.

There are life-scripts,[20] which are general ideas about how for example migrants should tell the real and true story of the migrations. In the history study circle, the participants reminisced and described the silent countryside in Haapajärvi. They remembered about who had migrated and where they had moved to. One participant was good at using computers and started to make searches on the Internet. Every time the study circle met, the participants came up with more and more migrants, and new searches were made on the Internet. The results were announced at the next meeting. Teamwork based on each individual member's personal memories forms the foundation of the association's collective memory bank about *haapajärviset* in the diaspora.

Without a thorough knowledge of Haapajärvi it would be impossible to follow through with the documentation initiated and carried out by the Mälardalenin Haapajärvi -seura. The participants of the history circle were all born in Haapajärvi and were very familiar with the area. This makes it possible for them to survey all the different villages and the central locality. They know all the kinship relationships very well and, at the same time, they have considerable knowledge about the people that migrated to Sweden. They have this knowledge because of their life experiences in Haapajärvi. The reservoir of knowledge about the locality among the members is obvious.

To Leave Something for the Future

The collective memory gathered in the association's documentation is one way for them to orientate themselves towards the future and the generations to come. Both the past and the present is seen as valuable for the group and thus preserved becoming part of the collective memory and of history. Many of the interviewees were convinced that there would be interest in Finland

and Sweden about the haapajärviset that had migrated to Sweden and their lives in Sweden and, therefore, in the material they had gathered.

Some of the interviewees thought that involvement with one's home community was more natural for the elderly than for the young. They were therefore not surprised by the lack of interest amongst young people for the association. Furthermore, they were convinced that the children and, more especially, the grandchildren of the haapajärviset will in time become interested in the Haapajärvi background of their parents and grandparents. They will also be curious about the Mälardalenin Haapajärvi-seura and Haapajärvi. According to these interviewees, this expected interest will not present itself until the children and grandchildren approach middle age, or maybe even later. "Middle age is the time for them to look back on their lives and search for their roots", says, for example, Erkki. Many of the interviewees think that adolescence is a time to look ahead whilst it is older people who look back to previous generations. Martti says that people in their thirties and forties are so caught up with everyday life that they simply lack the time for anything else. But, he says, the older a person gets the more he will look back. He is also convinced that genealogical research will increase among the Finns in Sweden. He says that many of the people born in Sweden with a Finnish background see themselves as Swedes. According to Martti, as well as many others, this is a consequence of being born in Sweden. To go to school in Sweden also contributes to the self-identification as Swedes, say some of the interviewees. They say that school plays an important role in the socialisation and identification as Swedes. The self-identification as a Finn is also weakened if one marries or co-habits with a Swede, according to many of the interviewees.

Many of the interviewees view the collective memory of the haapajärviset in the diaspora gathered together in the society's own study as a legacy for future generations. Many think that the association is going to die out due to its difficulties in attracting young people. Should the association cease to exist, the members will have handed down and left something valuable for posterity, in the form of this documentation. They are confident that posterity will appreciate this gift. The documentation is also a way for them to avoid being forgotten. They also strive to hold on to the right to define themselves, even if the association ceases to exist.

To Take a Place in History

The collective memory in the form of documentation can also be seen as a guarantee for a place in history. It is rooted in different epochs, and in the future, and in several places including Haapajärvi. The questionnaires concerning the haapajärviset in the Mälardalen area have been given to the Local Heritage Society in Haapajärvi.

The current chairman of the association talks about the purpose of the documentation:

Well, the main purpose was to find out the numbers, how many of us are there. We will, of course, never find an exact number, but we will get an approximate figure. ...But we are going to stay in touch with everybody in the future. That is the most important thing. ...

The questionnaires and answers are filed in Haapajärvi. But I believe that they are going to be worked up into a broader text about the haapajärviset in Sweden. I hope it will result in a small book as well. Or that, in describing the history of Haapajärvi, this will get a special department, or a new historical chapter about the emigrated haapajärviset, especially the haapajärviset in Sweden.

Apart from the ambition to facilitate contacts with the haapajärviset in the diaspora, the Mälardalenin Haapajärvi-seura wants to be recognized as part of the history of Haapajärvi and, indeed, the whole country, through their documentation. The association has actively worked to gather knowledge that otherwise might be lost. The association wants to be visible and take its place in the history of Haapajärvi and to contribute to their collective memory in Sweden, but also to be a part of the collective memory in Haapajärvi. Their ambition is to show that even though they left the home community and live far away they are still present in Haapajärvi. Their project also shows that Haapajärvi as memory and community lives on with many people in other places outside its purely geographical location. Narratives from the home community migrated together with the haapajärviset from Haapajärvi to Mälardalen. The migrant narratives about life outside Haapajärvi are already part of the history of Haapajärvi back in the home community. The questionnaire strengthens their position in that history. Since the collected memories are linked to Mälardalen it will never be a neutral place.[21] The inquiry will of course also be part of Swedish history and its connection with Haapajärvi.

The purpose of the documentation is, according to Hilkka, to shed light on and correct the picture of the Finns in Sweden. She says:

There are a lot of people in Finland who believe that we Finns here in Sweden are some kind of lower class citizens. But that is not true. We were not met and have never been treated that way. We have been appreciated and our work has been respected. In many ways. But I think, that people who do not enjoy living in Sweden would not enjoy living in Finland either. It depends on you and your attitude.

Both the above quotations show that the association, through its members, wants to present its own image of life in Sweden. They want to speak up and tell their story. The members want to take part in constructing their history. The collective memory is passed on, in the group, through documentation and narratives. Memory is not only a reconstruction of the past, an account of experiences, or control over the present, the collective memory helps people to orientate themselves towards the future.[22] Through their work, however, the members select what will eventually enter their history of their community.[23]

It is the migration history that the members of the Mälardalenin Haapajärvi-seura have choosen to write. With their questionnaire's questions, the members are selecting the categories of memories which will be collected from the haapajärviset in Sweden. Their study focuses mainly on the haapajärvisets' relations to Haapajärvi and Finland, a sense of belonging. A considerable number of the collected narratives deal with identifications, the respondents', their children's, or their grandchildren's. Basically, the study focuses on how the respondents, their children, or grandchildren identify themselves as Finns, Finns in Sweden, Swedes or all of it, or something else.

In the postmodern era, many groups wish to shape and make manifest their own history.[24] This exercise in oral history, this documentation written and collected by the haapajärviset in the diaspora, is one of several ways to contribute to the history of Haapajärvi. Their history project shows that people with origins in the same place can live in different locations all over the world and still identify themselves with their home community. Their historyproject reclaims a place in history for those people who migrated from Haapajärvi in the sense that they refuse to be excluded from the community in Haapajärvi, to be "lost".[25] People living in Haapajärvi call themselves haapajärviset as do the active members of the Mälardalenin Haapajärvi -seura even though they sometimes indicate a difference between the two by emphasizing that they are the emigrated haapajärviset. They all identify themselves as haapajärviset, but their experiences of being a haapajärvinen vary.[26]

What is it about our time that makes people search for their "roots" or engage with the past in this way? The historian Eric Hobsbawm suggests that people can not resist positioning themselves in their own ongoing lives as well as in the lives of their families and groups, they can not resist comparing today with yesterday. This is why people today have cameras and video recorders.[27] For the same reason we also engage in genealogical research. Richard Jenkins argues that people have always asked questions about identity. But the way people talk about identity is historically and culturally specific. The communications technologies of today are important in this matter.[28] Searching for one's "roots" and discussions about identity in connection with the past takes place not only in times of trouble and disruption, but also when social crisis seems remote.[29]

The majority of the interviewees were convinced that their association will eventually cease to exist due to the fact that the children and grandchildren of those who once migrated from Haapajärvi to Mälardalen do not identify themselves as either haapajärvinen or as Finns. Perhaps, as Martti believes, people with Finnish backgrounds in Sweden will become interested in family genealogy and start visiting archives and seeking relatives in Finland, in the future. Family genealogy is a very popular and fast-growing leisure activity within Europe, including Finland and Sweden.[30] Perhaps Martti is right. Perhaps future generations will be interested in the background of their parents and grandparents. If that time comes, there is a lot to find in Haapajärvi.

NOTES

1. Haapajärviset refers to people from Haapajärvi. Haapajärvinen is the singular form.
2. Beck 1998, 101.
3. Cohen 1997, 184.
4. This article is part of my doctoral thesis.
5. Hockey & James 2003, 3.
6. Pilcher 1995, 81.
7. See also, for example, Nyman-Kurkiala 1999; Kuosmanen 2001; Snellman 2003; Hareven 2000.
8. See Akaoma & Öhlander 2002.
9. Jaakkola 1984, 26.
10. See Hareven 2000, 31–76.
11. Jenkins 2003.
12. Cohen 1997, 184–187.
13. Närvänen 1994, 187–198.
14. Malkki 2001, 56.
15. Bergman 2002, 219.
16. Hareven 2000, for example, 3 and 321.
17. Hall 1999, 231–243.
18. Hall 1999, 231–243.
19. According to information received from Tarmo Kärnä, Mälardalenin Haapajärvi-seura.
20. Frykman 1992, 261.
21. See Bergman 2002, 224.
22. Närvänen 1994, 195.
23. Hobsbawm 2001, 21.
24. Aronsson 2000, 14.
25. See Telinkangas 2005.
26. Jenkins 1996, 24.
27. Hobsbawm 2001, 38, 52.
28. Jenkins 2003, 9.
29. Knuuttila 1998, 206.
30. Hockey & James 2003, 7.

SOURCES

Akaoma, Helena & Öhlander, Magnus 2002. Inför pensionering. En intervjustudie med immigranter. Underlagsrapport för äldreberedningen SENIOR 2005. Accessible www.senior2005.gov.se (Accessed on 2002-06-02.)

BIBLIOGRAPHY

Aronsson, Peter 2000. *Makten over minnet. Historiekultur i förändring*. Lund: Studentlitteratur.
Beck, Ulrich 1998. Vad *innebär globaliseringen? Missuppfattningar och möjliga politiska svar*. Göteborg: Daidalos.

Bergman, Anne 2002. Lokalhistoria som berättartradition. Anne Eriksen & Jan Garnert & Torunn Selberg (eds). *Historien in på livet. Diskussioner om kulturarv och minnespolitik.* Lund: Nordic Academic Press.

Cohen, Robin 1997. *Global diasporas : an introduction.* Seattle: University of Washington Press.

Frykman, Jonas 1992. Biografi och kulturanalys. Tigerstedt, Christoffer & Roos, J. P. & Vilkko, Anni (eds.). *Självbiografi, kultur, liv.* Levnadshistoriska studier inom human- och samhällsvetenskap. Stockholm: Brutus Östlings Bokförlag Symposium.

Hall, Stuart 1999. Kulturell identitet och diaspora. Eriksson, Catharina & Eriksson Baaz, Maria & Thörn, Håkan (eds)1999. *Globaliseringens kulturer. Den postkoloniala paradoxen, rasismen och det mångkulturella samhället.* Nora: Bokförlaget Nya Doxa.

Hareven, Tamara K. 2000. *Families, history, and social change: life-course and cross-cultural perspectives.* Boulder, Colorado: Westview Press.

Hobsbawm, Eric 2001. *Om historia.* Stockholm: Prisma.

Hockey, Jenny & Allison, James 2003. Social *identities across the life course.* Basingstoke: Palgrave Macmillan.

Jaakkola, Magdalena 1984. *Siirtolaiselämää. Tutkimus ruotsinsuomalaisista siirtolais-yhteisönä.* Vammala.

Jenkins, Richard 2003. *Social identity.* London: Routledge.

Knuuttila, Seppo 1998. Paikan synty suomalaisena ilmiönä. Alasuutari, Pertti & Ruska, Petri (eds) *Elävänä Euroopassa. Muuttuva suomalainen identiteetti.* Tammerfors: Osuuskunta Vastapaino.

Kuosmanen, Jari 2001. *Finnkampen. En studie om finska mäns liv och sociala karriärer i Sverige.* Hedemora: Gidlunds förlag.

Malkki, Liisa 1997. National Geographic: The Rooting of Peoples and the Territorialization of National Identity Among Scholars and Refugees. Gupta, Akhil & Ferguson, James (ed.) *Cultural Power Place. Explorations in critical anthropology.* Durham, N.C.: Duke University Press.

Nyman-Kurkiala, Pia 1999. *Att flytta bort och hem igen. Sociala nätverk i kedjemigration.* Umeå: Boréa Bokförlag.

Närvänen, Anna-Liisa 1994. *Temporalitet och social ordning. En tidssociologisk diskussion utifrån vårdpersonalens uppfattningar och handlingsmöjligheter i arbetet.* Linköping: Linköpings universitet.

Pilcher, Jane 1995. *Age and generation in modern Britain.* Oxford: Oxford University Press.

Snellman, Hanna 2003. *Sallan suurin kylä – Göteborg. Tutkimus Ruotsin lappilaisista.* Helsinki: Suomalaisen Kirjallisuuden Seura.

Telinkangas, Sisko 2005. *Tuskanpunaisesta sinivalkoiseen. Lähestymistapojen, näkökulmien, välineiden etsintää syrjäisen maaseudun tutkimiseen.* Tampere: Acta Universitatis Tamperensis.

The Making of New Finland

TERHI WILLMAN

Urbanized Karelians

K arelians were forced to leave their homes in the region ceded to the Soviet Union as a consequence of the Second World War. The evacuation of some 410,000 inhabitants from this region to new homes further west received wide publicity. Resettlement changed not only the way of life and culture of the evacuees, but also the culture of the places to which they moved.[1] Despite this change, the heritage upheld by the Karelian evacuees continued to thrive in other parts of Finland, drawing strength from the act of evacuation. The Karelians consciously preserved their Karelian heritage by collecting traditional lore and recording their own history. The Karelian Association founded in 1940 was also dedicated to the preservation of the cultural heritage and sought to further the interests in Finland of the Karelians forced to leave their home regions. The parish societies and associations founded by the evacuees set themselves the important task of preserving and recording the culture of the people from the ceded Karelian territory.[2]

The starting point of my research, and, indeed, a major frame of reference for it is the construction of the Finnish nation that had begun in the nineteenth century and that reflected concepts of Karelia, that had been created by educated circles in Finland. According to these circles, there existed a separate Finno-Ugrian nation wedged between two other nations, the Finns and the Russians. The significance of Karelia as a major fountainhead of the national cultural heritage was also stressed. The collective self-understanding of Karelian evacuees during the Second World War also drew widely on concepts of Karelian culture that had emerged in the nineteenth century.[3]

In fact, the evacuation of the Karelians during the Second World War no longer affects the Finnish nation to the same extent that it used to. The ranks of the evacuees are growing thinner. The construction of a Karelian identity has been joined by new modes of identity construction among the evacuees. The new groups formed by evacuees increasingly draw their substance from their wartime experiences, not just their Karelian origins. The various associations that suffered because of the war attract many Karelian evacuees.[4] The evacuee identity is constantly changing and being moulded in the process.[5]

A vast amount of evacuee research has been carried out in Finland from the perspective of the construction of the Karelian identity, and although the concept "Karelian" has acquired numerous manifestations, it seems still to

143

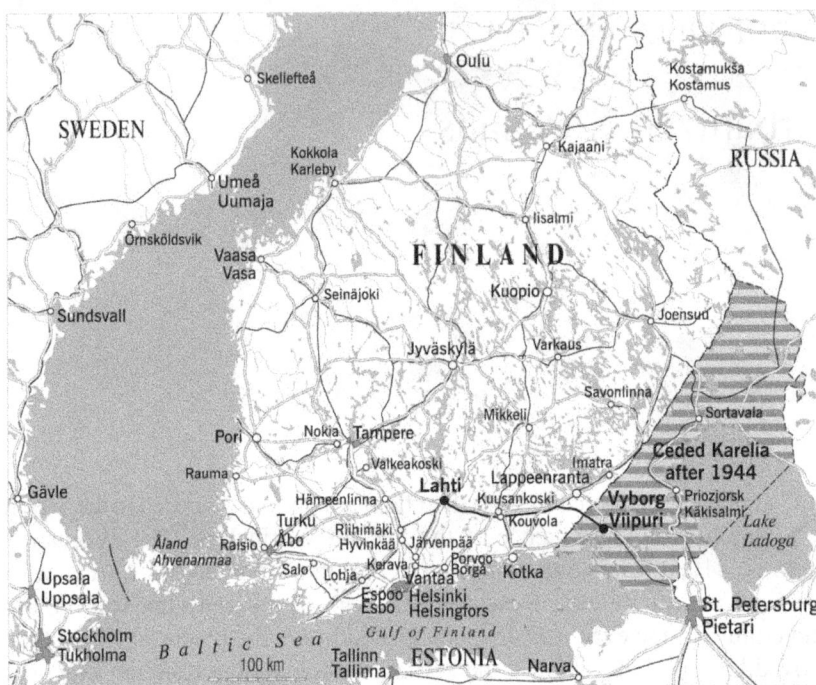

The railway line between Lahti and Vyborg had particularly important role in the evacuation and resettlement of the urban Karelians. Most of the people from Vyborg moved to the largest Finnish towns, and as far as is known, 5,000 of them to Lahti. A few hundred of the Karelian newcomers were from suburb Vyborg's Tienhaara.

be a serviceable one. There is also a danger of examining the evacuees from too narrow a perspective, from the Karelian perspective alone. The emphasis on this perspective over that of the Finns evacuated from Lapland may be the result of purely political interests.[6]

"Karelian" as a concept still carries a strong collective identity in Finland today. Deconstructing the concept may provide a further means of examining the manifold experiences of evacuee communities and the individuals in them. The concept of identity covers not only family, job, profession, locality, gender, and age but also ethnic, religious, national, and political identities. On the other hand, identities are not uniform and lasting. Their constant transformation and flexibility and the objects used for identification are characteristic of post-industrial society.[7] A Karelian does not represent just one ethnic identity. Ethnic identities in Finland are different and they depend on situation.[8]

According to the widely-quoted study *Modernity and Self-Identity* (1991) by Anthony Giddens, "self-understanding is subordinated to the more inclusive and fundamental aim of building/rebuilding a coherent and rewarding sense of identity".[9] On the other hand, the search for self-identity is a modern problem.[10] Hence, the individual has the ability to maintain a plausible story about himself/herself. According to Penny Summerfield,

144

oral history invites attempts to reconstruct the self as a coherent whole.[11] A Finnish folklorist Laura Aro has researched narrative identity in a Finnish Karelian Village. In her study, she points out that the need for coherence is typical in reconstructing narrative identities. On the other hand, she asks, whose identities they were.[12]

Evacuees have, in the past few years, often also been examined from the perspectives afforded by the "Karelian memory culture" and "Karelian stories"[13] associated either with the former lost home region, especially with the traditions of the countryside, or with the war. My assumption is that a special urban perspective exists in addition to the prevailing ones. The study of the cultural manifestations of evacuees is made even more interesting by their connection with community practices and customs in today's urbanised way of life.

Massive folklore collection projects have given thousands of evacuees the change to influence the picture given of them. The views of the ambiguous evacuees in particular have been vital to the definition of the evacuee. It has been in the interests of the urban evacuees to identify with the narrative told by their agrarian counterparts. True, the overall picture of the evacuee has been constructed partly by ethnologists and partly through amateur research, art, entertainment, journalism, and the official accounts of history. Scholars have also engaged in lively interaction with the evacuees of their research.

The identity of the local urban community I have examined is founded on communal experiences in the former and present home region. The community's past has been constructed by collecting and publishing individual memories of childhood and youth and by reiterating them. Personal experiences merge in stories of the past with historical events. One of the results of this has been the construction and establishment of a community in what has become a new home town. On the other hand, the published narratives have helped to diversify the one-sided image formed in the public eye of the evacuee as being fundamentally Karelian and hence agrarian.

Very little research has so far been carried out into the experiences of urban evacuees. The evacuees have been the topic of academic research ever since the early 1950s. Recent research has made a special point of establishing the attitude of the individual evacuee to his former home region in an urban environment. Studies have been conducted into how evacuees from Vyborg speak of their former home town and into the way the Karelians have become localised.[14] Much thought has been devoted to the similarity found in the narratives of Karelians describing visits to their former home region and to topics not mentioned by Karelian evacuees in relating their memories. On the other hand, it must be remembered that the Karelian perspective dominated the debate on evacuees and related issues for many years in Finland. Evacuees have been addressed via resettlement and adaptation to the agrarian way of life, and the Karelian evacuees' experience accordingly fits the stereotypes of agrarian culture in particular. My interest has been in the relationship between the Karelian cultural phenomenon (the transfer of agrarian tradition, adaptation narratives) and evacuees' experiences in urban localities.

My article is concerned with the identity of an urban evacuee community in the town of Lahti, in other words, the evacuees' story of their local community since the Second World War. My material consists of narratives, photographs, publications, and other items such as documents produced by this local community. Using these, I will discuss how the construction of this urban Karelian evacuee community compares with the prevailing, seemingly agrarian and even homogeneous evacuee experience. Let us call the object of my research the urban Karelian evacuee community as distinct from evacuee communities of rural origin, identifiable as Karelian.

This article is based on my ongoing doctoral research, the ontological approach of which displays the influence of constructivism. In examining the past, the constructivist also addresses the present. The past is constructed and recollected on the present's terms. According to constructivist thinking, a narrative not only follows and summarises, it also precedes and organises experience.[15] My research does, on the other hand, also employ a cultural-analytical approach, according to which, phenomena cannot be taken for granted or regarded as normal. One of the tasks of cultural analysis is to determine what people mean when they say and do certain things, and what words and achievements are independent of their personal intentions.[16] As an ethnologist, I am not looking for an objective truth but a subjective one.[17]

The Miracle of Karelian Resettlement: A Short History of the Myth

A Finnish ethnologist Pirkko Sallinen-Gimple described the miracle of Karelian resettlement in Finland in her doctoral dissertation in 1994.[18] Under the interim peace treaty signed in September 1944, Finland was obliged to cede about twelve percent of its territory to the Soviet Union[19], most of it in Karelia, and on the outer islands in the Gulf of Finland, and in the districts of Salla and Petsamo in Lapland. In addition to ceding territory, the Finnish Government had to resettle about 420,000 people within the borders of the now smaller country.[20] The Land Acquisition Act came into force in 1945 and the Karelian evacuees were able to influence its content. Under the Act, evacuees and ex-servicemen were entitled to land, as were war widows and farm workers who had lost their jobs. Resettling the agrarian Karelian evacuees was felt to be morally important.[21] Nearly half of the Karelian evacuees (190,000) came from non-farming circles.[22]

Rehousing the agrarian population in areas prescribed by the resettlement plan was a sizeable operation. In the eyes of the agrarian evacuees, the allocation of farms took far too long – years. Peace brought extensive migration of people within Finland and emigration. The evacuees travelled south, east, and southeast.[23] There were a lot of difficulties for urban people who represented the industry of ceded Karelia, which were put aside during the resettlement. The main focus was on solving the problems of agrarian people.[24]

The jobs available in the towns and the better training and earning potential attracted townsfolk not specifically covered by the resettlement plan. The only obstacle to movement into the towns was the shortage of housing. Help was sought from people and relatives already familiar from the previous evacuation in 1939–1940.

By the beginning of the 1950s everyone had been resettled. Land for the purpose came primarily from that owned by the state, but also by means of voluntary purchases and expropriation. Some was donated by farm owners. The majority of Finnish farms were not subject to expropriation. There was a lively debate over the viability of farms affected by expropriation, and this was a cause for general concern among both those who had lost lands and those who had been settled on them.[25]

Farms in Karelia had always been small, and the post-war resettlement policy further increased the predominance of small farms. They had been favored by agricultural policy ever since the liberation of the crofters in 1918.[26] The politics of the first half of the 1950s continued to favor the small farmer. Forestry brought in welcome additional income, since the small farms alone were not able to guarantee a viable income.[27]

Familiar and Unfamiliar Karelian Urban Culture

Lahti, the home of my research community, is a town in Southern Finland. It is the biggest town in the province of Päijät-Häme. Until the Second World War it was still only a little town of 27,000 inhabitants, but its population was greatly increased by evacuees from Karelia and by migrants from other parts of Finland as a result of industrialisation after the war. Some 10,000 Karelian evacuees moved to Lahti,[28] which is on the railway line from Riihimäki to St. Petersburg, more than half of them from the town of Vyborg, which had almost 80,000 inhabitants. The 1950s and 1960s was a period of the rapid growth for the Lahti.[29] The town also received people from Viipuri's suburbs like Tienhaara, the home of an estimated 3,000–5,000 or so people in 1939.[30] Most of the people from this area moved to Finland's largest towns, and as far as is known, only a few hundred of them moved to Lahti.[31] When I began my research, I was already familiar with Lahti. It was the home of my grandmother, a Karelian evacuee, and my grandfather's family came from the town.[32] Before embarking on my fieldwork in Lahti, I also acquainted myself with interviews of rural evacuees from ceded Karelia.[33]

The urban Karelians of my research are a local community that moved to Lahti from the Viipuri suburb of Tienhaara. An active community, it nowadays consists of only few dozen people. They are united by their former home in the ceded area of Karelia, their experience of evacuation, and a lifetime of urban living. Many of them nowadays identify themselves both as Lahtians and as Karelians.

"Karelia" has, since the Second World War, often been associated in the public eye with official organisations and communities and has in this sense become institutionalised. In collecting my material I have been an insider, and in analyzing it I have tried to look beyond the material. Ethnologists in Finland have often researched topics with which they are personally familiar and that are close to them by reason of family background, occupation, or place of residence. Studying a familiar phenomenon is thought to give the researcher a head start in seeking to understand it. The cultural-analytical approach further underlines the ethnologist's ability to operate at various cognitive levels ranging from the abstract to the concrete. Society and the individual, the past and the present are all important subjects for analysis. Distantiation is therefore essential, though exceedingly challenging when the phenomenon is close to the researcher. I myself come from an area defined as Karelia, from a part of Karelia that was not ceded to the USSR and I later moved to the town where the people I am studying live. I have experiences similar to those of many of the Karelian evacuees and of cultural features common to our native region, such as the dialect spoken within the family and certain culinary traditions. I may possibly have had similar "newcomer" experiences to those of the urban Karelians when they first moved to their new town. On the other hand, the phenomenon I am studying has many elements alien to me. The people upholding the Karelian ethos belong to a different generation. I do not have their experience of having to leave Karelia or their understanding of what it means to be Karelian. Their ideas of what constitutes Karelian were constructed and moulded among people cherishing their native heritage long before I was born. The Karelian ethos reflecting this heritage now manifest in the town of Lahti is both familiar and unfamiliar to me – a typical state of affairs for the cultural analyst. Hence, I do not regard the topic as posing any more of a research problem than any other commonly recognisable phenomenon in Finnish society with its increasingly global culture.

The Evacuee Community in the Town of Lahti

The urban Karelian evacuee community[34] I have chosen to study, namely, "the former Tienhaarans in Lahti", may be regarded as a typical. It appears to have been activated later than most other parish societies. Its emergence as a *community* was not, however, a coincidence. People began getting together in the early 1980s when they approached retirement. The urban Karelian evacuee community was an offshoot of a national network. Meetings within the national network were first held in the early 1960s and more regularly in the 1980s and 1990s. Some members of "my" urban Karelian evacuee community have also been active in the national network. They still meet once a month at a restaurant frequented by pensioners.

As part of a national network, the local community is similar to other evacuee groups that seek to preserve Karelian culture, such as the local branches of parish societies. They have held regular meetings. Exchanging news has been extremely important, as has evoking memories of the home region. They have also received members' letters from the national community network inviting them to join outings to their former home region and to contribute to books about it. However, it was not until the 1970s that the collecting of Karelian reminiscences began to spread; this was also the decade in which members of the community began attending events at their house "Karelia House". The operations of the national community have acquired the nature of an association, with fund-raising for communal projects. The local community from Lahti and its active members appear to play a leading role in these activities.

The continued existence in Lahti of a community of former Tienhaarans from Vyborg can be assumed to be the outcome of emotional ties that have developed and strengthened over the years. The roles in the community of the nine persons I interviewed appear to have become more established with the passing of time. Communications within the community, such as the organisation of monthly meetings, have mainly been the concern of Silja[35] and her partner Olavi, and another member Helena, who lives alone. They also have all been active members of the national network. They maintain regular contacts with other members of the larger community living elsewhere in Finland, other former Tienhaarans. Other active members of the local community have been the "Susi driver brothers", the "Luukkonen girls", siblings, and a widow Marjatta, who spent her entire working life as a post-office clerk. There are also other former Tienhaarans, their husbands, wives and widows.

It is easy to see that they knew one another while they were still living in Vyborg. They went to the same school or were former neighbors. Yet their mutual interaction only became established later in life, in adulthood. Many evacuees ended up in Lahti, albeit by different routes. In Lahti they all were members of the local community and national network. Their sense of belonging together has been reinforced by their generation's experiences, but one might ask what else possibly? More or less they have had an urban way of life and been involved with collective activities in the town. The next generation, such as children and grandchildren, seem to fall outside this community. Some members of the subsequent generation do join trips to the former home region, but they do not attend the regular monthly meetings. The community operates according to the way of life its retired members. Probably, when the time comes for the older members to depart, there will be no one to take over in the community.

Many from the community have helped to edit publications of memoirs about the former home region. Olavi, Helena, and another girl from Luukkonens, have contributed narratives to these books, and an even larger network all over Finland has sent in material for various picture books. Recording the past became a joint project for the national network, and the former Tienhaarans, back in the 1980s. The first documents were, so far as is known, collected in the previous decade, when gathering Karelian traditions became popular. The results of small-scale efforts at collecting photographs and interview projects provided material for programme items at mass meetings of the national network in the 1970s. The collections resulted in four local heritage books in the 1990s and 2000s, and the authors and editors of the books were mostly members of the national network living in the Helsinki region. The documentation of the communal past seems to have been very significant for the local community, too. It has supported and strengthened the feeling of community by providing an opportunity to get together with former neighbors and acquaintances now living elsewhere.

These four local heritage books constitute a chronicle that former Tienhaarans themselves have produced. The titles of the books translat into English as *The historical suburb of Tienhaara and its manors* (1990),

The urban Karelians' journey "west" – Vyborg Tienhaarans from Lahti made a trip by train to Vyborg in 2005. For them the sight of the train stop of Tienhaara suburb is a symbol of the old home. Photo: Terhi Willman.

Tienhaara in pictures (1996), *Tienhaara – that's where we lived* (1997) and *Tienhaara during the Continuation War* (2001). The books trace the life of the former suburban community from childhood to on its "never-ending evacuee journey". There are no accounts of life in Lahti. *Tienhaara in pictures* (1996),[36] for example, is really a photo album in book form and was produced as a joint voluntary effort. Group photos are typical of the book: families gathered round a table on a special occasion, neighbors and families sitting on steps, pupils in the school yard, workers outside the factory, youngsters enjoying their hobbies. The photos show new buildings, technical facilities, and gardens with apple trees grafted by the local Martta Association[37]. They seek to express the development and progress then taking place in Karelia. They have also helped the community to absorb the narrative and its later telling. They were invariably brought out at every interview. In the second book, former inhabitants of the suburb describe what was best about Tienhaara. It is described as "a nice place to live in", "the most western suburb of Vyborg", and "a harmonious place where neighbors got on well with one another and where there was a strong sense of belonging".[38]

The publication of all kinds of books about their former region also seems to have helped develop participation in the community. It has usually been the custom to arrange some kind of reception in conjunction with a book release where it has been possible to meet other members of the larger national network. The books have also occupied a prominent symbolic place in the private lives of members of the local community. These books have pride of place alongside other local heritage books on the bookshelves of many homes. The books are a way for the owners to exhibit their origins. To the researcher they reveal that the person in question is involved in the construction of a collective identity.

The local community has constructed a history of its own aside from the national network of the former Tienhaarans. An unpublished album shows photos taken at meetings of the national network and outings, "pilgrim journeys"[39], to the former home region.

The national network has an important role in the activities of the community. Reports of these outings have, whenever possible, been presented to other members of the community either at joint meetings or in articles in the magazine Karjala (Karelia). Over the years, the places visited have observed an almost stereotypical order and feature in the unpublished photo album: the memorial in the former suburb, the cemetery, the school, the beach where people went swimming, and the former home. The album of photos of the visit must be important to the local community because it is preserved with great care. Sometimes the collective photo album will be brought out and perused during the monthly meetings.

The local heritage books and photos have been a means of constructing and highlighting the neighborliness of the community in its former home region. Many of the members of my community also live within short walking distance of one another in their new home town Lahti. The physical proximity of their homes is not, however, sufficient grounds for the existence of the community. Shared experiences, and the sharing of them by talking about them, are equally important. Talk at the meetings is often about people who were important to the community.

Many of the former inhabitants of Tienhaara were also important to narrators. These *key individuals* were mentioned both in the local heritage books and in the interviews with members of my community. One person frequently mentioned was the former Tienhaara primary school teacher. He had been "popular with the girls" in particular while still in Vyborg; he could imitate the cries of birds and appeared on national radio after the war. The published narratives and interviews also mentioned well-known artists and local business folk. People were clearly proud to have known them. The books of memoirs and collective records, such as press cuttings and photo albums, create a picture of a suburban community in which everyone knew everyone else. For decades talking about certain people had also helped to create and maintain a collective past and community. These key individuals represented values considered important by the community today. The compilers of the local heritage books may also be regarded as important persons. People obviously trusted their opinions and knowledge of the former home region, since my interviewees urged me to consult them.

One element of the Karelian stereotype is nostalgia for a sort of golden age where everything was better than it is now. Many researchers consider the longing for a former home region to be culturally and socially acquired.[40] The significance of longing is concretely manifest in speaking of key individuals. These are used as a means of enhancing the significance of the places mentioned in the narratives and of ordering the collective past related to them. The narratives of the local community may be illustrated by means of a theory borrowed from Immanuel Kant according to which modern man has a desire to gain access to the objects of his knowing and longing and also achieves his objective via narratives, descriptions, and texts.[41] The objects of longing are, in this case, the people and places important to the community, and they can be accessed via narratives, descriptions, and texts.

The Urban Karelians' Journey West

The books by the urban Karelians I examined provide only a few accounts of evacuation during the Winter War (1939–1940). People said more about the evacuation in the interviews, and even preferred this topic to speaking about life in the new locality. Barry Curtis and Claire Pajaczkowska have explained how a journey is a typical narrative symbol:

> Narratives of loss and retrieval are particularly significant, not only in terms of leaving home and returning, but in the profoundly imbricated structures of narrative and subjectivity. Narrative structure itself can be regarded as an intro-subjective journey. Through narrative the subject self is allowed a regressive splitting – into fragmented component selves – and is offered forms of identification for subsequent reintegration.[42]

In this case the accounts serve to construct the community, since the journey seems to reinforce the community's experience of being on the move. In telling of the former home region, they are travelling in time.[43] The members of my community often used the word "evacuee" when speaking of themselves.

The actual evacuation is an important experience – a major element of the narrative plot of the agrarian evacuees.[44] In the light of my material, the telling of the journey is also important for their urban counterparts. The typical narrative speaks of searching for other members of the family, and about transporting belongings and cattle. At first, the narrated memories gave the impression of being episodic,[45] isolated accounts of events and required several readings before they could be identified as part of a larger narrative corpus. Narrators from Tienhaara use such metaphors as road and railway routes. The starting point of the community's evacuation lay at an important traffic junction. The means of transport used for the evacuation is also a salient detail of the accounts. One male interviewee spoke of his family's experience of evacuation:

> It [an evacuee journey] began when the last trains came. *They* [family] went. Anything you could get on the train, all the cows. We had two cows at the time. And then this boy and mother, *they* took them there. *They* couldn't take any of the sheep. *We* had to leave a calf, and so *the others* went. Then *my father and I* collected up what we could in a crate. *I* made some evacuation crates, just with bare planks, and chopped some up. Then the train came. "Now *we* can

The documentation of the communal past seems to have been very significant for the local community of Vyborg Tienhaarans in Lahti. Books about their former region seem to have helped develop participation and remembrance of the past in the national network of Vyborg Tienhaarans. Photo: Terhi Willman.

go." It was eleven o'clock when we left. Then onto the train, and *we* kept looking, and I wondered whether *they'd* make it, if *they'd* catch the passenger trains. Then I changed onto a passenger train. I couldn't find *them*. Then off at Kouvola. And from there of course, *we* had to go to Uusikylä. *We'd* been billeted at Kokemäki. And so *Dad and I* went to Kokemäki. And *we* took a ram and a sheep or that ram and the calf had to be taken to the knacker's. *We* managed to get the sheep on a farm near the station. And then back onto the train. On *we* went to Lahti, and from Lahti by bike over to Uusikylä. *We* went searching to see if we could find [the family] there. And there *they* were in a house given by some Swedes on Lake Sylvi. There was Mum milking the cow and then *we* were there for two weeks.

The narrator was a young boy at the time of the experiences he described. He also describes the experience of his family. The narratives of the Viipuri suburbanites are very reminiscent of those of the agrarian evacuees. Children and youngsters attended to the transportation of cattle and belongings.[46] The urban evacuees might also have taken cattle with them. The accounts reveal the various means of transport employed. Some went on foot, others on bicycles, kick-sleds, horses, lorries, private cars, or trains. The reports of the urban Karelians also trace a mental journey, [47] experienced and lived, between the former and present home region, the topography of which consists of remembered roads, and railway lines. Typical features of the narratives were mentions of precise moments in time, such as months, dates and hours of the day. These are a means of giving the narratives credibility and comparing experiences.

The time spent on the journey allowed the evacuees to experience their home in a new way, through the experience of temporariness. Agnes Heller the philosopher claims that the home and home region only became focal points in life with the emergence of western societies and modern man. The idea of the home was thus made possible by movement away from, and back to it.[48] Movement and temporariness were also greatly to the fore in the evacuation experience. The narrative structure also makes the journey, being on the move, easier to construe.[49] Though the achievement of a consistent and unfragmented self through the telling of such stories is problematic.[50]

The local community describes its movement towards the past. In the community, the past is connected with a particular direction. Thanks to the local heritage books, it is possible to travel to a home that was somewhere "in the west". The narratives of my interviewees do not bring out the eastern location or eastern culture of their home region.[51] For them, the west does not, however, mean merely a point of the compass; it also carries metaphorical meanings. Does the prosperity or progressiveness of Tienhaara represent the west? *Tienhaara as a western suburb* is described via referring to the numerous jobs there were in industry and trade and such things as the good transport service. The way in which past events are recalled and presented as history in the Tienhaarans narration, may be particular to European or western thought.[52]

In the published texts of the Vyborg Tienhaarans, "west" also refers to a general image of Vyborg after 1917, when Finland had become independent, and the industrial, urban way of life was a salient feature of their descriptions of the town.[53]

> At Tienhaara, as indeed everywhere in Finland, there were, in the 1920s–1930s, strong differences of political opinion and class conflicts between people that were dispelled in time and that vanished completely under the threat of the Winter War. We have, in compiling this work, tried to avoid emphasising these aspects and to restrict ourselves solely to describing the history and normal way of life in Tienhaara in the years of peace and war.[54]

One marked feature of the published narratives is the absence of class conflicts.[55] This undoubtedly does not reflect the personal experiences of all who lived in the area. Though the publications do mention a local workers' hall, a civil guard hall, and the activities associated with it as something of a norm. The influence in the area of the workers' movement and its members is not underlined in the same way as, for example, the influence of the civil guard movement. The presence of multiple and "challenging" discourses makes a coherent story problematic.[56] It is obvious that not all members of the community subscribed to such uniform political ideals and in the same spirit as the writers of the local heritage books lead us to understand. All of them do not try to avoid emphasising strong differences of political opinion.

Above all the "west" metaphor in the context of Vyborg expresses the industrialised, urbanised and capitalist face of Karelia. "The west" can thus be conceived of as a historical construct. Stuart Hall has pointed out that East and West have never been free of myth and fantasy. The west is as much an idea as a fact of geography.[57] The significance of key individuals in the construction of a communal "west" appears to be exemplary. Their opinions have formed the coordinates on a sort of memory chart from which narrators take their bearings. As if by mutual agreement, the former Tienhaara is described as being the most western suburb of Vyborg, and this recurs in the interviews.

The idea of the west includes agrarian features with in a national context. "The west" is referred to implicitly in the interviews. The influence of the metaphor of the west in my community explains the interviewees' descriptions of instances of "madness" in the former home region as something peculiar to the East.[58] One interviewee described his deep astonishment at a building put up by the Russians on marshy land near his former home on precisely the grounds that it was a crazy thing to do: "People just don't do that. When you think about it, however you look at it, it's just so mad!"

The opposition of the west and east signify crazy reverse images. The accounts of evacuation given by my community may be likened to, say, a film tape shown in reverse. By symbolically rewinding the past in their narratives, people are trying to repair a line of development they feel has been severed. The nostalgia for Karelia felt on an imaginary level is a means of providing symbolic protection against outside assault[59], from "East", by describing the "West". An attempt is made through narrative to retrace a line that has been broken in the direction the narrators assume it would have taken. The narrative structure permits the description of development, growth, and change. The narrative about the journey home has, for members of the local community, also permitted them a therapeutic experience of their own history and culture at a symbolic level.[60]

The Ethnological Backcloth to the Story of Agrarian Karelia

The narratives of the Vyborg Tienhaarans about their former home region manifest features of both an agrarian and urban way of life. The attempt to establish an image of a homogeneous suburban community by describing its agrarian features tends to overshadow the social nuances and differences of the population living there, such as the rural and urban poor. Research into the

Karelians can also be said to have emphasised the equality and homogeneity of the Karelian evacuees. Judging from the interviews I conducted, the experiences of the people who once lived in the suburb of Vyborg and ended up in Lahti are in line with the prevailing image of "agrarian Karelian evacuees", even though many of them were from a town. To what extent have I, an ethnologist, adopted and taken with me into the field and used in my interpretations, the assumptions and theories that were built into the discipline at early stage?

In the nineteenth century the Karelians were often described by the authorities and by other official actors. The image of the wretched conditions, from poor housing to a subnormal mental capacity, of the "eastern" inhabitants of the Karelian Isthmus and the Karelian border regions was not as a rule complimentary. According to Hannes Sihvo, the authors of the earliest ethnological descriptions also contributed to the construction of this image.[61] The latter half of the nineteenth century saw a rise in ethnological interest in Karelia. After Finland became independent in 1917, visiting the relatives in the east was no longer so easy. Research was confined to Finland and fieldworkers headed systematically for the provinces and local communities such as villages.[62] By studying the Karelians, ethnologists helped to draw attention to the polyvocal nature of the nation at the time. Some subjects such as the controversies, class differences, or the poverty of peasantry were avoided by researchers for decades.[63]

All in all, what do people mean in speaking of "ethnological research", especially with reference to the Karelians? Hannu K. Riikonen has suggested that the pictures of people at work in *Karjala muistojen maa* (1940) and *Rakas entinen Karjala* (1942) edited by Olavi Paavolainen display a marked "ethnological" interest.[64] Hence the ethnological interest directed at Karelia during the Second World War also included an examination of the everyday work of individual Karelians. Not until the end of the 1950s did ethnologists turn their attention to the Karelian evacuees, and specifically the agrarian evacuees and their experiences of resettlement. The Seurasaari Foundation which supports ethnological local heritage research in Finland, organised a questionnaire on the subject in 1957. A summary of the results was published in a leaflet put out by the Foundation the following year. Not until the late 1980s did scientific monographs on the topic begin to appear in any number.[65] The main question posed by the project was: how did the Karelians and other Finns regard one another during the resettlement period? In other words, did the Karelians notice anything about the local inhabitants which they considered strange, and vice versa?[66] In a way the questionnaire took a stand on the misunderstandings between the evacuees and the local rural population. The misunderstandings were viewed mainly as comic, and they were explained as resulting from the collision of cultures.[67] Looking back, many Karelian evacuees said it was a difficult time for them. They were not permitted to speak of the loss of Karelia. The "correct" way in which the Karelians and their losses were publicly spoken of in Finland was also influenced by Finland's foreign policy and policy of friendship with the Soviet Union. [68] The need to talk about Karelia was channelled into a literary memory culture the foundations for which had already been laid during the war.[69] Fiction has for the most part dealt with the experiences of the agrarian evacuees.

A project led by professor Niilo Valonen, an ethnologist, has revealed that in studying the Karelians in 1950s, ethnologists stepped into the furrow already ploughed by sociologists. Heikki Waris, a sociologist, and his team had conducted an extensive research project some ten years earlier. The findings of this study were published in 1952.[70] In particular the study was concerned with the adaptation of the evacuees. It was conducted by with the help of then current sociological methods, with questionnaires and interviews and addressed the ongoing change in society by taking a special look at the status of the evacuees who had been resettled in towns. There also seems to have been some division of labor between the disciplines: the sociologists making a broader study of the problems of a society in the throes of industrialisation, while the ethnologists debated the rural perspective.

Not until the late 1960s did Finnish ethnologists begin to show an interest in urbanisation and industrialisation alongside agrarian folk culture. Until then, folk culture was not, for example, taken to include the clergy, artisans, or the landless population. That Finland's agrarian past could be regarded as harmonious even as late as the 1980s has since been criticised.[71] Agrarian culture was the basis of a harmonious Finnish culture until 1939.[72] Through the Karelians, the agrarian Finland view became even more emphasised after the wars. It was tempting to draw parallels between the evacuees, harmonious rural regions, and the Karelians. This over-exaggerated focus on the Karelians as the embodiment of agrarian culture was in harmony with the general line of research prevailing in ethnology.

The Karelian Community and Urban Individuals

The experiences of the Karelian evacuees have always been examined in an agrarian context. The fact that the evacuees came from Karelia meant that their experiences came to be identified as those of agrarian evacuees. The ethnological angle meant focusing on agrarian work, and the change in rural culture from the perspectives of the community and its adaptation.

In 1948 Heikki Waris asked in a questionnaire whether the Karelians would assimilate with other Finns. Nowadays, the members of my urban community stress that they are evacuees and Finns. Some make a point of their Karelian background and their agrarian features. During the war they fled the area twice: once during the Winter War of 1939–1940 and again at the end of the Continuation War in 1944. People were also forced to move from place to place during the war, if for no other reason than because of the threat of military action. The period from 1944 to the 1960s was a significant one for the construction of the Karelian evacuee identity, and preceded the primary construction of my community of Vyborg Tienhaarans. Local heritage associations intent on preserving the memories of the parishes in the part of Karelia that had been ceded published books of memoirs. These stories were reinforced in films and literature and thus kept alive. They had a therapeutic effect on those who had lost their homes in the countryside.

Karelian evacuees still reflect on the painful relationship they had with the rural inhabitants who received them. By being in the news, the agrarian evacuees made their voice heard in society and in Finnish cultural circles. The concept of the agrarian Karelian evacuee that emerged reflects the opposition of town and country characteristic of the war years. This opposition seems to have been an international phenomenon that became particularly marked during the war. The idealistic image of lost country villages with their harmonious landscapes subsequently cherished by the Karelians also ties in with the nation's reconstruction project – in times of hardship, rural regions represented continuity and harmony, and the hope of peace. The towns were seen mainly as being conducive to an unhealthy way of life and thus as a threat to the nation's unity.[73] Urbanisation and industrialisation had already become realities in Finland from the 1950s onwards.

Ethnological studies carried out in a spirit of preserving Karelian culture are for their part developing and even solidifying the image of the evacuees as being homogeneously agrarian. The reason for this lies not only with in the discipline but also in the needs manifest in society and culture which the solidifying process has served. There has been a serious debate in Finland about agriculture and urbanisation, and about the sweeping structural change that this has entailed, and the rural traditions, which ethnology has helped keep in the spotlight, have satisfied a need in our increasingly urban society. Individual and sometimes controversial urban memories and experiences that challenge the Karelians' memories remained in the shadow. The published narratives help to maintain the social cohesion of the community, thus keeping it alive.

The narratives of urban Karelians have served as a tool for talking things over and for collective remembering, and they have, at the same time, broadened the picture to include people from other Vyborg suburbs who ended up all over Finland. The community is reconstructed in the present by producing history. Meetings and joint excursions have created the prerequisites for this. The construction of the community may also be regarded as an outcome of urbanisation, as a consequence of which the community has to strengthen the uniqueness of its identity in relation to the surrounding society. The same themes to some extent recur in the interviews, such as the experiences of the agrarian evacuee in the stereotypical, ideal Karelian narrative.[74]

The focal element in the collective narrative is a description of the actual evacuation. The visit to the former home in Karelia seems to be the former journey and evacuation westwards in reverse. The narrated journey may be likened to a film reeled backwards and forwards between two points that strengthens the local community. The actual journey is what unites all the evacuees, agrarian and urban alike.

The control of the Karelian community in relation to the experiences of the urban individual poses a further challenge for the researcher, who must constantly decide where the border lies between the community and the individual when interpreting the past. It is, also necessary, in my view, to throw light on the practices by which communities and institutions have influenced the construction of individual identity in an urban environment.

And it is precisely on the terms of the consistent narrative of the community that the more individual experience of the urban Karelian appears to be constructed.

Translated by Susan Sinisalo

NOTES

1. Sallinen-Gimpl 2005, 25.
2. Waris et al. 1952, 315; Sallinen-Gimpl 1994, 311; Raninen-Siiskonen 1999, 195–199.
3. Raninen-Siiskonen 1999, 285–286.
4. There are several national and local associations in Finland concerned with people who had difficult experiences during the wars 1939–1945.
5. Giddens 1991, 54; Woodward 1997, 11–12.
6. Lähteenmäki 1999, 8.
7. Bauman 2001, 152.
8. Ruotsala 2002, 382.
9. Giddens 1991, 75.
10. See Giddens 1991, 74, 76.
11. Summerfield 1998, 253.
12. Aro 1996, 51, 296, 301, 302, 308. A Finnish ethnologist Laura Aro refers to the concept "narrative identity" used by Guy A. M. Widdershoven. Widdershoven, Guy, A. M. 1993. The Story of Life, Hermeneutic Perspectives on the Relationship Between Narrative and Life History. The Narrative Study of Lives. Vol. 1. Eds. Ruthellen Josselsson and Amin Lieblich. Newbury Park et al.: Sage Publications. Pp. 1–20.
13. For example Lehto & Timonen 1993; Raninen-Siiskonen 1999; Armstrong 2004; Loipponen 2005.
14. Ståhls-Hindsberg 2004a; Ståhls-Hindsberg 2004b.
15. Hyvärinen 1998, 329.
16. Ehn & Löfgren 2004, 150.
17. Snellman 2005, 20.
18. Sallinen-Gimpl 1994, 23.
19. Roiko-Jokela 2004, 27–28.
20. The rest of the evacuees went back to their home regions, which were not ceded to the Soviet Union.
21. Roiko-Jokela 2004, 35–37.
22. Laitinen 1995, 86.
23. Roiko-Jokela 2004, 32.
24. Soikkanen 1970, 446–445.
25. Roiko-Jokela 2004, 41–50.
26. Mylly 2005, 165.
27. Mylly 2005, 167.
28. Hassinen & Heinonen 2005, 9–10.
29. Vihola 1996, 261, 268.
30. Ahtiainen & Fontell & Sormunen 1990, 11.
31. There is no official information available about the population which moved from Tienhaara to Lahti. 116 in Lahti have participated in meetings of the national network

"the former Tienhaarans in Finland" during the years 1979–2004. Probably a small minority of former inhabitants of Tienhaara have been active in meetings.

32. It is quite typical that the family background of the researcher has an effect on the topic of the research. Hanna Snellman refers to a book "Etnologiska visioner"edited by Lena Gerholm, which was published in 1993. After the publication of the book, self reflection on the part of the researcher has been a dominant practice in in Finland. Snellman 2005, 16.

33. I worked as an interviewer and co-ordinator in a co-operation project "Karjalaisista siirtokarjalaisiksi" conducted by Department of Ethnology in Helsinki University and Karjalan Liitto (Finnish association of Karelians) in 2000–2002 led by Ph.D. Sanna-Kaisa Spoof. I got many ideas and developed the research problem "urban karelians" based on this material.

34. I interviewed nine people in 2004–2005. They came from Tienhaara in Vyborg and are now living in Lahti. In the following chapters, I will refer to interviews with former Tienhaarans in Lahti, and to my field work notes about interviews and meetings with interviewees. I will refer to other documents mentioned in the text in order to analyze the construction of the local evacuee community in Lahti.

35. I have changed the names of interviewees, so that they are unidentifiable.

36. The names of the author's edition memory books of the former home district "Tienhaara" in Finnish are "Tienhaara Viipurin kaupunginosa kartanoiden keskellä" (1990); "Viipurin Tienhaara kuvien kertomana" (1996); "Viipurin Tienhaara – siel myö asuttiin" (1997); "Viipurin Tienhaara – jatkosodan aikana" (2001).

37. The Martta Association was a local household association for women.

38. Viipurin Tienhaara – siel myö asuttiin 1997, 9.

39. Members of the local community first travelled to their former home region ceded to the Soviet Union (later Russia) during the 1960s. Later on, from the end of 1980s, "free journeys" to their home region, for example, to the suburbs of Vyborg, became popular with them. Liisa Lehto and Senni Timonen have written about "the pilgrim journeys of Karelians," Lehto & Timonen 1993, 100–101.

40. Latvala 2005, 50; Korkiakangas 1996, 38.

41. According to Agnes Heller, "Kant made a distinction between 'knowing the world' and 'having a world'. The opening up of infinite space, on the one hand and the discovery of the unknown territories on Earth, on the other hand was at first a revolution in knowing the world. Learned men and women began to see the world and their place in the world in a different light." Heller also continues: "The world in-distance enflames imagination, just as it also elicits nostalgia, curiosity, the wish to be there, the wish to expand the world that we have. The hunger for letters, stories and descriptions is also the hunger to fill the gap between the world that we know and the world that we have." Heller 1999, 186–187.

42. Curtis & Pajaczkowska 1994, 199, 212.

43. Lehto & Timonen 1993, 97.

44. The importance of the evacuee journey in narratives has changed. At first it was a reflected in fiction after the Second World War. For example, the Finnish author Unto Seppänen published book named "Evakko" (translated in English "An Evacuee") in 1954. The film an Evacuee was made in 1955 and the manuscript of the film was based on the book. See Sedergren 2002, Evakko – elokuva ja romaani karjalaispakolaisista. http://www.ennenjanyt.net/3-02/evakko.htm.

45. Korkiakangas 2005, 134.

46. The theme was common in many of the interviews with agrarian evacuees, which I collected in the project "Karjalaisista siirtokarjalaisiksi."

47. See also Lehto & Timonen 1993, 94; Vilkko 1998, 27–29.

48. Heller 1999, 193.

49. Rapport & Dawson 1998, 28.

50. Summerfield 1998, 253.

51. For example Armstrong 2004, 50.

52. Armstrong 2004, 50.

53. Could "west" in this case be thought of as referring to the values of the White faction that won the Civil War of 1918? This hypothesis would require broader investigation. See also Fingerroos 2004.

54. The citation of the book has been translated in English for this article. Ahtiainen & Fontell & Sormunen 1990, 7.

55. See also Ahtiainen & Fontell & Sormunen 1990, 147–148.

56. Summerfield 1998, 253.

57. Hall 1992, 276–277.

58. I have heard several stories of "experiences of madness in Russia" during my fieldwork. Similar stories were also told also to interviewers in the project "Karjalaisista siirtokarjalaisiksi".

59. Armstrong 2004, 132.

60. See also Curtis & Pajaczkowska 1993, 215.

61. Sihvo 1998, 450.

62. Kirveennummi & Räsänen 2000, 9, 13.

63. Fingerroos 2004, 402. Fingerroos refers to the article by Nina Sääskilahti. Nina Sääskilahti 1997. Kansa ja tiede. Suomalainen kansatiede ja sen kohde 1980-luvulle. Tutkimuksia 31. Jyväskylä: Jyväskylän yliopisto, etnologian laitos.

64. Riikonen 1995, 112.

65. Heikkinen 1989. Tarja Raninen-Siiskonen has listed all the important studies on this subject before 1999 in her doctoral thesis. Raninen-Siiskonen 1999, 18–23.

66. Seurasaari 1957/2 -questionnaire.

67. Seurasaari 1958/1 -questionnaire.

68. Pernaa 2005, 196–197.

69. For example, female authors such as Eeva Kilpi and Iris Kähäri have written about the experiences of evacuees. Raninen-Siiskonen 1999, 232–234.

70. Waris et al. 1952.

71. Apo 1984.

72. Latvala 2005, 179.

73. For example, Rose 2004, 200, 203, 208.

74. About the rhetoric of Karelians, see also Raninen-Siiskonen 1999, 68.

SOURCES

Unpublished sources

Notes of field work in Lahti 2004–2005.
Photo-album owned by the former Tienhaarans in Lahti.
List of members of national network owned by the former Tienhaarans in Finland.

Interviews

Author's interviews to nine persons representing the former Tienhaarans in Lahti in January 2005.

Printed sources

Ahtiainen, Eelis & Fontell, Heikki & Sormunen, Tapio [1990]. Tienhaara. Viipurin kaupunginosa kartanoalueen keskellä. [Helsinki]: Entiset tienhaaralaiset.

Viipurin Tienhaara – jatkosodan aikana 2000. Sormunen, Tapio (ed.). [Helsinki]: Entiset tienhaaralaiset.

Viipurin tienhaara kuvien kertomana 1996. Sormunen, Tapio (ed.). [Helsinki]: Entiset tienhaaralaiset.

Viipurin Tienhaara – siel myö asuttiin 2001. Sormunen, Tapio (ed.). [Helsinki]: Entiset tienhaaralaiset.

Seurasaari 1957/2 [Published questionnaire of the Seurasaari Foundation].

Seurasaari 1958/2 [Published questionnaire of the Seurasaari Foundation].

Internet sources

Sedergren, Jari 2002. *Evakko – elokuva ja romaani karjalaispakolaisista.* http://www. ennenjanyt.net/3-02/evakko.htm.

BIBLIOGRAPHY

Apo, Satu 1984. *Kansankulttuurimme kaksi kuvaa.* Kotiseutu 1:6–10.

Armstrong, Karen 2004. *Remembering Karelia. A Family's story of Displacement during and after the Finnish War.* Berghahn Books: New York & Oxford.

Aro, Laura 1996. *Minä kylässä. identiteetti haastattelututkimuksen folklorena.* Suomalaisen Kirjallisuuden Seuran Toimituksia 650. Suomalaisen Kirjallisuuden Seura: Helsinki.

Bauman, Zygmunt 2001. The Individualized Society. Polity Press: Malden (MA).

Curtis, Barry & Pajaczkowska, Claire 1994. Getting there: travel, time and narrative. Robertson, George & Mash, Melinda & Tickner, Lisa & Bird, Jon & Curtis, Barry & Putnam, Tim (eds), *Travellers' tales: Narratives of home and displacement.* Futures, new perspectives for culture analysis. Routledge: London & New York.

Ehn, Billy & Löfgren, Orvar 2004. *Kulturanalyser.* Gleerups: Malmö.

Etnologiska visioner. Femton forskare reflekterar kring sitt ämne. 1993. Gerholm, Lena (ed.), Carlssons: Stockholm.

Fingerroos, Outi 2004. *Haudatut muistot. Rituaalisen kuoleman merkitykset Kannaksen muistitiedossa.* Suomalaisen Kirjallisuuden Seuran Toimituksia 985. Suomalaisen Kirjallisuuden Seura: Helsinki.

Giddens, Anthony 1991. *Modernity and Self-Identity.* Polity Press: Padstow.

Hall, Stuart 1992. Where and what is 'the West'? *Formations of modernity.* Hall, Stuart & Gieben, Bram (eds), Polity Press in association with The Open University: Cambridge.

Hassinen, Esa & Heinonen, Jouko 2005. *Satavuotias Lahden kaupunki.* Lyhyt historia. The City of Lahti at The Century Mark. A Brief History. Lahden kaupunginmuseo & Lahden satavuotisjuhlatoimikunta: Lahti.

Heikkinen, Kaija 1989. *Karjalaisuus ja etninen itsetajunta: Salmin siirtokarjalaisia koskeva tutkimus.* Joensuun yliopiston humanistisia julkaisuja 9. Joensuun yliopisto: Joensuu.

Heller, Agnes 1999. *A Theory of Modernity.* Blackwell Publishers: Oxford.

Hyvärinen, Matti 1998. Lukemisen neljä käännettä. Hyvärinen, Matti & Peltonen, Eeva & Vilkko, Anni (eds), *Liikkuvat erot. Sukupuoli elämäkertatutkimuksessa.* Vastapaino: Tampere.

Kirveennummi Anna & Räsänen, Riitta 2000. *Suomalainen kylä kuvattuna ja muisteltuna.* Suomalaisen Kirjallisuuden Seuran Toimituksia 777. Suomalaisen Kirjallisuuden Seura: Helsinki

Korkiakangas, Pirjo 1996. *Muistoista rakentuva lapsuus. Agraarinen perintö lapsuuden työnteon ja leikkien muistelussa.* Kansatieteellinen Arkisto 42. Suomen Muinaismuistoyhdistys: Helsinki.

—— 2005 Muistoista tulkintaan – muisti ja muisteluaineistot etnologian tutkimuksessa. Korkiakangas, Pirjo & Olsson, Pia & Ruotsala, Helena (eds), *Polkuja etnologian menetelmiin.* Ethnos-toimite 11. Ethnos ry: Helsinki.

Laitinen, Erkki 1995. Vuoden 1945 maanhankintalain synty, sisältö ja toteutus. Laitinen, Erkki (ed.) *Rintamalta raivioille. Sodan jälkeinen asutustoiminta 50 vuotta.* Atena: Jyväskylä.

Latvala, Pauliina 2005. *Katse menneisyyteen. Folkloristinen tutkimus suvun muistitiedosta.* Suomalaisen Kirjallisuuden Seuran Toimituksia 1024. Suomalaisen Kirjallisuuden Seura: Helsinki.

Lehto, Liisa & Timonen, Senni 1993. Kertomus matkasta kotiin – karjalaiset vieraina omilla maillaan. Laaksonen, Pekka & Mettomäki, Sirkka-Liisa (eds), *Kauas on pitkä matka. Kirjoituksia kahdesta kotiseudusta.* Kalevalaseuran vuosikirja 72. Suomalaisen Kirjallisuuden Seura: Helsinki.

Loipponen, Jaana 2005. Pako, koti, Lahti. Willman, Terhi & Huovila, Marja (eds), *Karjala Lahdessa.* Palmenia-kustannus: Helsinki.

Lähteenmäki, Maria 1999. *Jänkäjääkäreitä ja parakkipiikoja. Lappilaisten sotakokemuksia 1939–1945.* Historiallisia tutkimuksia 2003. Suomen Historiallinen Seura: Helsinki.

Mylly, Juhani 2005. Asutuspolitiikasta suureen muuttoon – pientila-Suomen kuihtuminen. Pernaa, Ville & Niemi, Mari K. (eds), *Suomalaisen yhteiskunnan poliittinen historia.* Edita, Kleio: Helsinki.

Pernaa, Ville 2005. Ystävyyspolitiikan aika: Suomi Neuvostoliiton naapurina. Pernaa, Ville & Niemi, Mari K. (eds), *Suomalaisen yhteiskunnan poliittinen historia* Edita, Kleio: Helsinki.

Raninen-Siiskonen, Tarja 1999. *Vieraana omalla maalla. Tutkimus karjalaisen siirtoväen muistelukerronnasta.* Suomalaisen Kirjallisuuden Seuran Toimituksia 766. Suomalaisen Kirjallisuuden Seura: Helsinki.

Rapport, Nigel & Dawson, Andrew 1998. Home and Movement: A Polemic. Rapport, Nigel & Dawson, Andrew (eds), *Migrants of Identity. Perceptions of Home In a World of Movement.* Berg: Oxford & New York.

Riikonen, Hannu K. 1995. *Sota ja maisema. Tutkimus Olavi Paavolaisen 1940-luvun tuotannosta.* Suomalaisen Kirjallisuuden Seuran Toimituksia 633. Suomalaisen Kirjallisuuden Seura: Helsinki.

Roiko-Jokela, Heikki 2004. Asutustoiminnalla sodasta arkeen. Markkola, Pirjo (ed.), *Suomen maatalouden historia III. Suurten muutosten aika. Jälleenrakennuskaudesta EU-Suomeen.* Suomalaisen Kirjallisuuden Seura: Helsinki.

Rose, Sonya O. 2004. *Which people's war? National Identity and Citizenship in Britain 1939–1945.* Oxford University Press: Oxford & New York.

Ruotsala, Helena 2002. *Muuttuvat palkiset. Elo, työ ja ympäristö Kittilän Kyrön paliskunnassa ja Kuolan Luujärven poronhoitokollektiiveissa vuosina 1930–1995.* Kansatieteellinen Arkisto 49. Suomen Muinaismuistoyhdistys: Helsinki.

Sallinen-Gimpl, Pirkko 1994. *Siirtokarjalainen identiteetti ja kulttuurien kohtaaminen.* Kansatieteellinen arkisto 40. Suomen muinaismuistoyhdistys: Helsinki.

—— 2005 Karjalaisten ja hämäläisten kohtaaminen Hämeessä. Willman, Terhi & Huovila, Marja (eds), *Karjala Lahdessa.* Palmenia-kustannus: Helsinki.

Sihvo, Hannes 1998. Karjalainen kulttuuri ja kulttuuri Karjalassa. Nevalainen, Pekka & Sihvo, Hannes (eds), *Karjala Historia, kansa ja kulttuuri.* Suomalaisen Kirjallisuuden Seuran Toimituksia 705. Suomalaisen Kirjallisuuden Seura: Helsinki.

Snellman, Hanna 2005. *The Road Taken. – Narratives from Lapland.* Kustannus-Puntsi: Inari.

Soikkanen, Hannu 1970. Luovutetun työväenliikkeen historia. Tammi: Helsinki.

Ståhls-Hindsberg, Monica 2004a. Vyborg – Town and Native Place. Åström, Anna-Maria & Korkiakangas, Pirjo & Olsson, Pia (eds), *Memories of my Town. The Identities of Town Dwellers and Their Places in Three Finnish Towns.* Studia Fennica Ethnologica 8. Finnish Literature Society: Helsinki.

—— 2004 Town, language and place. Åström, Anna-Maria & Korkiakangas, Pirjo & Olsson, Pia (eds), *Memories of my Town. The Identities of Town Dwellers and Their Places in Three Finnish Towns.* Studia Fennica Ethnologica 8. Finnish Literature Society: Helsinki.

Summerfield, Penny 1998. *Reconstructing women's wartime lives.* Manchester University Press: Manchester and New York.

Waris, Heikki & Jyrkilä, Vieno & Raitasuo, Kyllikki & Siipi, Jouko 1952. *Siirtoväen sopeutuminen. Tutkimus Suomen karjalaisen siirtoväen sosiaalisesta sopeutumisesta.* Otava: Helsinki.

Vihola, Teppo 1996. Lahden historia 3. Lahden talouselämän historia. Lahden kaupunki: Jyväskylä.

Vilkko, Anni 1998. Kodiksi kutsuttu paikka. Hyvärinen, Matti & Peltonen, Eeva & Vilkko, Anni (eds), *Liikkuvat erot. Sukupuoli elämäkertatutkimuksessa.* Vastapaino: Tampere.

Woodward, Kathryn 1997. Concepts of Identity and Difference. Woodward, Kathryn (ed.), *In Identity and Difference.* Open University & Sage: London.

Åström, Anna-Maria & Korkiakangas, Pirjo & Olsson, Pia 2004. (eds), *Memories of my Town. The Identities of Town Dwellers and Their Places in Three Finnish Towns.* Studia Fennica Ethnologica 8. Finnish Literature Society: Helsinki.

LEENA LOUHIVUORI

The Journey to the Seventh Floor

On the 15th of December 1962 over 2,000 people, of which more than 1,000 were children, moved during one single day into three council houses in Helsinki city suburb of Koskela. On the yard, there was one desk at which sat just one council worker who handed out the keys in exchange for a signature. There was a long queue for the keys, and people fought in the queue. The elevators did not work that day. The apartments were intended for families with lots of children. Previously, the families had lived in small houses – often without indoor water pipes or lavatories. After that struggling it was a real joy to receive a new modern apartment which had all those amenities. The new residents came from "barrack-villages" nearby, from other parts of Helsinki, and from the countryside, mainly from Eastern and Northern Finland.[1]

These three houses were called because of their color the Yellow (also Brown), Blue, and Red buildings. Collectively, they were also called "Kuntsit"; that is, an abbreviation of the street name Kunnalliskodintie. Three big high buildings, each of which had nine entrances and seven floors, were quite an impressive sight in Helsinki in the beginning of the1960s.

This article introduces a group young people and traces their life from adolescence onwards in these buildings, in one of the first suburbs in Helsinki from 1962 to 2002. The focus is on the beginning on the first decades up to the middle of the 1980s. The study is interested in how the residents formed the character and identity of the suburb of Koskela. What was the spirit of Koskela? Why do Koskela people always say "because of the spirit of Koskela", generation after generation?

Fathers and Sons

In Finland, the period after the Second World War was a time of rebuilding and rehabilitation in both spiritual and physical sense. Plenty of work was available. Migration from rural areas to the cities was continuous, especially to Helsinki. At the same time, migrants from Karelia had to be relocated quickly. Twenty-four thousand new inhabitants moved annually to Helsinki in the period 1946–1950 and after that, an average 10,000 new inhabitants

165

arrived every year. These were huge numbers in proportion to the number of residents in Helsinki, which was about 300,000 after the Second World War. Finland can be called an industrialised society only after the 1960s or 1970s.[2] In other Western countries, industrialisation had already taken place at the beginning of the twentieth century, and, for example, Sweden became industrialised as early as the 1910s. Simultaneously collaboration between the Nordic countries and pressures from Europe for a welfare society demanded clear-cut measures. It is good to remember that due to its rapid industrialisation, Finland also experienced a cultural change of the same speed and magnitude.

The traditional structure of the city began to crumble. Accommodation, work, and traffic dictated a city structure in accordance with working life. The bourgeoisie, or the middle-classes, and the workers settled down in their own areas. Urbanisation had started. The Olympic Games of 1952 gave it a final push and polished the architectural picture of the city.[3]

Having acquired recognition as a welfare state, Finland lived happily during a period of continued economic growth from the 1980s to the 1990s. Both Finland and its people lived far beyond their means. The depression at the beginning of the 1990s was the most severe in Finland's history. From a situation of almost full employment and a shortage of labor, the country changed, experiencing mass unemployment. The bank crisis seriously affected a country in debt and a people in indebt. Following the depression, came poverty, which still holds sway today at the beginning of the twenty-first century.[4] According to Vesa Puuronen, Finnish society today is more unsafe, more unequal and more unjust than it was at the end of the 1980s – only the base skeleton of Finland's welfare society remains.

The country has moved from the poverty of the post-war period to the poverty of the depression from the banking crisis. The payment of the war indemnities and rescuing the banks actually cost an equal amount. Furthermore, Finland had to prepare up in the 1990s in order to qualify for the EU. Finland became a member of the European Union in 1995. In spite of all this, and thought it all, the people of Koskela lived their own lives amidst these cycle of social and economic change. People were crammed into Koskela and this gave the area a character of its own.

The focus of this study is on generations, a difficult concept in itself. The word comes from the Latin verb generare – to produce one's own kind (genus). Later generation was connected to the generations of a family.[5] In this study, it is used in the sense of a common shared experience.[6] It is interesting to use generation in its Latin meaning – to produce one's own kind. On one hand, all the members of a common collective have experiences of their own. Experiences cross each other's path, meet, and continue on their way. On the other hand, these experiences produce stereotypes of stories, myths and constructions of life stories about the time shared together. These collective experiences produce constructions of collective life stories. Generation after generation, the inhabitants of a suburb share the lives and experiences but also create an identity of themselves and the character of the suburb.[7]

Gangs, poverty and slums have been studied since the 1940s, from Chicago to London.[8] Professor Åke Daun started a new approach to studying the

Koskela boys from 1963. Photo: Leena Louhivuori's collection.

suburbs by asking the residents of suburbs "how is the life somewhere there near the centre?"[9] This research tradition has continued in Sweden. Nowadays, due to immigration policy, research into segregation and ethnicity and suburbs has been in the spotlight.[10] In Finland, the history of urbanisation has been more a question about migration within the country. After 1990, the research point of view have changed to focus on immigration.[11]

Living in a suburb and sharing the experience of living in a very special suburb such as Koskela, where the residents were selected only on social grounds, has a special kind of character or stigma attached to it. The residents of Koskela's council houses on Kunnalliskodintie are very conscious about the stigma they have.

Suburb as a Field for Fieldwork

As a research method, I have used the ethnographical fieldwork method; interviewing, observing, photographing, discussing, filming, and using fieldwork diaries.

The first stage in studying the Koskela's inhabitants began in 1984 with the main focus on young people. These youngsters found a great deal of unity and identity through an extreme form of heavy punk rock music. In a field investigation inspired by Margaret Mead, these young people were first instructed to handle cameras in order to take photographs of themselves

The spirit of Koskela. Photo: Leena Louhivuori's collection.

in situations reflecting normal life in Koskela during 1984–1986.[12] As a result of this ethnographical fieldwork, I have produced a public photograph exhibition, a photograph book, and a fictional "gangster movie" together with a group of teenagers from Koskela.

The second stage involved ethnographical fieldwork, and, at the same time, the arrangement of a 40 year anniversary village party in Koskela. In 2002 the youngsters of the first-stage had become grown-ups and were now fathers themselves. The fathers of the first stage youngsters were interviewed as well; those fathers who were still alive. The children of the first-stage youngsters were also interviewed. So there is some material collected from "father-son-father" relationships.

During 2002–2003 I conducted 80 interviews altogether. The main emphasis in this study is on the key individuals of the first gang from the 1960s as well as on the gang of the 1980s and their leading figures. The third group is the children of the boys who have been in both gangs, focusing on fathers and sons. The fourth important group of interviewees is composed of other family members, that is, mothers and sisters.

The theoretical enquiry has changed since the first research stage. Working with the material – interviews, diaries, transcripts, and photographs – has introduced new perspectives to my research. The concept of cultural analysis has also changed in the course of these twenty years. The Swedish ethnologists Billy Ehn and Orvar Löfgren acknowledge that the model of cultural analysis started to develop as result of various studies. Especially in the field of research between disciplines (Cultural Studies), the model of cultural analysis has developed and acquired new concepts. In particular, collaboration between ethnologists, sociologists, and anthropologists has produced a new model of cultural analysis in which the concept of culture is questioned. Further more, it has also been asked whether it is meaningful to study culture as a separate empirical phenomenon at all.[13] A need has arisen to understand societal, historical, and contemporary phenomena in everyday life together.

The moral, ethical, and judicial questions have remained. In itself, writing about poverty demands a lot from the researcher. Moreover, the ethical dilemma in writing this study lay in the fact that the life of the gangs included a lot of things that were illegal and criminal but that were part of the praxis of youth culture. The researcher has changed as well over the intervening twenty years. There is obviously much that is hidden and unspoken which will inevitably emerge, from the research material, and be seen as practices of everyday life when the subject is youth gangs, youth cultures, poverty, suburbs, and survival.

The Spirit of Koskela and the Character of a Suburb

When these rental apartments of the city of Helsinki first appeared in 1962 in areas outside the city center, in Koskela and its neighbourhood, one can only imagine what other kinds of phenomena started to appear. In those days, children were put out to play in the yard, and surviving out there was if anything a struggle. This is said to be the beginning of "the spirit of Koskela" and also the beginning of the Koskela gangs.[14]

The first signs of new youth generation and new youth culture could be seen in Helsinki after the middle of the 1950s. Teenagers adapted and admired the youth culture which arrived from England and America, the so-called western youth cultures. References to an undisciplined generation and "hithats" began to appear.[15]

The new youth culture was in Finland to stay. The media started to follow the phenomenon from the very beginning. According to the media, the center of the city was dangerous for every one, especially for newcomers from the countryside. Young people started to seek out and occupy places of their own, for example, the stairs of the old student house and the park near Eino Leino's statue. It was soon noticed by some that these gatherings produced restlessness and disquiet. This restlessness soon led the evermore confrontations between the police and young people. A vicious circle was created without an any apparent solution. Rock, grass, and love produced problem adolescents, and they in turn produced youth problems. This new youth generation adapted English and international youth culture as their own culture. And education for this international youth culture came through rock music, movies, and television – not school. At the same time, at the beginning of the 1960s, politics came to the school and school adolescents started their political careers.[16]

From the big baby boom of that period a different kind of youth generation grew up – suburban youth. They were conscious about being different in this way. They were living in a suburb which was far from the city center,

169

isolated, and without any services. And they understood why they were living in that area. Over half of the residents were not adults. These children and young people grew up in the yards of council houses. They have their own rules and strategies for managing.[17]

It was noticed that the youth problems of the suburbs and the policy of building suburbs were two sides of the same coin. This linkage was noticed at the beginning of the 1970s by both the municipal authorities and politicians and by the media. The youngsters of the suburbs ensured that outsiders could not come into their suburb. The suburb was their territory. It was obvious that these suburbs started to become centers of "bad life". That was one kind of dialogue between the youngsters and the media.[18] It was often portrayed as if the youth had been the biggest problem for all the suburbs since 1960. Other problems included quarrelling neighbors, unrest in the yard, insecurity, stealing, the bad condition of the apartments, the lack of services in the area, and, for several families, financial hardship.[19]

The Spirit of Koskela – Stigma and Character

According to my fieldwork, the most important thing for Koskela's youngsters were friends. They had the biggest significance. The trustworthiness of friends was especially important; whom to trust and whom not. The traits of a good friend were constantly reiterated. School was a place they avoided. They were either in special classes, taken in to custody in a children's home, or were hiding in the forests and in the city until they were 15 years of age. They wanted to start work was as soon as possible. They lied about their age in order to get a job. In those days, anyone could immediately get work on construction sites without having any schooling. Leisure time was a time when all sorts of things could be done together. There was drinking, playing games, stealing, use of drugs, driving cars, bodybuilding, and fishing.

Home and family were the same thing, or separate, depending on the situation in life. Family usually meant mother and siblings. Home was a place to sleep if one's keys had not been confiscated as a form of punishment. Home also included a father, for a few of them. Father was someone who had performed great deeds and who had survived through everything in life. He was the strongest and wisest person they knew. Only, it was a shame that he often left and sometimes, did not return at all. The relation to one's own residential area was a state of mind reminiscent of the love one had for one's own native region. Even all the stones and stubs were known by heart. Places were named according to what had happened there – and so renamed. The center, "stadi", was a place where one went during the weekends to meet other youngsters. At these moments, other youth was categorized. Girls were sought after and there was fighting with other gangs. The girls were categorized with thoroughness and devotion. They were talked about, they were dreaded and despised. Films were usually watched on video. The same films were watched repeatedly, and preferably with friends. Heavy music filled the hifi-systems. Concerts were well prepared for. Clothes were designed.

Twenty years later these youngsters looked back at the time in Koskela and in the gang. Their fathers spoke about their childhood and adolescence

The Koskela boys 1963. Photo: Leena Louhi-vuori's collection.

in Koskela, and how they see it now, in 2002. What kind of phenomena was produced by the youth culture of the suburb of Koskela in the 40 years of its existence?

Poverty as Subculture and Resource

During the time of my research, Finland went from almost full employment to mass unemployment. The classical division of society between the bourgeoisie and the working class had changed. After the depression in 1990 there were the employed and the unemployed. The content of everyday life, dreams and hopes have remained quite similar and this ability to understand others in the same situation. The common experience of living in this suburb has unified the residents. Koskela people accepted and understood other residents in Koskela. They shared the same situation and same experience. Comparing the different kinds of materials from the first stage of my research with all the alternative phenomena of youth culture one can argue that – this was all designed to conceal their poverty and keeping outsiders out.[20]

171

The content of a life in Koskela also manifests itself in its own special way. In Koskela, the family has always been especially important. The pride of the poor and the hiding of their poverty from the wealth of the surrounding area has entailed a different type of creativity. Social contacts and mutual networks have been extremely significant, especially during a period of rapid social change, and where in principal no-one can be trusted except oneself.

In addition to a collective memory, a collective amnesia began to emerge from the interviews of the second stage. What was talked about and what was left unsaid. It was as if there was a general agreement. The suppressed topics did not relate to crime but poverty. There was mutual working-class solidarity and agreement that there was a constant shortage of money, and the little there was often imbibed straight away.[21] Oscar Lewis has argued that poverty creates a different culture. Poverty manifests itself in everyday life. Living in poverty produces and creates a subculture of its own within the main culture and society. And if someone wants to research this subculture, she/he has to study its language and its way of life, its identity, dreams, hopes, and aims.[22]

A collective memory of the past and the collective, common time of being child and adolescent in Koskela was a unifying experience through all these research stages. A collective way of understanding without the need to talk was obvious. It soon became apparent that "we in Koskela" are different from other city people. Before urbanisation and the building of suburbs, all the city people lived in the center of the city. Newcomers had been living in the country. That time was different. Suddenly people "like we in Koskela" had been gathered together in a concentrated area, and that concentration can be seen in the architecture, in attitudes, and in the neighbourhood. To survive in this concentrated area, the children and young people created their own kind of society, the gang. The spirit of Koskela was essentially the will to survive. The gangs kept outsiders away. Gangs provided a sense of security, strength, and coming together. With time it was transformed in to a myth about a heroic common collective childhood and surviving against the surrounding society. It was a way of constructing an identity.[23]

Life in the suburb was, at the same time, both a resource and a burden. Occupying spaces and places is part of youth culture. The way young people occupy certain places is different if they come from the suburbs or the center of the city. Occupation manners differ in time to time as well. The time that has elapsed from the beginning of the Koskela suburb until 2002 has transformed values, attitudes, and manners, even creating their exact opposites. Some phenomena have disappeared and whilst some new ones have been created.

The identity and character of Koskela, the so-called spirit of Koskela, has been transformed over these intervening forty years – over the course of its existence. A lot has happened during this period. Some of the places have been renamed. The local history has disappeared along with the story tellers, and the names do not mean anything to the new generation – but the stories live on. The local history of a suburb is different from the local history of a native region but there are some similarities. Organizing the village party and the forty year anniversary party of Koskela was like living the local historyof the native region of Koskela.

Youth culture since the sixties has changed, as well. The Koskela youngsters did not swallow everything from the main youth culture. Of course, there was lot they did not understand at the beginning of the sixties because of the English language and the distance from its original real context. But there was a lot in youth culture which they really despised – which they did not adopt. This western youth culture was filtered and transformed many times. At first, phenomena were imitated, and young people lived in the spirit of common western youth culture. What was understood is a different thing. At the time, imitating and varying its meaning was one way of passing the time, like an amusement. They started to be interested in and even create rock music, movies and stories. It was like the situation of immigrants in the sense that the immigrant little by little engages with the main culture but filters out whatever is not suitable.[24] Second generations always exist somewhere in between the past and the future.

A concentrated area such as Koskela creates a very special life. Young people created gangs for themselves in order to survive and keep outsiders out of the area. The journey from the cellar to the seventh floor with all the luxuries of modern life was, at the beginning of the sixties, a dream come true. Later that modernity resulted in another reality: poverty.

NOTES

1. Sculman 2003, 62–63; Pulma 2003, 111–115; Louhivuori 2005, 163–165.
2. Alestalo 1980, 102–107;Talve 1980, 310–318; Helve 1987, 62–63; Schulman 2003, 97–98.
3. Schulman 2003, 74–78; Pulma 2003, 123–131.
4. Pulma 2003, 329–336; Puuronen 2004, 14–22.
5. Williams 1987, 140.
6. Gerholm 1990, 112–116; Tuominen 1991, 45–49; Virtanen 2001, 22–24, 33–35.
7. Gerholm 1990, 121–122; Louhivuori 1988 17–22; 2005; Pulma 2003, 251–256.
8. See Helanko 1953, 117–121; Lewis 1970, 11–13.
9. Daun 1974, 13–14; Interview with Å. Daun in 2004 by Leena Louhivuori.
10. Arntsberg 2001, 31–32.
11. Honkasalo 2005, 251–256.
12. Louhivuori 1988, 31–32.
13. Ehn & Löfgren 2001, 8; Frykman & Gilde 2003, 16–24.
14. Louhivuori 1988, 41.
15. Heiskanen & Mitchell 1985,10–19 ; Pulma 2003, 242–279.
16. Heiskanen & Mitchell 1985 48–66; Louhivuori 1988, 11–13; Pulma 2003 329–335; Hoikkala & Laine & Laine 2005 11; Roos 2005, 53–102.
17. Louhivuori 1988, 40–47; Louhivuori 2005, 164–165, 177–178.
18. Louhivuori 1988, 49–51; Louhivuori 2005,163–166; Pulma 2003, 257–270.
19. Heiskanen & Mitchell 1985, 15–17, Louhivuori 2005, 164–165; Pulma 2003, 257–266.
20. Louhivuori 1988, 112–117; Louhivuori 2005,177–179.
21. Louhivuori 2005,177.
22. Lewis 1970, 13–15.

23. Louhivuori 1988, 112–117; 2005,164; Pulma 2003, 262–266.
24. Snellman 2003, 223–2

SOURCES

Fieldwork in Koskela.
Interview with Åke Daun 11.11.2004.

BIBLIOGRAPHY

Alestalo, Matti 1980. *Yhteiskuntaluokat ja sosiaaliset kerrostumat toisen maailmansodan jälkeen. Suomalaiset. Yhteiskuntarakenne teollistumisen aikana.* Juva: Otava.

Arnstberg, Karl-Olov 2001. Segregation – processer och konsekvenser. Arnstberg K-O & Ramberg I (eds) *I stadens utkant. Perspektiv på förorter.* Hägersten: Mångkulturellt centrum.

Daun, Åke 1974. *Förortsliv. En etnologisk studie av kulturell förändring.* Stockholm: Prisma.

Ehn, Billy & Löfgren, Orvar 2001. *Kulturanalyser.* Malmö: Gleerups.

Frykman, Jonas & Gilje, Nils (eds) 2003. *Being There. New Perspectives on Phenomelnology and the Analysis of Culture.* Latvia: Nordic Academic Press.

Gerholm, Lena 1990. Generation som erfarenhet och konstruktion: En etnologisk betraktelse. Blehr, Barbro (ed.), *Femtiotalister. Om konstruerandet av kulturella generaioner.* Carlssons: Uddevalla.

Heiskanen, Ilkka & Mitchell, Ritva 1985. *Lättähatuista punkkareihin.* Keuruu: Otava.

Helanko, Rafael 1953. *Turun poikasakit.* Turun yliopiston julkaisuja 46. Turku.

Helve, Helena 1987. *Nuorten maailmankuva.* Kansalaiskasvatuksen Keskus. Tutkimuksia ja selvityksiä 1/1987.

Hoikkala, Tommi & Laine, Sofia & Laine, Jyrki 2005 (eds). *Mitä on tehtävä? Nuorison kapinan teoriaa ja käytäntöä.* Helsinki: Loki-Kirjat.

Honkasalo, Veronika 2005. Methodological considerations on doing ethnographic fieldwork in multicultural surroundings. *Mixed Methods in Youth Research.* Helve, Helena (ed). Tampere: Finnish Youth Research Network.

Lewis, Oscar 1970. *Fem familjer. En studie av fattigkulturen i Meksiko.* Stockholm: Tema/Rabén & Sjögren.

Louhivuori, Leena 1988. *Koskelan pojat – Tutkimus jengikulttuurista.* Kansalaiskasvatuksen keskus. Tutkimuksia ja selvityksiä.

—— 2005 Writing personally and speaking ethnographically about methodology. Helve, Helena (ed.), *Mixed Methods in Youth Research.* Finnish Youth Research Society. Publications 60. Tampere: Juvenes Print.

Pulma, Panu 2003. I skuggan av tillväxten. Schulman H, Pulma P. & Aalto S. (eds), *Helsingfors stads historia efter 1945.* Helsingfors stad.

Puuronen, Vesa 2004. *Suomalainen hyvinvointiyhteiskunta tienhaarassa. Karjalan tutkimuslaitoksen raportteja* 8/2004. Joensuun yliopisto.

Roos, J. P. 2005. Missä he ovat nyt? 60- ja 70-lukulaiset aktivistit 2000-luvulla. Hoikkala Tommi, Laine Sofia, Laine Jyrki (eds), *Mitä on tehtävä? Nuorison kapinan teoriaa ja käytäntöä.* Helsinki: Loki-Kirjat.

Schulman, Harry & Pulma, Panu & Aalto, Seppo 2003. *Helsingfors stads historia efter 1945*. Helsingfor stad.

Snellman, Hanna 2003. *Sallan suurin kylä – Göteborg. Tutkimus Ruotsin lappilaisista* Helsinki: Suomalaisen Kirjallisuuden Seura.

Talve, Ilmar 1980. *Suomen kansankulttuuri*. Helsinki: Suomalaisen Kirjallisuuden Seura.

Tuominen, Marja 1991. *"Me kaikki ollaan sotilaitten lapsia." Sukupolvihegemonian kriisi 1960-luvun suomalaisessa kulttuurissa*. Helsinki: Otava.

Virtanen, Matti 2001. *Fennomanian perilliset. Poliittiset traditiot ja sukupolvien dynamiikka*. Helsinki: Suomalaisen Kirjallisuuden Seura.

Williams, Raymond 1987. *Keywords*. A vocabulary of culture and society. Glasgow: Flamingo.

TARJA KYTÖNEN

Five go to Finland

Enid Blyton (1897–1968) was one of the most popular children's authors in Great Britain in the twentieth century. She wrote hundreds of books, many of which were translated into several languages and loved by children around the world. Well, maybe not everywhere. For example, pop singer Madonna shocked the British media when interviewed about her new children's book. She was asked if she had been a Blyton fan as a child. But she had never heard of Blyton.

Madonna's ignorance is not surprising, since Blyton, though popular in Europe and Australia, was never popular in the USA. According to Index Translationum, a translation database maintained by Unesco, Enid Blyton was fifth on a list of the world's most translated authors between 1979 and 2002, right on the heels of V. I. Lenin![1] Blyton appears in the "top ten" of most translated authors in a variety of countries: she is the first in Germany; second in Austria, Portugal, and Indonesia; third in Finland; fourth in Spain, France, Sweden, and Turkey; fifth in Island; seventh in Greece; and eighth in the Netherlands and Slovenia.

Although the Index Translationum database favors authors who write (or wrote) lots of books, it nevertheless shows how widely Blyton's books were published, even after her "prime time" in the 1950s and 1960s. Blyton was, no doubt, a very international writer, even if she was not that "international" in her life.[2]

Enid Blyton wrote over 600 books including poetry books, picture books, adventure and school stories, plays, non-fictional books for children, books about pedagogy. She also ran two magazines, *Sunny Stories* and *Enid Blyton's Magazine*, for which she wrote all the contents. In her most productive period, from the 1940s to 1950s, she published over 30 titles per year. Some critics suspected that there must have been an army of writers behind the popular brand "Enid Blyton", but there was not. She wrote intuitively and in a manic way, spending most of her life writing. Her first full-length adventure story, *The Secret Island*, in 1938, started a parade of adventure books: the most popular being The Famous Five, the Secret Seven, the Adventure, and the Mystery series. There was also a very popular character, especially in the UK, called Noddy, a pixie, whose adventures were the subject of countless picture books.

Enid Blyton was essentially an English author, who actually traveled outside England only a couple of times. Her most beloved adventure books portrayed a stereotypical land of endless amounts of moors, caves, and ginger beer. The stories were set in contemporary (1940s and 1950s) England; however, the social structures and, for example, gender roles, represented rather a nostalgic dream of Blyton's childhood days, the Edwardian age.

Over the years, Blyton's books were accused of many things; for example, xenophobia and classism. In the 1970s especially, her books were condemned for depicting foreigners as criminals or, at least, suspicious characters. David Rudd, in his research of Blyton's books, has refuted this.[3] Rudd's point is that Enid Blyton's books do not represent the "isms" she has been accused of, because readers do not notice them in her books. While Rudd's arguments are based on reader-response criticism, another argument, sometimes heard, is relativistic; Blyton simply lived and wrote in a racist and classist time and place, and, thus, her books contained elements of these.

I would like to take a more historically oriented view, as I believe a book can represent and act as a mediator for all sorts of ideas and "isms", even if the target audience does not consciously recognize them. John Stephens, in his book *Language and ideology in children's fiction*, argues that "a narrative without an ideology is unthinkable: ideology is formulated in and by language, meanings within language are socially determined, and narratives are constructed out of language." In addition, the author might well be unaware of the beliefs and assumptions reflected in the text.[4]

This is why literature, and especially popular literature, makes an important and interesting subject for historical research. It is not only the text, but also the response to it on many levels (reviewers, readers, the literary establishment), which can reveal a lot about the society and culture around it.

I find it fascinating to think how Enid Blyton's books, which represented a twisted and nostalgic view of Britain, were admired by children in so different a country as Finland. Children liked the books, there is no doubt about it, as will be shown later in the article. The aim of this article is to analyze the reception of Blyton's books from the "adult viewpoint". As an example, I will use the reception of the Famous Five series. How did the professionals: literary critics, librarians, and other people interested in children's literature, evaluate the books? How did the response change between the 1950s and the early 1970s? Was the response in Finland similar to that in Great Britain?

Five Fall into Adventure

In 1950, when the first Enid Blyton book, *The Island of Adventure*, was published in Finnish, Finland was still an agrarian country; a country on the verge of urbanization and economic prosperity. In popular culture, the center of gravity had already started to move towards the West. In the case of popular literature, this had already occurred in the 1920s and 1930s when the focus had changed from the Nordic countries and Germany to the Anglo-American world.[5] All in all, in the fifties, Finland was a mixture of the old and the new: many young people still worked in agriculture as their grandparents had done, while some tried to rock around the clock to the tunes and trends of American youth culture.

Then, in 1952, a fresh breeze blew in from the west in the shape of *Donald Duck* magazine. The importance of *Donald Duck* for Finnish children cannot be overestimated; even today, it is the best selling weekly magazine in Finland. Other comics, as well as movies, and, later, television came to challenge books as the main media for children's amusement.

However, Blyton's books did not represent modern American trends, but a more traditional older society, with strictly defined social classes and virtues. The books resembled more the popular books from the early part of the twentieth century, for example, Edith Nesbit's *Five Children and It*[6], or, in Finland, the children's fiction written in the 1920s and 1930s, in that the values appreciated were good manners, self-discipline, justice, honesty, and physical health.[7]

The 1950s saw a change in children's literature: the didactic aspect, common in the 1940s, diminished, more books were translated, and, generally, the genre received more attention from publishers and the newspapers.[8] The content of the books changed too. Children's literature that librarians, teachers, and the critics acknowledged involved themes of growth; personal development, and the ability to resolve a crisis. The typical hero was an exceptional character, slightly rebellious and defiant, the kind of guy who gets wiser in difficult situations.[9] Moral education was also involved. For example, Toini Havu, a literary critic in the leading Finnish newspaper, *Helsingin Sanomat*, said that the ideal type of fiction for the young encouraged chastity and the striving for objectives.[10]

If book awards represented the views of adult readers, a survey conducted in 1950 revealed a contradiction between adult and youth responses. The Finnish author Eino Arohonka conducted a reader survey for his doctoral thesis, which, however, was not accepted by the University of Helsinki. Päivi Heikkilä-Halttunen, who has made several studies on Finnish children's literature, argues that one of the reasons (the others being personal and political conflicts) why Arohonka's doctoral thesis was not accepted was that he handled quite popular light reading in his study, and that was too much for some of the academics.[11]

Arohonka based his research on over 4,000 questionnaires answered by secondary school pupils in spring term 1950. Though extensive number of pupils, this research represents only a minority of Finnish youth, as in those days only a limited number of children went to secondary school. Nevertheless, the research gives some insights into what Finnish schoolboys and girls read. The boys' favorite books involved action and adventure: Finnish adventure novels, the *Tarzan* series, *The Three Musketeers*, *Robinson Crusoe*, and *The Mysterious Island*, while the girls' favorites dealt with Victorian family ideals: classics like *Emily of New Moon*, *Anne of Green Gables*, *Little Women*, and *The Secret Garden*, as well as Finnish school stories.[12] Perhaps, not surprisingly, the children's favorites rarely coincided with the books appreciated by the literary establishment in Finland. The disparity in views can be seen by the results of the annual Topelius awards, a major prize in Finland given to the authors of children's literature, and the

Anne at Kirrin Cottage. A drawing by 8-year-old Terhi Willman, one of the authors of this anthology, in 1979.

results of Arohonka's questionnaire. None of the authors who received the award between 1949 and 1951 appeared on the children's favourite list at all, although some had a few "votes".[13]

The first Blyton book was just about to be released in Finnish when Arohonka was researching his PhD. The results of Arohonka's questionnaire show that in 1950 one might have had a strong horizon of expectations for new adventure stories. After all, many of the foreign books on the favorite list had been written in the nineteenth century and had been translated into Finnish many decades earlier. Furthermore, on the girls' list the focus was on family and school stories, the only adventure books on the list were written by Alexandre Dumas and Zacharias Topelius, a famous Finnish, nineteenth century author. Considering the favorites in 1950, Blyton's adventure books probably appeared as different and new, with a group of children as the heroes, and with two girl characters, too.

Five Have a Wonderful Time

Legend has it that most of the public libraries in England would have liked to ban Blyton in the 1950s. Both Sheila Ray and David Rudd have disproved this and argue that even if some librarians actually could have banned her books, a talk in the 1970s and 1980s of a moral panic is exaggerated.[14] Nevertheless, the question "is Blyton good for my children?" was asked by more than just a few parents, librarians, and teachers in England.

A drawing inspired by Blyton's book The Sea of Adventure. A drawing by Terhi Willman, 1979.

Blyton's aim was to be the storyteller for all age groups, so that English children could grow together with her books from toddlers to teenagers. "I myself love all ages, and write for every age from two-and-a-half to the teens", she wrote in an article in the *New Statesman*, in 1959.[15] Blyton's objectives were realized. According to Sheila Ray, Blyton headed all kinds of surveys carried out amongst British children from the end of the 1940s onwards.[16]

This evoked a negative response especially amongst librarians and teaching professionals in England. In England, Blyton's books were criticized for mediocre plots, weak characterization, and an unimaginative use of language. The most critical reviewers thought the books could ruin a child's literary taste.

Blyton wrote hundreds of books, but only about sixty were published in Finnish. Her books were published in Finland by series. At first, the four books in the *Adventure* series were published by publishing company WSOY between 1950 and 1954. From 1956 to 1964 publishing company Tammi published all twenty-one *Famous Five* books. Tammi continued with the *Mystery* series, fourteen books between 1962 and 1967, and with the *Secret Seven* series, fifteen books between 1973 and 1977. Besides these series, two *Noddy* books were published in Finnish in 1962, with the original pictures and texts. In the 1990s, thirteen more Noddy books, in revised versions, were published. Only a couple of Blyton's fairy-tale books were ever published in Finnish, and none of the school series, *Mallory Towers*, *Naughtiest Girl*, and *St Clare's*, were ever translated into Finnish.

Without more detailed research, it is impossible to say why only the adventure series were published in Finnish. Maybe the school story market in

Finland was already full, or the genre itself a bit old-fashioned. After all, the most popular Finnish school stories for girls were written in the 1930s. The reason why Blyton's picture books or fairy-tales were not a success in Finland can be deduced from the few reviews which were written about the Noddy books.[17] The critics mentioned that the books were formal, plain and not at all innovative; all in all quite boring.[18] Considering this, it is not surprising that Otava, the publisher, decided not to reprint the books. However, Blyton's adventure books became very popular in Finland, from the first, *The Island of Adventure*, in 1950, to the *Secret Seven* series published in the 1970s.

In 1960 IBBY Finland (the Finnish division of the International Board on Books for Young People) organized a questionnaire survey of children's favorite books. This survey included statistical data from seventeen libraries and two hundred eighty-four questionnaires. Unlike Eino Arohonka's survey in 1950, this time the questionnaire was sent to boys and girls going to elementary school; thus, the respondents came from a more socially heterogeneous background. The result of the 1960 survey was self-evident: now the children's favorite author was Enid Blyton.

A librarian, Kaija Salonen, from IBBY Finland, presented the research and gave the opinion of a professional in children's literature about Enid Blyton:

> Hopefully, Blyton serves only as supplementary reading, as a passing narcosis. For those who read many other books, Blyton is of no harm, just a waste of time. However, those who only consume Blyton, will get literary deficiency, and might be infected by an epidemic of mediocre and light reading.

She did not hide her opinion that Blyton's books were rubbish and that the children should be guided to read better books.[19] The opinion that very popular books were like weeds in the garden of literature could be found in many articles in *Kirjastolehti*, the professional magazine for librarians in Finland. Blyton's books are referred to as trash, weeds, light, and poor. Children were not blamed for this. Instead, blame was seen to lie elsewhere: the publishers, the funding, or rather lack of funding, of libraries, and the lack of information about good literature.

Five Have Plenty of Fun

For a closer look at on what Finnish newspaper critics made of Enid Blyton's books, I will now analyze the reception of the Famous Five books in Finnish newspapers and magazines. Twenty-one books from the series were published in Finland within nine years, and there were at least 53 reviews of the Five books (some reviews included several titles).

Overall, the initial response seems to have been ambiguous: approximately half of the reviews were positive, one third negative, and the rest were somewhat neutral. Usually, the first time a reviewer read one of Blyton's books, the response was good, but when more titles were published, and the adventures of the four children and a dog continued on the same track, the reviewer got tired of the books. Even if one or two were good, to have twenty-one similar stories was considered boring.

The negative critics used similar words as their colleagues in England: mediocre, weak, dull, and passive. They complained about the repetitive pattern of the books. On the other hand, the positive reviewers found many good qualities; for example, the stories were fun and cohesive, and they were imaginative, had lively characters and freshness.

As a whole, the language in the books did not get much attention from the Finnish critics. Only five reviews out of fifty-three noticed language at all: one critic said that the vocabulary was limited, and the four others that Blyton's language was fluent. Again, without closer examination, it is difficult to say how true to the original texts the Finnish translations are. Lea Karvonen was usually credited as the translator, but actually, this was a collective pseudonym used by a group of translators.

How then did the Finnish critics respond to the Englishness of the books? Few reviewers mentioned that the stories were set in England. In one of the most negative reviews, written about *Five on a Treasure Island*, in *Lapsi ja Nuoriso*,[20] a magazine published by the Central Union for Child Welfare in Finland, the reviewer referred to an Austrian Richard Bamberger, a children's literature professional and one of the founders of IBBY[21], who had also criticized Blyton for being too "English" to be read outside England. To this the Finnish reviewer wrote that the books' Englishness did not seem to bother Finnish children, as they were recommending Blyton to each other and inquiring about her books in libraries.

In another review, about *Five on Kirrin Island again*, in *Kansan Uutiset*,[22] a left wing newspaper and the main organ of the People's Democratic League of Finland, the reviewer commented favorably on the humor and lively narrative, but suspected that the setting was a bit too pompous for Finns. The reviewer referred to Quentin Kirrin's (George's father) profession as a scientist, and to the fact that the family had given a whole island to their daughter, George.

A reviewer in *Keski-Pohjanmaa*, a provincial newspaper, writing about *Five have plenty of fun* noted: "Despite the story being set in England, Finns, not only children but also adults, gladly read these adventures".[23] This review was thoroughly positive, but still the reviewer pointed out that the story was set in a foreign country and used the word "despite". It appears that the foreign setting of the books was recognized, and some reviewers thought it might estrange the readers, which could be good or bad, depending on the reviewer's opinion. In addition, the economic conditions, the wealth, of the children in the stories were mentioned, but only in some reviews.

How about the positive reviews: what made the Famous Five books good? The characters seemed to be one of the reasons why the critics liked the books. The children were seen as lively and brave, and the friendship amongst the children was regarded as positive. George, the girl who wanted to be a boy, was also considered a fresh and successful character in the stories.[24] The reviewer in *Kirjastolehti*, the librarians' magazine, found it especially satisfying that, in *Five on a Treasure Island*, the friendly attitude of the three other children had a positive influence on George's character.[25]

Most of the reviewers seemed to think a children's book was good if it provided good models and examples for the young. Good teamwork, friendship and liveliness were definitely seen as good model qualities, but so was the sense of justice that some of the reviewers highlighted. A reviewer in *Aamulehti*, a right-wing regional newspaper, looked for reasons why children liked the Famous Five books so much. The reviewer thought the explanation for their popularity lay in the friendship and sense of adventure to be found in the books and that "the honest fight for justice and truth appeals to the readers' incorruptible sense of justice".[26]

A sense of justice is a very interesting theme in Blyton's adventure series in general, as all the books handle crime and catching criminals. The only slightly critical and humorous comment on the justice aspect of the books was made in *Helsingin Sanomat*, the largest newspaper in Finland, in a review about *Five fall into Adventure*, with the reviewer commenting "the uncomplicated handling of the criminals probably corresponds to the expectations of the age group: let the bad lot get their just deserts".[27] Here the reviewer noticed the black-and-white moral of the books, but took a humorous stand on it.

However, it is interesting that the very real problems and dark tones that appeared in the stories did not come through in the reviews. For example, the book *Five go off to Caravan* includes an orphan circus boy, Nobby, who is abused by his guardian. Nobby is described as dirty, quite simple, but a kind person, and the children become friends with him. On several occasions, it is clear that the guardian, the villain of the piece, has beaten him up and that the boy is in constant danger.

The two reviews written about *Five go off to Caravan* said that the book was interesting, fun, and full of cheerful excitement. The reviewer in *Aamulehti* noted that, "The young are probably interested in the adventures of the Five, and even if the events connected to the circus are part of a joyful and innocent holiday, all the same, an educational lesson is included".[28] It is unclear what the educative message in the story the reviewer referred to was, but the terms joyful and innocent pointed to something nice and sunny, just like the Blytonesque world was interpreted to be. Beating a child did not belong to that world, even if it was part of the plot.

Even if a third of the newspaper reviews criticized the stories, the general feeling of the reviews was very light and uncomplicated. Was it simply a case of uncomplicated, simple books receiving uncomplicated criticism? On the other hand, was it reflective of Finnish society in the 1950s and early 1960s with its clear and straightforward views on good and bad, right and wrong? This might explain why there were no comments on the obvious violence in the books.

In addition, women's status in society had still to change, although it was not uncommon for Finnish women to be employed. That could be the reason why none of the reviews commented on George's identity problem, wanting to be a boy. A tomboy character was not new in Finnish literature, but still it looks like none of the reviewers seriously considered George's wishes.

Five Get into Trouble

David Druce has made an interesting comparison by analyzing the structure of Ian Fleming's James Bond novels and Enid Blyton's books. His conclusion is that in both, the interaction of the characters is invariably depicted as a series of hostile confrontations, which alter from rage to frustration to the triumphant paying-off of old scores.[29] For the Five, "justice" always triumphs in the end, when the police thank the children for being so clever and take the criminals off to jail. In the Famous Five's world, no court is needed, as long as there is the police.

After reading one or two Famous Five books, the adult reader notices at once when a criminal is introduced: he looks suspicious and is definitely different from the rest. His (the villains are usually male) features might be ugly or otherwise strange, maybe a flat nose, weak jaw, small eyes, or then he can be almost animal looking. On the other hand, the criminal can have cold blue eyes too, as in *Five go Adventuring again*, in which the bad guys are probably German spies.

If Blyton used stereotypical images of foreigners and roma, was it racism or xenophobia, or was it just because she lived in a racist time? According to Finnish historian Jouko Jokisalo, racism is built-in in the foundations of modern western society, and the connecting of beauty and esthetic with morals and intelligence was rooted in the Enlightenment.[30] The idea that European, western man, is substantially above the others was also standard in Blyton's times.

This did not diminish the critical tone that began to appear, for example, in England, in the 1960s. The amount of writing about children's books grew, and the objects of criticism changed: now the critics were concerned about the stereotypes of race, sex, and class that were found in children's books.[31]

In Finland, the 1960s meant change too. The countryside started to empty as the young moved to cities or emigrated to Sweden. By the 1970s Finland had become urbanized and many large and small changes had occurred. The level of education started to rise, and the social security system and gross national product both grew. Culturally the 1960s meant renewal too. The new young intellectuals were politically on the left and many started to criticize western, especially American culture.

Comments on children's culture and children's literature started to build up, in Finland, too. At the end of the 1960s and the beginning of the 1970s, several books were published that took a clear stand on children's literature. In 1968, Tammi (which was also Blyton's publisher) published a small book, a collection of articles, that can be translated as *Cultural kitsch for children* (*Kulttuuririhkamaa lapsille*). It was a plea for children's culture. What is interesting in the articles, is that both western, Anglo-American, and children's literature in the Eastern block were criticized. Western children's literature was criticized especially because it was seen as strengthening conservative and bourgeois culture and old-fashioned gender roles in society.[32]

In 1968, the annual meeting of IBBY Finland's Oulu division included a discussion about the Famous Five books. A librarian Irja Tervo started the discussion by saying how difficult it was for a librarian when parents came and asked what children liked and the librarian had to say the Famous Five books. Tervo continued by criticizing the Famous Five books, because they included double standards; parents demanded manners that were, in her opinion, hypocritical, and abandoned their children in boarding schools, servants were depicted as being stupid, and the children were arrogant, snobbish, and mean towards more clumsy and slow-witted people.[33]

Compared to the newspaper criticisms written between 1956 and 1964, Tervo's comments were completely different. The Famous Five books were not seen as boring, or funny and adventurous, now the focus was on social inequality and on the characters' behavior. This was common for the new way of discussing children's literature.

In another book about children's literature, *Child and a book* (*Lapsi ja kirja* 1972), Märta Tikkanen, a famous Finnish author, wrote about the prejudices in Blyton's books. Tikkanen argued that the image of society presented in the books was "dreadful", that the sense of justice and the attitude towards felony was black-and-white, and that the children were xenophobic and greedy. Parents had double standards, both neglecting their children and demanding correct manners. Tikkanen argued that the worst aspect of Blyton's books was the way the reader was included into being passive. "Blyton never asks the reader to consider the background of the criminal, or how he is handled after the crime, nor does she ask the child to consider her/his own feelings about the criminal, the police, his/her parents or about society".[34] Similar thoughts to Tikkanen's can be found in a Swedish children's literature guidebook, *Reading for children* (*Läsning för barn* in 1973). Swen Wernström pointed out that the rogues, in adventure stories in general, are usually in accordance with middle-class society's idea of suspicious characters.[35]

The standards for what was right and correct had changed, and this could be seen in the critics aimed at the popular children's literature. Much of the critic towards Blyton was also a critic towards middle-class standards. Had the class struggle moved over to children's culture, or was the society simply more open to see the texts in a different way? The legal concepts probably were not changed, but maybe the sense of justice was.

These same questions are visible also in the academic world, or at least in the students thoughts. For example, Marja-Ilona Tynell wrote her master's thesis in the University of Helsinki, about the reception of Famous Five books, in 1971. She analyzed the reasons for the massive popularity of Blyton's books, and found out the following; the books were extremely easy to read, the morale and social values were simplified and it was easy to identify oneself in those. Still, the most important reason for popularity was, according to Tynell, the amount of adventure in the books.[36] Tynell also noticed the aggressive tones in the stories: The children treated criminals sometimes very violently, and their attitude was very strong and exclusive. They lived in a society with only the right or wrong thing to do, and the children always did the right thing.[37]

Tynell's thesis is an example of how the discussion about Blyton was now also an academic concern. It is also a good example of attempts to analyze the reasons for the popularity of Blyton's books, and to explore the reader experience together with the actual content of the stories.

Five Go Adventuring Again

Whilst people professionally interested in children's literature, and other culturally oriented observers continued to discuss these problems, children continued to read Blyton into the 1970s. However, Blyton's books were not the only popular adventure books for children, as many other series were published in Finland in the 1970s too. Two of the most important series were *Alfred Hitchcock and the three investigators* books (46 titles from 1972 to 1989), and the *Nancy Drew* mysteries (100 titles from 1972 to 2001).

Currently, in 2006, neither the Famous Five nor Blyton appear at the top of the favorites' list, but the books are still read and being reprinted. The publisher Tammi has released new "old" versions of the books, with the same cover pictures as the first editions, and the same texts. These reprints might attract nostalgic adults, but are also being read by many children, even if detective stories are no longer the number one genre in children's literature. Catching criminals has been replaced by witchcraft and magic. Fantasy is the most popular genre in contemporary Finnish children's literature and J. K. Rowling now occupies the same position Enid Blyton once did. When the first Harry Potter book was published in Finnish in 1998, there was quite a lot of discussion about children's literature, and whether Rowling was a "good" writer or not. Still, the tone of the discussion was much milder than in the late 1960s and early 1970s.

However, as I mentioned earlier, Blyton is not dead and buried yet. Here are some extracts from book reviews, written about the Famous Five books by young Finnish readers between 2004–2005 as part of a reading project in Northern Karelia.[38]

> This book is just one example of Enid Blyton's marvelous books, which always have a fantastic plot and well-invented characters.
> The book was great. It is quite thrilling.
> This book has an absolutely machinelike plot. If you want to be thrilled, read this. It is so good you have to read it at one go.

NOTES

1. "Statistics on the whole Index Translationum database. 'Top 50' Author". Index Translationum www page http://databases.unesco.org/xtrans/stat/xTransStata?VL1=A&top=50&lg=0 . (Accessed in March 31, 2006.)
2. The general biographical information on Enid Blyton in this article is based on Barbara Stoney's book *Enid Blyton*. Stoney's book is the only comprehensive biography of Blyton.
3. Rudd 2000, 94.
4. Stephens 1992, 8–9.
5. Hellemann 1988, 93–94.
6. Nesbit's book was one of Blyton's own favorites as a child.
7. Hakala 2003, 77–81.
8. Huhtala & Juntunen 2004, 76–77.

9. Heikkilä-Halttunen 2003, 169.
10. Kirjastolehti nro. 4/1953. 46 vsk.
11. Heikkilä-Halttunen 2000, 251–255.
12. Heikkilä-Halttunen 2000, 339–341.
13. Heikkilä-Halttunen 2000, 342.
14. Ray 1982, 48–49.
15. Blyton 1959, 649.
16. Ray 1982, 38.
17. The two Noddy books published in Finnish in 1962 were *Noddy meets Father Christmas (Nyökky tapaa joulupukin)* and *Noddy and his Car (Nyökky ajaa autoa)*.
18. HMS, "Nyökky ja joulupukki", Kotimaa December 21, 1962. Kauko Kula, reviews in Kauppalehti September 14, 1963 and August 24, 1963. "Kuvakirjoja satuikäisille", Maaseudun Tulevaisuus, March 7, 1963. "Lasten ja nuorten kertomakirjallisuus", Kirjastolehti 2–3/1963. Lukija, review in Kansan Työ February 1, 1963. M-a-t-a, "Satuja", Helsingin Sanomat September 8, 1963. "Kuvakirjoja satuikäisille", Maaseudun Tulevaisuus, March 7, 1963.
19. Salonen 1962, 10; Salonen 1963, 194–195.
20. Untitled anonymous review, Lapsi ja Nuoriso 7–8 / 1956.
21. The International Board on Books for Young People, founded in Zurich, in 1953.
22. "Syksyn nuorisokirjoja", Kansan Uutiset August 31, 1958.
23. YJK, "Viisikon seikkailut", Keski-Pohjanmaa April 15, 1962.
24. "Nuorisokirjoja", Vihuri, 16/1956. Vihuri was the chief organ of the Social Democratic Youth Association of Finland.
25. Henry Granfors, Kirjastolehti 6/1956.
26. K. H, Aamulehti April 7, 1960.
27. To-Ti-nen, "Viisikkonelikko", Helsingin Sanomat May 17, 1960.
28. ö-ö, Aamulehti June 11, 1958.
29. Druce 1988, 160–163.
30. Jokisalo 1999, 36–39.
31. Ray 1982, 68.
32. Ambjörsson & Ikonen 1968, 17–25.
33. "Mikä Viisikoissa viehättää", Kaleva May 17, 1968.
34. Tikkanen 1972, 109.
35. Wernström 1973, 135–136.
36. Tynell 1971, 39–41.
37. Tynell 1971, 88.
38. "J. Jokisen eväät" web page http://jjokinen.jns.fi/etu.htm. Accessed in November, 2005

SOURCES

Unpublished sources

Tynell, Marja-Ilona 1971. *Lukijakuntatutkimus Blytonin Viisikon sosiaalisista suhteista.* Master thesis, Department of Finnish language and literature. University of Helsinki 1971.

Newspapers

Aamulehti 1958, 1960
Helsingin Sanomat 1960
Kaleva 1968
Kansan Työ 1963
Kansan Uutiset 1958
Kauppalehti 1963
Keski-Pohjanmaa 1962
Kirjastolehti 1963, 1956
Kotimaa 1962
Lapsi ja Nuoriso 7–8/1956
Maaseudun Tulevaisuus 1963
Vihuri 1956

Published sources

Ambjörsson, Gunilla & Ikonen, Tuula 1968. Lastenkirja yhteiskunnallisena säilyttäjänä. Ambjörsson, Ikonen & Vaijärvi (eds), *Kulttuuririhkamaa lapsille*. Helsinki: Tammi.

Blyton, Enid 1952. Writing for Children. *New Statesman* 9.5.1959.

Salonen, Kaija 1962. "Hauskoja tempauksia, jännittävää, kehittävää. Nuoret kertovat mielikirjoistaan", *Helsingin Sanomat* 25.3.1962.

Salonen, Kaija 1963. "Mitä nuoret lukevat?", *Lapsi ja nuoriso* 6–7/1963.

Tikkanen, Märta 1972. Ennakkoluulon sanakirjat. Blytonista ja sarjakirjoista. Kari Vaijärvi (ed.), *Lapsi ja kirja*. Helsinki: Weilin+Göös.

Wernström, SVEN1973. Yngre människor som jagar bovar... Ambjörnsson, Gunilla & Strömstedt, Margareta (eds), *Läsning för barn*. Stockholm: Bonniers.

BIBLIOGRAPHY

Druce, Robert 1988. *This day our daily fictions. A comparative study of the writings of Enid Blyton and Ian Fleming*. Delft: Eburon.

Hakala, Hellevi 2003. 1920- ja 1930-luvun nuortenromaani: pyryharakoita ja sankaripoikia. Huhtala, Liisi, Grünn, Karl, Loivamaa, Ismo & Laukka, Maria eds), *Pieni suuri maailma. Suomalaisen lasten- ja nuortenkirjallisuuden historia*. Helsinki: Tammi.

Heikkilä-Halttunen, Päivi 2000. *Kuokkavieraasta oman talon haltijaksi. Suomalaisen lasten- ja nuortenkirjallisuuden institutionalisoituminen ja kanonisoituminen 1940–50-luvulla*. Helsinki: Suomalaisen Kirjallisuuden Seura.

—— 2003: 1940- Ja 1950-luvun klassikot ja Patikkamatka maalta kaupunkiin. Huhtala, Liisi, Grünn, Karl, Loivamaa, Ismo & Laukka, Maria (eds), *Pieni suuri maailma. Suomalaisen lasten- ja nuortenkirjallisuuden historia*. Helsinki: Tammi.

Hellemann, Jarl 1988. Käännöskirjallisuuden vuosisata. Nuorteva, Jussi (ed.), *Kirjan rantaviiva*. Helsinki: Gaudeamus.

Huhtala, Liisi & Juntunen, Katariina 2004: *Ilosaarten seutuvilta. Lasten- ja nuortenkirjallisuuden historiaa ja tutkimusta*. Helsinki: BTJ Kirjastopalvelu Oy.

Jokisalo, Jouko 1999. Suvaitsemattomuuden perintö, valistus ja rasismi. Isaksson, Pekka

& Jokisalo, Jouko (eds), *Eriarvoisuus, valistuksen lupaus ja rasismi*. Helsinki: Suomen Historiallinen Seura.

Ray, Sheila 1982. *The Blyton Phenomenon. The controversy surrounding the world's most succesful children's writer*. London: Andre Deutch Ltd.

Rudd, David 2000. *Enid Blyton and the Mystery of Children's Literature*. London: Palgrave Macmillan.

Stephens, John 1992. *Language and ideology in children's fiction*. London: Longman.

Stoney, Barbara 1974. *Enid Blyton*. London: Hodder and Stoughton.

Deep Roots

Deep Roots

PÄIVI MARIA PIHLAJA

A Northern Science

In 1757, a Finnish-born scholar Johan Arckenholtz (1695–1777), who had for a long time worked in Germany, published a polemical article against views that had been advanced by the French editors of the *Journal Encyclopédique*. The problem concerned the history and origins of the Finns and their northern neighbors, the Sámi (Lapps in the language of contemporaries). The two were often – as Arckenholtz now emphasized – confused with each other. Arckenholtz was trying to fight against suppositions that were derived from second-hand information and which in his view, had distorted the image of the Finns. Interestingly, he portrayed the problem as a problem of communications between the "Center" and *les pays plus éloignés du Centre,* the periphery of European scholarly networks.[1]

During the eighteenth century, several scholarly papers were published that ambitiously declared as their goal the unification of the famous new "Republic of Letters". This name is used to describe the new sphere of publicity that in many ways crossed state borders. It unified Europe through an ever-growing production and circulation of journals, books, correspondence, and other forms of literary production. This new sphere was to a great extent learned and scientific. An important part in this development was played by the emerging network of new scientific academies. This was the moment when, it has been said, the so-called "international scientific community" was born in its first form.[2] Arckenholtz's article and the questions it raised were connected to this same process. How had the Kingdom of Sweden, which at that time included the Grand Duchy of Finland, become part of this community?

It is clear that the Swedes often bitterly resented the superiority of these centers of the western world of science – whether in terms of equipment, funding, or scientific publications. The Swedish astronomer Fredrik Mallet argued that "the Astronomy of the French is as if they were building up a whole Wardrobe of Sciences. In Sweden it has nothing more than overcoats…".[3] This is why the relationship of the *Vetenskapsakademien,* the Royal Swedish Academy of Sciences, with academy circles in Paris can also be of great interpretative value and allow us to study the level of access of the Swedes to this new European network. It must be admitted that scientific circles around the British *Royal Society* and some German universities were of similar, or even greater, importance to certain Swedes as center of western science. However, the *Académie Royale des Sciences* of Paris (founded in 1666), was the most effective and powerful society in Europe, and, unlike the Royal Society in London, the number of its members and correspondents was strictly regulated, in order to promote their "quality". This is why being elected to the *Académie des Sciences*, especially for foreigners, was regarding as reaching the highest level of the international scientific community.[4]

I will use Paris in order to study the integration of scholars in Sweden (including Finland) into this new international network, as well as the means they used to take their place in it. This invites us to examine how they may have seen their position in this community, and what were the topics that were brought up for discussion when forming ties with foreign colleagues.

According to the new contextualist views towards science, scientific activity provides an arena for interesting developments that concentrate not just on discussions on the immutable laws of nature, but also on "external" interests, cultural practices, and goals. Rather that just a tool in power conflicts inside a society, scientific activity can be studied as a tool for creating new "national" self-images and as a sphere where stately and national interests meet on an international level.

The Problematic Relationship between Northern Studies and Scientific Exchange

In Sweden, the "scientific society movement" that historian James McClellan III writes about[5] can be traced to the beginning of the eighteenth century. A small group of savants around Uppsala University formed a private scientific society called the *Collegium Curiosum*. New scientific activity arose all over the country: in Finland, the Royal Academy of Turku (Åbo), where Arckenholtz had received his education, was the center for wide-ranging scientific and utilitarian concerns. However, it must be acknowledged that during this period the centers best known to foreign scholars were the institutions established in Uppsala and Stockholm. The Uppsala scientific society had an interrupted existence, although it was later embraced by the King. It gave way to *Vetenskapsakademien,* the new national science academy founded in Stockholm in 1739, but persisted in a more cosmopolitan spirit since it published its Acts in Latin. *Vetenskapsakademien* was in some ways closer to certain new utilitarian tendencies as a result of which its attention was turned towards the national context. Still, it also became a kind of central bureau for scientific exchange, regulating and supporting international contacts which before had been grounded on a more individual basis. In Europe, the new academies superseded in many ways the old universities that were in decline. In Sweden, however, this juxtaposition was not as hard, as the circles of the learned men were in many ways the same and overlapping. In the Finnish part of the Kingdom, circles around the Royal Academy of Turku played a similar role as the new societies elsewhere.[6]

It is striking how – as Sweden was creating more and more institutional ties with other European centres – interest in scientific matters seems to have been increasingly directed towards to the northernmost parts of the country.

Many articles published in the *Vetenskapsakademien*'s own publication dealt with circumstances in the North, often with its economic potential. In Finland, the Royal Academy of Turku directed a lot of attention towards the northern parts of the country and Lapland. This growing interest in the northern and boreal parts of Scandinavia in the Swedish realm has usually been explained as a result of internal concerns, within the utility project that turned attention "inwards". In the Great Northern War (1700–1721), Sweden's position as a Baltic power had been lost to Russia. In the words of historian Lisbet Koerner, the state now "had to make do with the heartlands that Sweden had managed to retain".[7] In this new situation, the North had to be "found" and exploited to compensate for the fertile lands that had been lost.

However, institutionalised science developed a dual role. Although it had utilitarian aims, it wasn't simply national or inward-looking. As the scientific quest became fashionable throughout Europe and, indeed, one of the most important activities of the era, taking part in scientific investigation became a quest for glory, which a country and its prince could only attain by participating in the search for universal progress within the European *Republic of Lettres*.[8] We can but note how convenient this turn to the fashionable natural sciences, this embodiment of the nation's glory, must have been for Sweden at a time when its military "great power" status had just collapsed. This is echoed in a letter of the Uppsala society, in 1719, which, seeking the support of the King, stated that the base of its motivation was, to "be able to serve the fatherland and bring it to fame among foreigners, as before in heroism and braveness, now also in learning and in sciences".[9]

Even though the centrality and over-emphasizing of Paris has been criticized in studies concerning the eighteenth century and can not be accepted uncritically, the general attitude of the age was captured by Jonas Jacob Björnsståhl who – on a study trip to Paris in 1769 – described Paris as "the stading point that you can with right understand as the Centre for all Arts and Sciences, not just in Europe, but in the whole World".[10] In Björnståhl's depiction, we see Paris depicted as a kind of "calculation centre"[11] of the type of Bruno Latour – a center where information and specimens from all over the globe are brought and collected, the accumulation of information giving it a power position and the licence to interpret the world and its phenomena. This is quite close to what science seems to have meant for Count Carl Gustav Tessin, who compared scientific activity to the making of a clock, with Sweden as a workman, or an artisan, providing the pieces of "raw material" or pieces of a mechanism, which the great men of learning (or "clock makers") in the centers would then "put together" – that is, form into larger theories.[12]

What then marked the role of the Swedes in scientific exchange? What kind of materials were they providing for European colleagues? It has been noted that the authors of various Swedish works that had been translated into other languages were not always considered as great scientists in their own country or in later times. In explaining why their texts were interesting to foreign scholars, the value of these texts has been attributed to their practical and utilitarian interest.[13] This may be true in certain situations but not in all of them. First of all, while the utilitarian sciences were still in great

195

vogue in the *Vetenskapsakademien*, other European academies were already turning their attention towards more theoretical questions.[14] Moreover, in those other countries no direct, concrete benefits were to be expected from texts concentrating on economic and local questions. The secretary of the *Vetenskapsakademien* P. W. Wargentin (1717–1783) pointed out that it was not always possible to export utilitarian discoveries to other environments. In 1750 – when the Swedish and French science academies agreed to exchange their official publications – Wargentin apologized to the theoretically-oriented Parisians that they would hardly find the Swedish publication interesting, as practical findings dominated and, moreover, were "applicable only in our climate".[15] One might have thought that the presence of Northern themes in Swedish works would have reduced the foreign interest in their practical findings.

Given what has been said above, it is surprising that, instead of hiding away these particularly northern subject matters, the Swedes were, on the contrary, focusing a lot of attention on them as they were making their findings public in an international context. Why was the North now discussed so often, and why was it ultimately interesting for foreigners?

Geographical Hierarchies: The North Seen as an Obstacle to Scientific Thinking

There is also another factor why it is surprising to see that the "North" was so often the subject of discussion. As Sweden wished to appear as a country of science, prejudices among European colleagues forced the northerners to play down ideas dealt with their specifically Northern environment and climate. In the minds of these continentals, the Swedish realm was, because of its northern position, endowed with certain negative attributes; attributes that lead to disadvantageous conclusions regarding its image as a learned nation. This makes it even more surprising that the North should have acquired in the eighteenth century an increasingly central place in scientific exchange.

In pointing to the intellectual and political divisions that typically affected the European "Republic of Letters", Françoise Waquet and Hans Bots have also noted that a *climatic* division, or "geographical hierarchy", was one of the disintegrating factors dividing the European scientific community. In the minds of contemporaries, climate forged the scientific community into hierarchical "intellectual orders" (*ordre intellectual*). In this period, science, learning, and culture were still closely connected to the effects of sun, warmth and an agreable southern climate. Culture – understood in both its meanings as agriculture and civilization – was thought to be able to develop only in the warm and fertile lands of the South, which allowed people to be idle and engage in intellectual pursuits instead of struggling for their daily existence. As for other physiological and environmental arguments, it was thought that southern conditions equipped men with an inner constitution that yielded a lively mind and imagination – whereas the North could hardly "produce" great intellectuals. This general idea was so strong that even in scientific biographies it was hinted that scholars could escape this fatalism

A vignett presenting the Sun and used by the Académie des Sciences in its publications. In Suites des Mémoires de l'Académie des Sciences, 1731. Finnish National Library.

by traveling to more favorable environments – an interesting point of view given the popularity of European journeys and *Grand Tours* in this age. [16]

The North, on the other hand, had a different fate. Not seen as a cradle of intellectual activity, it was traditionally seen as a cradle of *physical* excellence producing hardy soldiers, new incarnations of the Goths who had plundered Europe, and had been integrated into Swedish self-imagery during the wars in the seventeenth century when Sweden was a great power. In these traditional "climate theories", popular in the eighteenth century, the northern cold supported physical talents at the cost of intellectual ones. This was a real problem for scholars and intellectual who came from the North. For example Christopher Polhem (1661–1751), an active member of the Uppsala society, observated in 1730 that "the Foreigners ... have already for a long time thought that they could, in their own interests, make our Swedish Nation believe that our climate would not be suitable to Arts and Sciences".[17]

By renewing and developing the views of traditional "gothic" history that celebrated the warrior spirit of the ancient Swedes, Olaus Rudbeck had made a new step. At the turn of the seventeenth century, he had argued in his gigantic *Atlantica* that it was not just herds of warriors but *culture* too that had come to Europe from the North. By studying old Finnish, Swedish, and Sámi words and traditions, he argued that Sweden was the child of the mythic *hyperboreans* who had worshipped Apollo, the divinity of science, and he identified its old kings with ancient explorers known from antique myths.[18]

It is symptomatic that, of all his excesses, in the eyes of reviewers on the continent of Europe, this theory that Sweden was the cradle of knowledge and science seemed to appear the most plausible.[19]

At the beginning of the 18th century, the Swedes had tried in many ways to prove that Sweden shared Europe's cultural patterns and emblems. They also used these *universal allegories* to prove the country's suitability for scientific activity. The common imagery concerning the necessity of sun and warmth as the basis for culture can also be seen in the use of the Sun and Apollo as universal symbols for learning, and, interestingly, in connection with the image of the "Sun King". The King of Sweden now had to prove that he was entitled to this pan-European allegory. This lead to a new innovation in Sweden – the use of the famous midnight sun of Lapland as the proof that the Swedish King was the "true" Sun King. Charles XI travelled to Northern Sweden in 1695 to see the midnight sun. The event was an allegorical meeting between one "eternal might" and another, and suggestive of an old idea of a Kingdom where the sun never set. The following year, the king sent a scientific expedition to Lapland to observe the refraction of the midnight sun's rays. The scholars who took part in this expedition were to publish a book on their findings in Latin that was destined for the scientific community in Europe. At the same time, the expedition, with its ambitious aims, underlined the scientific aspect of Rudbeck's argument that science could flourish in the North – and even had its earliest origins there. Scientific discoveries and the glory of the state were thus closely connected.[20]

Also for science, the midnight sun of Lapland was brought into the picture in order to explain that the north's nature allowed Sweden a special type of development. For Rudbeck, the midnight Sun had been one of the most importance pieces of evidence that the origin of the European myths lay in the North, as the sun cult of the Sámi was proof of this identification with the ancient "hyperboreans".[21] But the Sun and its meanings were also considered on the physico-environmental level. Northern scholars used the northern sun as a symbol for knowledge, to explain that "great minds" could also be produced in the North. Polhem argued that in the North, just as the sun was present for half a year and then absent for half a year, so in Sweden you could find both great geniuses and quite stupid people, the two "extreme values": but the "sum" of these two extremes was still the same as in the southern countries (where the intellectual abilities of individual were more of the "median" value).[22] This was why the prejudiced views expressed against the possibility of science in the North did not apply. In similar vein, the long summer days were also mentioned in economic discourse, as compensating for the lack of warmth during the other seasons and, therefore, also as evidence of habitability and agricultural pursuits even in Lapland.[23]

In these discussions, it was still a question of allegories and symbols shared with the rest of Europe. However, at the end of the seventeenth century, we can note an interesting change: a shift from the universal allegory of the sun towards more particular, "northern" allegories that began to appear on stately, and, later, also scientific emblems. They seem to side with the new scientific interest in Northern nature. The Pole Star soon replaced the Midnight sun as a royal emblem. The tendency was felt even in the symbols of the new scientific institutions of the so-called era of Liberty. When, for instance, the *Academie des Sciences*'s publication printed on its pages the allegory of Sun/Apollo, the *Vetenskapsakademien* chose for its seal the Pole Star, shining its light of learning from the North.[24] Whether this was a consciously-made choice or just the reflection of a generalized trend, it seems that now – instead of trying to take over universal symbols and explain that Sweden had all the attributes traditionally thought to be the prerequisites of culture and scientific progress – the northerners started to emphasize the *difference* of the North.

How the North Became a Scientific Resource

We have already mentioned the growing interest in Sweden in the eighteenth century towards the northern parts of the country. In this trend, scientific, practical, and economic interests were to a great extent intertwined. Moreover, the Swedes seemed eager to discuss the North and its phenomena – although, as we have seen, there were many reasons why it might have been sensitive subject for them.

The most famous case of the Swedes using their Northern experience before their continental colleagues was that of the naturalist Carl von Linné (Linnaeus) (1707–1778), who completed a journey in Lapland before continuing his travels in Europe. Linné's travels in the North are still a high point in Swedish science studies. Linné had, in fact, justified his journey to the North in terms of the interest it would have for foreigners: he explained that it would provide "curious and rare naturalia as their Africa ever has (…) No Catalogus Plantarum could be more admired by foreigners than a Flora Laponica".[25] After this, Lapland was often, if not visited, at least mentioned by Linné and many other Swedes when forming ties with foreign colleagues. Lapland served as the setting for some of the most important scientific projects conducted in Sweden. One of the most well-known expeditions of this time took a similar course only a few years later, as a group of French astronomers travelled to Lapland to study the shape of the earth. The expedition received a lot of attention in Europe. Astronomical projects in Sweden before and after this event indicate that similar plans had been cherished for a long time in Sweden, and had been seen as Sweden's chance to repair its scientific reputation.[26]

Another Swedish naturalist, perhaps second in importance only to Linné, the entomologist Charles De Géer (1720–1778) made no less use of Lapland as a key word when contacting his famous French colleague René Antoine Ferchault de Réaumur. He referred to the fame of the Pierre-Louis Moreau de Maupertuis expedition to Swedish Lapland in 1736–1737, which had caused a lot of talk in Paris, noting the interest that had been aroused in Paris by a lappish insect brought back by Maupertuis. De Géer promised to provide "more specimens from the North where the winter reigns with such dominion", underlining how different the climate in Sweden was compared to the "*climat douce de la France*".[27] The willingness to emphasize the harsh northern climate is quite a contrast to the above-mentioned tendencies to play down the effects of the cold in order to prove Sweden's suitability for scientific endeavour.

In 1732, Carl von Linné had travelled in Lapland and studied its flora before going on a long study trip in Europe. In the frontispiece of Flora Lapponica, published in Holland in 1737, Linné portrayed himself as a Sámi in a fanciful landscape of Lapland.

Many of the Swedes who entered the *Académie des Sciences* as members, and came from various fields of natural studies, seem to have been somehow connected to the study of the North and used this experience when introducing themselves to foreign colleagues. In the eighteenth century, before science was professionalized, memberships of an academy was seen as a measure of one's career. Recognitions by the *Académie des Sciences* were, it can be assumed, a particular honor.[28] Already during the early years of the Uppsala scientific society, it was considered important to publish topics that could be of use to foreign colleagues in their work in the society's acts [29] – mainly alluding to the Royal Society in London and the *Academie des Sciences* in Paris. In Sweden, Svante Lindquist had noted how, already in Uppsala circles in the 1710s and 1720s, there seems to have been an awareness that observations tied to northern phenomena would be easier to publish abroad.[30] We can therefore ask whether the "northern" topics selected for French translation indicate a sort of "strategy" on the part of the Swedes: it seems that the Swedish scholars had noticed that the specificity of the Swedish climate might be useful for their career. We will see that many of the writers who received attention in France were often physically located on the northern edge of Europe: this seems to have increased interest in their observations abroad, even if the authors were not regarded particularly highly as "scholars" in their own country.[31]

In French translations of Swedish scientific publications, there were a large number of authors who published observations and works specifically on northern phenomena. These include writings on the types of ovens used in northern countries; Anton Rolandson Martin's journey in 1758 to Spitzberg in the Arctic Ocean, and his studies on the effects of temperature on the human body.[32] Of particular interest, in collections as well as in the *séances* of the *Académie des Sciences* in Paris, were Anders Hellant's observations in Tornio and surrounding regions in Lapland, and he later produced a great amount of observations on various phenomena, including astronomy and temperature.[33] Hellant had worked as a translator on the French expedition to the Arctic Circle in 1736–1737.

It seems that these men, who were not always rated highly in their own country and did not become well-known later in science history, received a certain interest abroad because of their arctic milieu. But why would this particular type of information interest the French? Seeking to explain the French interest in northern topics simply in terms of their exotic nature in unconvincing. Unlike the preceding century, science was no longer about strange items kept in cabinets of curiosities: scientific enquiry now received its justification and meaning as evidence of universal laws, portraying the conformity and predictability of nature.[34] To come to valid conclusions on such matters, however, there was a need for experiments and observations from as large a variety of circumstances as possible. But, as the French *Encyclopédie* put it, the best that a French chemist could do when "wishing to know all the effects of (…) warmth on different substances (…)" was "to place his laboratory between a cold store and the furnace of a glazier". The scope of experiments was limited in France by the fact that no constant, severe cold temperature could be produced or maintained "*dans nos climats*".[35] This is where the Swedes must have seen their chance. For example, one of the most celebrated Swedish scholars of this time was a professor of experimental physics and the successor of Wargentin as secretary of the *Vetenskapsakademien*, J. C. Wilcke (1732–1796), whose scientific claim to fame was based on his observations on an old question in physics, namely the forms of snow and the nature of temperature, which were conducted during the winter in his own courtyard whilst he was gardening.[36]

Observations and specimens unique to the northern edge of Europe and brought or sent to Paris from provided French scholars a foundation on which they could make assumptions about most general philosophical issues. Climate and its effects were often a subject for discussion, as well as a significant explanatory factor, in various scientific questions from the history of man to physics, medicine, or political theory. Therefore, the small insects brought to Réaumur from Lapland invited the great naturalist to contemplate the necessity of revising generally accepted theories concerning the effects of climate and the works of nature.[37] The way that the French translators read and translated works, which were from the Swedish point of view more "practical", are emblematic. Swedish writings concerning northern

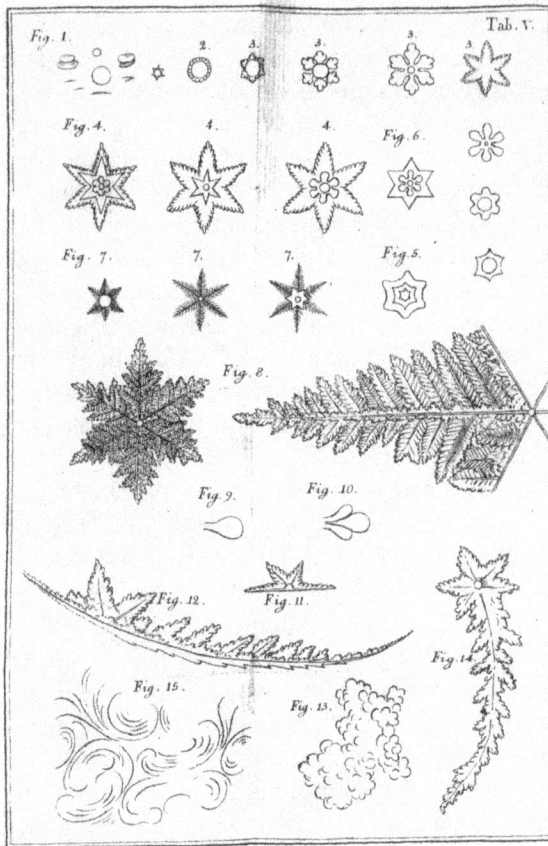

J. C. Wilcke's studies on the formation of ice. Published in Kongl. Vetenskapsa-kademiens Handlingar 1769 (Apr–Jun), appendix 5.

ovens were not read by French men of learning in order to build a house with efficient heating: such writings, as well as experiments done in Finnish saunas, could be read by the French for physiological evidence on how the human body reacts to temperature in general – or if climate theories which, for example, associated cold with hardiness, did or did not apply.

Correspondents were essential for receiving information needed when building up general "doctrines", following the inductive method that was favored over scholastical "hypotheses". It was, therefore, the Baconian method that made correspondents, able to report their observations "on the spot", so valuable for scientists. For example, Marat the younger asked the *Vetenskapsakademien* to conduct certain optical experiments for him because in Sweden, "during one part of the year, the sun is longer over the horizon".[38] Northern nature with its extreme conditions served as a big *natural laboratory*.

To describe the astronomical "system" of eighteenth-century Europe, a Swedish historian of science Sven Widmalm used a model by an American historian of technology Thomas P. Hughes where the relationship of different centers is understood as working towards a common endeavour, the system itself consisting of a main centre as well as specialized under-systems that act in concert for a mutual goal. According to Widmalm, the international astronomy projects of the eighteenth century, which demanded comparable observation data from all around the world, made Sweden a *nordic sub-system*, offering specialised data for the needs of the whole.[39] Astronomy is perhaps the field where the need for joint activities was most manifest.[40] But this viewpoint might well be extended to other fields, and Sweden understood as taking its place in a new field of cooperation concerning its northern specialities.

A common denominator in Swedish texts is that they are often related to the northern location of Sweden as a unique place for performing experiments and observations. In astronomy, the Swedes had spoken of the extraordinary suitability of their "hyperborean skies" for astronomical observations.[41] In the first scientific publication of the Uppsala circle *Daedalus Hyperboraeus* the stated aim was to "show our land to be more fruitful for the performance of experiments that the others".[42] Now the Swedes had, it seems, noticed that northern phenomena were the means to make this goal a reality. The scholars tended to emphasize the northerness of the country, so as to take over a sphere where they could act as experts in the eyes of their continental colleagues. It could be said that the North itself became a specialized field of scientific activity. Instead of denying the effects of cold and dark winters, scholars and scientists started to study them as physical phenomena that could not be examined anywhere else, and in this way discovered the North as a scientific resource.

New Means to Refute the "Intellectual" Climate Theory?

The optimistic utilitarianism of the eighteenth century has been seen as the heir to Gothic dreams, depicting Sweden as a promised land, perfect for habitation and even agriculture. Swedish historians like Jacob Fredrik Neikter embraced, in the latter part of the century, the Montesquiean climate theory which provided an opportunity to maintain the associations of the North with ideas of physical strength, liberty, and heroism. However, it seems that for the scholars and scientists who practiced natural philosophy, this theme was not favored. The reason was one we have already mentioned: the assumption of the unfavourable effects of the cold on one's intellectual disposition. Instead, they stated that climate theory, which claimed that there was a certain determinism in the "spirit" of different nations, had to be refuted as inaccurate. Wargentin regretted a conclusion that, unfortunately, deprived the Swedes of their supposed gothic virtues – but comforted his fellow countrymen by arguing that this refutation allowed the Swedish input to science to be seen in a better light.[43]

It is an interesting thought that the value of northern studies was changing attitudes in that science and the North could be seen not only as mildly compatible entities, but as supportive of each other. At the same time, the "periphery" seemed to begin to challenge as interpretations made in the center, on the basis of direct observation and not just reasoning. For instance, the attitudes and information found in, and promoted by, compilations such as the *Encyclopédie* or *Journal Encyclopédique,* had a critical reception in Sweden. The tendency of the French *philosophes* to put more emphasis on "spirited" or more or less wild interpretations and theories, at the cost of pure facts, was noted on several occasions, for example when Wargentin tried to correct mistakes in the article "Suède" in the *Encyclopédie.*[44] The author, chevalier De Jaucourt, expressed the typical relationship between the two, stating that, from the French point of view, lively *"reflexions politiques & morales"* had far more importance than individual facts. This also affected his decicion to use, for his article "Lapland", the brief remarks by Voltaire, and not the detailed Swedish account by Johannes Schefferus.[45]

It was against this interpretative attitude, wide speculations based on little evidence, that for example, Arckenholtz directed his criticism. Arckenholtz wanted journalists working in Europe to extend their correspondence networks "to the countries more remote to the centres" in order to get their facts right. The controversy between Arckenholtz and the editors was of course a small incident, but in my view could well illustrate the other side of scientific cooperation.[46] Knowledge of the North was becoming the business of local experts and their experiences. In Arckenholtz's view, the unification of the *Republic of Lettres* could be brought to perfection only by increasing the number of correspondents in remote areas such as Finland – only by "reaching out also to Countries more remote from the Centres"[47]

Conclusions

Observations from the North were integrated into the theories composed in the center, but the implications of these climate theories were not always approved by those northerners who hade taken part in the exchange. The introduction of climate theory in eighteenth-century Sweden has been studied in an interesting way by Carl Frängsmyr. However, the role of the Swedes in the formation of climate theories seems to be more complex, since these theories constantly drew upon evidence from writings that were distilled and delivered from the north; not just by northern travellers and eyewitnesses, but in diverse scholarly works.

This seems to have been the role of Sweden in scientific cooperation. The intention of the Swedish natural philosophers was to show that doctrines that suggested that difficult civilisation and learning was difficult in the North did not apply. It seems that as scientific cooperation began to develop in a European context, this was not just a process of unifying practices and goals – but a division of labor, where some sort of specialisation was in fact present, or even required. The willingness of the Swedes and Finns to find their place in this new arena for collaboration also seems to have brought up a culturally new sense of uniqueness.

NOTES

1. Arckenholtz 1761, 31–39.
2. McClellan III 1985, 45.
3. Letter from Fredrik Mallet to Lidén 27.2.1770. Heyman 1938, 201.
4. McClellan 1985, 17–20.
5. In the eighteenth century, a new sphere of action was being created for savants on a European level. These institutional forms of the famous *Republic of Letters* have been studied by James McClellan III as *the scientific society movement*. Approximately seventy official academies were established at that time in Europe. From the start, they had a strong international dimension and were considered colonies of the *Republic of Letters*. See McClellan 1985.
6. See for example, Lindroth 1997, 18–67.
7. Koerner 1999, 5.
8. During the joint ventures in astronomical years of the 1750s and 1760s, countries fought for the leading position. See for example Faivre 1966. In Sweden participation was seen as necessary for defending its "honor". For example, Letter from the Royal Academy of Sciences to His Royal Majesty 14.1.1767. Allm. verks. kollegiers m. fl. skrivelrser. Skrivelser till Kungl. Maj:t., VIII. Soc. Litt. Riksarkivet (RA, The National Archives of Sweden). Stockholm.
9. "att kunna tiena fäderneslandet och sättiä thet, såsom här tils för hieltemod och tapperhet, så och här efter för lärdom och wettenskaper uti beröm hos främmande nationer". Letter from the scientific society of Uppsala to His Royal Majesty, 17.11.1725. Allm. verks. kollegiers m. fl. skrivelrser. Skrivelser till Kungl. Maj:t., VIII. Soc. Litt. Riksarkivet (National Archives of Sweden). Stockholm.
10. Björnståhl 1780–1784, 74.
11 The term first used by Bruno Latour conveys the idea that centers of science actually gain in authority and interpretative power by their distance from the local reality. Latour 1987, 215–265, 212–213.
12. Tessin 1824, 221–222.
13. Holmberg 1939, iii–v.
14. Lindroth 1997, 94.
15. Letter from P. W. Wargentin to J.-N. Delisle 14.11.1750. Correspence of Delisle T. XI, 33a. Archives of Observatoire de Paris. Paris.
16. Bots & Waquet 1997, 77–78.
17. "Utlänningar (…) nog länge redan till sin goda fördel, tilltrot sig kunna inbilla wår Svenska Nation at wår Climat ej wore till konster och wettenskaper skickelig …" Polhem to Anders Johan von Höpken 29.11.1739. Letter 116. Polhem 1941–1946, 202.
18. Nordström 1934.
19. Eriksson 2002, 246.
20. Johannesson 1968, 89–129; Knapas 1994, 71–74; Seitz 1938, 89–116.
21. Eriksson 2002, 367, 376–377, 462; Nordström 1934.
22. Christopher Polhammar ad Emanuelem Swedbergium, Stiernsund d. 27 Martis 1717 (n. 35). Swedenborg 1907, 269.
23. See for example, Frängsmyr 2000, 27–66.
24. Johannesson 1968, 89–129; Knapas 1994, 71–74; Seitz 1938, 89–116.
25. Linnaeus to KVA, December 15, 1731; December 26, 1731. The Linnean

Correspondence. http://www.c18.org/pr/lc/, (Accessed on March 20,2005).

26. See for example Sydow 1962, 138–163.

27. Letter from Carl de Géer to R.–A. F. de Réaumur, 6.12.1744. Dossier biographique *De Géer*. Académie Royale des Sciences. Paris.

28. McClellan, 248–250.

29. *Bokwetts Gillets protokoll* 10.2.1721. Schück 1918, 43.

30. Lindquist 1998, 40–61.

31. Pihlaja 2005, 271–281.

32. "Observations faites dans un voyage au Spitzberg", "Chaleur des différentes parties du corps humaine", "Des bains chaudes en Finlande", Kéralio 1772, 176–178; 257–259, 314–316.

33. See Pihlaja 2005; Pihlaja 2004; Tobé 1991; Extract from the registers of the Musée de Paris addressed to "M. Hellant, Torno, Laponie". Wilcke, letters to unknown recipients. Kungliga Vetenskapsakademiens Arkiv. Stockholm; Procès-verbaux of the Academy of Sciences 5.3.1760. *Académie Royale des Sciences*. Paris.

34. Daston & Park, 208–210.

35. *Encyclopédie* 1757, Vol. VII, 320.

36. See for example Keralio 1772, 176.

37. Réaumur 1742, 312–330.

38. Marat to Wargentin 12.6.1779. Wargentin's incoming correspondence. Archives of the Royal Swedish Academy of Sciences. Stockholm.

39. Widmalm 2001, 321–337.

40. Faivre 1962, 98–124.

41. See Widmalm 1994, 34.

42. Daedalus Hyperboraeus 1716 (I), 10-12.

43. See C. Frängsmyr, 111–126 on the views of the astronomers Bengt Ferrner and P. W. Wargentin (the latter was also the secretary of the Stockholm academy).

44. Letter from Fr. C. Baer to P. W. Wargentin 31.8.1759. Wargentin's incoming correspondence. Archives of the Royal Swedish Academy of Sciences. Stockholm.

45. See the article "Laponie" in *Encyclopédie* 1765, Vol. IX, 287–288.

46. This study is based on the author's current doctoral dissertation project, with a preliminary title *Science under the Polar Star. Lapland and the Study of the North in European Scientific Discussions*. The research work has been pursued as part of a research project funded by the Academy of Finland, "Boundary Demarcation and Interaction in the North Calotte Area from the Eighteenth-Century to the Second World War" The leader of the project is Maria Lähteenmäki. (No. 177666).

47. Arckenholtz 1756, 4.

SOURCES

Unprinted sources

Allm. verks. kollegiers m. fl. skrivelser. Skrivelser till Kungl. Maj:t.
Riksarkivet (National Archives of Sweden). Stockholm.
MSS B1. Correspondance de Joseph-Nicolas Delisle.
Archives de l'Observatoire de Paris (Archives of the Observatory of Paris). Paris.

Wargentin's incoming correspondence; Wilcke's incoming correspondence. Letters from unknown recipients.

Kungliga Vetenskapsacademien arkiv (Archives of the Royal Swedish Academy of Sciences). Stockholm.

Dossier biographique De Géer; Procès-Verbaux.

Archives de l'Academie des Sciences (Archives of the Academy of Sciences). Paris.

Printed sources

[Arckenholtz 1761]. *Lettre aux auteurs du Journal Encyclopédique de Liége, au sujet des Remarques sur les Finnois où Finlandois, oú, en Reponse à ce qu'ils y onty avancé, on tâche de mieux déveloper l'Etat ancien & moderne des Habitans de la Finlande et de la Lapponie.* Frankfurt / Leipzig.

Björnståhl 1780–1784. *Resa til Frankrike, Italien, Sweitz, Tyskland, Holland, England, Turkiet, och Grekland: beskrifven af och efter Jac. Jon. Björnståhl (…) Efter des död utgifven af Carl Christof.* Gjörwell. Stockholm.

Daedalus Hyperboraeus 1716–1718.

Èncyclopédie, ou Dictionnaire raisonné des sciences, des arts et des métiers, par une Société de Gens de lettres. Paris 1751–1772.

Kéralio, Louis-Félix Guinement De 1772. *Collection académique, Composées des Mémoires, Actes, ou Journaux des plus Célébres Académies et Sociétés Littéraires Étrangères (…)* Vol XI. Paris / Dijon.

Polhem 1941–1946. *Christopher Polhems brev, utgiven (…) av Axel Liljencrantz. Lychnos-bibliotek 6.* Uppsala: Lärdomshistoriska Samfundet.

Réaumur, René Antoine Ferchault De 1742. *Mémoires pour servir à l'histoire des insects IV. Paris.*

Remarques sur les Finnois ou Finlandois. *Journal Encyclopédique*, Fevrier 1756.

Schück, Henrik 1918. *Bokwetts Gillets protokoll I-II.* Utgifna af Henrik Schück. Uppsala universitets årskrift 1918. Uppsala: Almquist & Wiksell.

Swedenborg, Emanuel 1907. *Opera quaedam aut inedita aut obsoleta de rebus naturalibus (…). I. Geologica et Epistolae.* Holmiae.

Tessin, Carl Gustav 1824. *Dagbok 1757. Utgifven af G. Montgomery. Stockholm.*

Internet Sources

The Linnean Correspondence.
http://linnaeus.c18.net/Doc/

BIBLIOGRAPHY

Bots, Hans & Waquet, Francoise 1997. *La République des lettres.* Belin: De Boeck.

Daston, Lorraine, & Park, Katharine 1998. *Wonders and the Order of Nature.* London: Zone Books.

Eriksson, Gunnar 2002. *Rudbeck 1630–1702: liv, lärdom, dröm i barockens Sverige.* Stockholm: Atlantis.

Faivre, Jean Paul 1997. Savants et Navigateurs. *Cahiers d'Histoire Mondiale*, Vol. 10, 1966.

Frängsmyr, Carl 2000. *Klimat och karaktär. Naturen och människan i sent svenskt 1700-tal.* Uddevalla: Natur och Kultur.

Hahn, Roger 1971. *The Anatomy of a scientific institution. The Paris academy of sciences 1666–1803.* Berkeley: University of California Press.

Heyman, Harald J. 1938. Fredrik Mallet ock Johan Henrik Lidén. Lychnos. *Årsbok för idé- och lärdomshistoria,* 270–308.

Holmberg, Arne 1939. *Kungl. Vetenskapsakademiens äldre skrifter i utländska översättningar och referat.* K. Svenska Vetenskapsakademiens årsbok 1939. Uppsala: Almqvist & Wiksell.

Johannesson, Kurt 1968. *I polstjärnans tecken. Studier i svensk barock.* Uppsala: Almqvist & Wiksell.

Knapas, Rainer 1994. Images of the North: the Pole Star and the Midnight Sun. *Landscape and northern national identity. Proceedings from a Seminar held at the Renvall institute of Historic Research, University of Helsinki Nov. 11ᵗʰ–12ᵗʰ 1994.* Helsinki.

Koerner, Lisbet 1999. *Linnaeus: nature and nation.* Cambridge: Harvard University Press.

Latour, Bruno 1987. *Science in action: How to Follow Scientists and Engineers through Society.* Cambridge (Mass.): Harvard University Press.

Lindquist, Svante 1988. Ett experiment år 1744 rörande norrskenets natur. *Kunskapens trädgårdar: om institutioner och institutionaliseringar i vetenskapen och livet.* Gunnar Broberg, Gunnar Eriksson, Karin Johannisson (eds). Stockholm: Atlantis, 40–77.

—— 1993. The Spectacle of Science: An Experiment in 1744 Concerning the Aurora Borealis. *Configurations,* Vol 1.1. The John Hopkins University Press, 57–94.

Lindroth, Sten 1997. *Svensk Lärdomshistoria III (Frihetstiden).* Norstedts: Södertälje.

McClellan III, James 1985. *Science Reorganized. Scientific societies in the 18ᵗʰ Century.* New York: Columbia University Press.

Nordström, Johan 1934. *De Yverbornes ö: Sextonhundratalsstudier.* Stockholm: Bonniers.

Pihlaja, Päivi Maria 2004. The study of the North in the Eighteenth-Century. Lähteenmäki, Maria & Pihlaja, Päivi Maria (eds), *The North Calotte. Perspectives on the Histories and Cultures of Northernmost Europe.* Publications of the Department of History, University of Helsinki 18. Inari: Puntsi, 25–37.

—— 2005. Sweden and l'Académie des Sciences. Scientific elites in 18th-century Europe. *Scandinavian Journal of History,* Vol. 30, No.3–4. Taylor and Francis, 271–285.

Seitz, Heribert 1938. Nordstjärnan, symbol för fosterland och snille. *Fataburen,* 89–116.

Von Sydow, Carl Otto 1962. Vetenskapssocieteten och Henrik Benzelius' Lapplandsresa 1711. Lychnos. *Årsbok för idé- och lärdomshistoria,* 138–163.

Tobé, Erik 1991. *Anders Hellant. En krönika om sjuttonhundratalets märkligaste tornedaling.* Tornedalica 49. Luleå: Tornedalica.

Widmalm Sven 2001. l'Espace scientifique scandinave. *L'Europe des Sciences. Constitution d'un espace scientifique.* Sous la direction de Michel Blay et Efthimios Nicolaïdis. Science ouverte. Paris: Seuil, 321–337.

OONA ILMOLAHTI

Teachers on Guard Against the East

In Europe the interwar period was a time of racial thinking. The old European nations had been founded on the ideas of nationalism constructed in the previous century. This also applied to the new nation-states formed after the First World War and as a result of the disintegration of the Russian and Austrian empires.[1] In one of these states, Finland with its small population, there was a need to find next of kin, racial relatives. An important motive in the search for the Finnish race was an urge to convince the western world that Finns were not of Asian or Mongolian origin but something much more developed, and, most importantly, European. This need, connected to the phenomenon of Finnish right-wing nationalism, created a bourgeois cultural movement, which attempted to create contacts with kinship nations.

In the nineteenth century, the Finns were defined by European race theorists as Mongols.[2] When Finland, an autonomous grand duchy, experienced two periods of Russification at the beginning of the twentieth century, the defense of Finnish autonomy also began to take on features from the race discourse: oppressive Russian policies – and later bolshevism – were seen as Asian barbarism and Russophobia became more widespread. After the Civil War, in 1918, the race question also acquired new political dimensions. Some Swedish-speaking scholars saw the Mongolian character of the Finnish-speaking people as one explanation of the war. Finnish-speaking savants were irritated by germanism and the allegations about the Mongolian origin of the Finnish people. Scholars, who followed closely the European scientific debate, tried to prove that the Finns did not belong to the Mongolian race.[3]

The Finnish nation was divided in the interwar period as a result of a bloody and traumatic Civil War fought in 1918 between left- and right-wing parties called the "Reds" and the "Whites" respectively. After the Civil War, won by the "Whites", Finnish nationalism was built largely on anti-russianism. Finnish historians have suggested that the portrayal of the Russians as the archenemy (perivihollisuus), which was powerful in the interwar period, was constructed rather late, namely in 1918, especially in white war propaganda even though hatred against the Russians' was described as an ancient emotion within the Finnic people. The white side started to use the term War of Liberty (vapaussota) to describe the Civil War, which indicated that it had been fought

Working-class children with their teacher in a class portrait from 1929. Picture from the Vallila elementary school, Helsinki.

against the Russians in order to maintain independence. By identifying the Reds with the Russians the enemy could be portrayed as unpatriotic.[4]

Nationalism has been a much contemplated subject in historical research. Many historians, such as Eric Hobsbawm, have defined nationalism as the principle whereby political and national units should be congruent. Hobsbawm sees nation-states as particularly young and modern constructions and suggests that many of the principles associated with the nations have been created consciously. He has argued that states, which have been understood as top-down constructions must also be looked at from the bottom up. It is important to ask how the masses adopted as artificial a form of identity as nationalism. Hobsbawm has emphasized that the thoughts of the silent masses are difficult to interpret. The idea of nationalism is that in a nation-state the citizens are supposed to put their obligations towards the nation above everything else. Why do people agree to this and what makes the nation-state worth scarifying everything else for and what attempts are made in order to get the masses behind the nation-state?[5] Hobsbawm has connected the concept of invented traditions – traditions that are presented as ancient can in fact be quite recent in origin and sometimes even invented – with nationalism and state building. In other words, various kinds of regularly repeated manners, practices, rituals, and symbols, which create an illusion of historical continuity, are used in order to create an image of an ancient, everlasting state.[6]

Research Frame

In the Civil War, civil servants, including elementary and secondary school teachers remained, for the most part, on the white side and Finnish elementary school teachers were seen in the public eye as protagonists of white Finland.[7] Finnish nationalism, the Fennoman movement,[8] had been built in the nineteenth century on the idea of the common people as the romantic core of the nation. For the Finnish-speaking educated classes, the Civil War meant the final[9] breakdown of this "integration" with the common people and a culmination of class conflict. This particularly affected ideological groups among the church and school system. The enlightened classes were divided in their approach: the right-wing view was to create a forceful national unanimity; the liberals, for their part, emphasized reform and conciliation.[10] Both of these views affected the school system.

In industrial societies the state-controlled comprehensive school has been an important factor in nation building and nationalism. Schooling is usually based on the values of ruling elites and politicians.[11] After the Civil War, public education was seen as an essential factor on the way towards a civilized, European Finland. A law of public compulsory education was enacted in 1921. It was mostly constructed by centralist parties, who wanted to strengthen democracy and prohibit the growth of extreme left- and right-wing influence. They saw compulsory education as a way to prevent societal chaos.[12] The National Board of Education determined that the elementary school (kansakoulu, literally people's school) should be a politically neutral conciliator, a balancing institution between the two sides.[13] Ultimately this meant following the policies of the winning bourgeois white side, which aimed at uniting all citizens in defense of the fatherland. It was up to the elementary schools to perform this task, and the working class movement became their ideological rival. The gap between elementary school teachers and working class families had widened as a result of the Civil War.[14] The teachers' alleged enemy was in the east, and Finnish identity was to be built on the contrast between east and west. The patriots felt that the Finno-Ugrians were the protectors of western culture against the dark and barbaric east.[15] This discourse was especially prominent in patriotic organizations such as the Academic Karelia Society (Akateeminen Karjala-Seura).[16] This cultural target also had expansionist tendencies – for many, the co-operation of the Finno-Ugrian people meant in fact uniting all the Finno-Ugrian language areas under one nation, Finland. The term used was Greater Finland (Suur-Suomi), which would also include territories inhabited by Finnic people.

The country's close neighbor Estonia was the main area to be approached in terms of Finno-Ugrian co-operation. For the Estonians, Finland was an obvious ally and some politicians had even planned a Finnish-Estonian union, or federation, in the period just before the countries gained independence. The Finns, however, did not need the Estonians as much as vice versa. After trying to form a so-called "union of border states"[17] with the Baltic countries and Poland, Finland withdrew from Baltic co-operation and turned to Scandinavia: mainly to her western neighbor Sweden.[18] Politically, Finland and Estonia remained quite distant from each other during the 1920s and 1930s due to various political problems.[19] There was, however, strong activity among the citizens aimed at developing co-operation and bringing the Finnish and Estonian people together, and the main engine of this effort, especially outside the academic world, were the Finnish-speaking schoolteachers. This

Teachers having a cup of coffee in 1932. Picture from the Vallila elementary school, Helsinki.

enthusiastic sense of kinship was exceptionally strong among the teachers in the capital city, Helsinki. The teachers also wanted to spread the ideas of the so-called kinship-movement[20] to their pupils and that way trough them to the whole nation.

This article discusses the kinship activity of Finnish teachers in the context of their occupation: how did the teachers' kinship-work manifest itself, what motivated it and how did this hobby relate to their teaching in elementary schools? After the Civil War the elementary school teachers' work was built on their larger-than-life task: uniting a deeply split nation and educating the common people in patriotic values. This task was especially important in the working class areas of the bigger cities, which were seen as potential growing places for dangerous – unpatriotic and communist – ideas.[21]

The teachers were supposed to be model citizens for the young nation. Their profession was seen more as a calling than a job and they were expected to act in an exemplar fashion round-the-clock. The teachers' occupational identities very largely formed at patriotic teachers' colleges, in which they studied at quite a young and receptive age. The schooling lasted from three to five years and all the students' actions were strictly regimented. Oili-Helena Ylijoki, a Finnish social psychologist, has suggested that studying is an identity-project, where students are socialized to the moral order and model story of the subject. She uses the concept of a moral order: in a social identity project, the individual person is attached to the traditions, values, beliefs, and modes of action of the community.[22] This happened for the teachers in the teachers' colleges. Elementary school teachers so thoroughly internalized their collective and personal model stories that they acted according to them in their spare time, as well. I assume that everything that teachers did outside their schoolwork was somehow related to their occupation. That is why it is possible to interpret their educational goals in the classrooms through their hobbies and interests.

Crossing the Gulf of Finland

The first phase in the cultural co-operation between Finnish and Estonian teachers occurred mostly due to the Estonian war of independence, in which

212

Teachers on a study trip in the 1930s. Picture from the Vallila elementary school, Helsinki.

4,000 Finnish volunteers took part. The war received a lot of attention on the part of the Finnish public. To promote the kinship issue a special Estonian week was arranged in Helsinki in January 1919. In Tallinn, a Finland's day was organized. The first, somewhat larger, attempt to strengthen cultural connections between the two nations was taken at the beginning of the 1920s, when the Estonian politician Jaan Tõnisson and the Finnish poet Eino Leino suggested the idea of teaching the other nation's language in primary and elementary schools. This suggestion did not materialize, but it was, however, possible to study Estonian in secondary school, teachers' colleges and universities.[23]

The best-known kinship-societies, such as the nationalistic Academic Karelia Society were formed among academics and university students. One of the most important organizations behind this kind of cultural kinship co-operation outside the academic world was the Association of Finnish Culture and Identity (also known as the Finnish Alliance, Suomalaisuuden Liitto, which was established in 1906) and its Department of Kindred Nations (sukukansa-osasto).[24] The first president of that department was Matti Pesonen, the inspector of Finnish-speaking elementary schools' for Helsinki.[25] Many elementary school teachers in the capital city were also members of the Association.

The first big manifestation of the teachers' co-operation was a Finnish-speaking schoolteachers' study trip to Tallinn in June 1919, when the first wave of enthusiasm for Estonia had been emerged because of the Estonian war of independence. Approximately 1,500 teachers from all over the country took part in this trip, and because of the number of participants the teachers were given the icebreaker Väinämöinen by the state to take them to Tallinn.[26] A group of Estonian teachers met the guests at the harbor with a brass band, and the visit was also noted in that day's newspapers. Some of the houses in Tallinn also put out flags to honor the Finnish visitors. The visit culminated in big celebrations at the Estonia Concert Hall, where refreshments were served, speeches given, songs sung, and hearts filled with feelings of kindred love. The farewell was wistful, and the teachers felt as if long parted sisters and brothers had found each other again.[27]

Estonian teachers made a return visit a few months later, when over a thousand elementary and secondary school teachers came to Helsinki. On these two visits the importance of kinship awareness in teachers as educators of the masses was brought up. Finnish School Counselor A. J. Tarjanne

213

emphasized the role of teachers in getting the two kindred nations closer together. He stated that the school system was an essential factor in creating ideals among the youth and that the teachers' work influenced the attitudes of young people towards neighboring countries. He suggested that teachers in Finland and Estonia should seek support from each other in their joint battle to civilize their countries. The Finnish Minister of Education Mikael Soininen for his part underlined the similarities between the two countries: the kinship of blood, the similar racial characteristics and national characters, the cultural heritage and the Lutheran faith. He also brought up the nations' common history as fighters against oppression and the Eastern giant, that is, Russia. Soininen praised the teachers' efforts: both countries had only recently (Finland in 1917, Estonia in 1918) gained political independence and the work of the teachers would also help to preserve that freedom. Only a civilized, enlightened, and spiritually healthy nation could uphold the gift of freedom, he declared.[28] Civilization was seen as the key to national independence and entry into the European family of nations, and that is why the schools' significance as the educator of the masses was emphasized.

The most profound manifestations of cultural co-operation were the Finno-Ugrian Culture Conferences organized in Finland, Estonia, and Hungary in the 1920s and 1930s.[29] The first meeting, on which the later conferences were built, was in fact a Finno-Ugrian school convention, held in Helsinki in 1921. It was initiated by Matti Pesonen, the inspector of Finnish-speaking public elementary schools' in Helsinki and was modeled on Scandinavian school meetings.[30] The main purpose of the teachers' convention was to create feelings of kinship and togetherness amongst the Finno-Ugrian teachers. They also wanted to strengthen their identities as legitimate citizens of Europe: in the welcoming speech it was proclaimed that the Finno-Ugrian peoples worked for the good of mankind and therefore should be accepted into the "brotherhood of Europe". Most of the participants were elementary school teachers: the secondary school teachers were conspicuous by their absence as usual, stated a writer in the Opettajain lehti (Teachers' Magazine).[31] This shows that it was precisely the elementary school teachers as the educators of the common people who found the kinship aspect important.

The Finnish people have often been said to have an arrogant and patronizing attitude towards the Estonians. This sometimes applied to cultural co-operation. For example, Finnish women's organizations approached the kinship issue thinking mainly how the co-operation could benefit the fatherland. Estonian women were organized later than their Finnish sisters and this created an imbalance in the relationship: Finnish women thought that their movement was more advanced than the one in Estonia and brought this up openly. The relationship can be seen as part of the Greater Finland ideology.[32]

The arrogant attitude of the Finns often seen in the Finnish-Estonian relationship did not, however, fully apply to the teachers. Professional interests provided a basis for mutual communication, as well. The Estonian school system, which was developed very rapidly after independence, was, especially in the 1930s, admired and looked up to. The Estonians were regarded as civilized survivors with an even higher cultural level than

Finland's, whose people had been lagging behind in the country's forests.[33] While Swedish-speaking teachers in Finland often turned to Scandinavia for influences, Finnish-speaking teachers followed educational developments in Estonia. They were especially interested in the writings of John Käis, an Estonian pedagogical reformist.[34]

At the turn of the 1930s some kinship enthusiasts worried about the level of interest the teachers were showing in their Estonian friends.[35] The co-operation between Finnish and Estonian elementary school teachers was, however, at its' most intensive in the 1930s. The fourth Finno-Ugrian Cultural Conference, held in Helsinki in 1931, received a lot of attention in Opettajain lehti, and teachers, especially in Helsinki, were active in organizing the conference. The teachers also had their own club, which met in the National theatre with 600 participants. A feast, which was funded mostly by teachers' voluntary donations, was organized by the Finnish Teachers' Association together with the Helsinki Teachers' Association.[36]

In October 1934, when the representatives of the Finnish Teachers' Associations visited the annual general assembly of the Estonian Teachers' Association, the two began to plan a treaty of friendship,[37] which was signed in June 1935 in Helsinki. It committed the teachers to get to know the one another's work by attending lectures and school exhibitions or by exchanging publications. The parties were to inform each other of their activities and the exchange of letters and trips were also recommended. Naturally, the teachers were also committed to spreading information about ideas of kinship in schools, newspapers, and other social circles.[38] Estonian-Finnish Teacher Days were arranged in Tallinn and Helsinki in the summer of 1935. These nine-day events consisted of lectures, exhibitions, demonstration lessons, and workshops. The purpose of these Teacher days was to familiarize teachers with the other country's methods of teaching and with the predominant trends in ideas, and in that way, improve professional skills and motivation in educating future generations. The same year many Finnish teachers also visited the Tartu school exhibition. The Finns were much impressed by the high level and rapid development of the Estonian school system and felt they had plenty to learn from their neighbors.[39]

Even though the kinship-enthusiasm can be seen simply as a hobby of a limited group of teachers, the importance of kinship-education was also recognized by the National Board of Education as well as the Finnish Teachers' Association. Official contacts with the Estonian teachers' organization were lively between 1928 and 1937. The Finnish Teachers' Association was represented at the Finno-Ugrian cultural congresses arranged in Budapest in 1928 and Helsinki in 1931, and participated in planning and organizing the events. In addition to general cultural congresses, the teachers of Finland and Estonia held specific kinship-days starting in 1935 in Tallinn and Helsinki, which were organized by the National Board of Education and different teachers' organizations. In 1937, an Estonian-Finnish School Gathering was organized; about 350 Estonians and 450 Finns took part.[40] The kinship-movement was a suitable activity for teachers, because it supported the nationalistic ethos the teachers were expected to possess.

The Poor Have No Fatherland?

Why did Finnish-speaking elementary school teachers hold the thought of kinship so dear? And most importantly, why was it so important that it had to be taught in schools? The answer lies – in addition to the teachers' patriotic self-image – in the Finnish elementary schools' character as a working-class school. Especially in the bigger cities such as Helsinki, the more well off put their children in to private schools, so-called preparatory schools, which were considered the best way into secondary school. The popularity of private schools in Helsinki was at its peak in the 1920s,[41] after the Civil War, when the city was deeply divided into winners and losers. The elementary schools were theoretically regarded as institutional means to rebuild national unity as the school of the whole nation, but in reality this was not the case. The schools were ideologically defined by the winners, yet most of the pupils, at least in Helsinki, were the offspring of the losing red side.

The elementary school was the main institution in socializing the working class. The teachers considered themselves as part of the Finno-Ugrian clan, which was part of western, civilized culture. Teaching kinship and national defense was, however, overshadowed by the working-class question and the fear of communism. It was regarded as essential that the whole nation stand behind the same patriotic values. The patriotic education of working-class families was sometimes problematic. While the wider reference group of Finnish-speaking teachers was self-evidently the western world and particularly the Finno-Ugrian family, the reference group of the working class and especially the labor movement was the international workers' community. The teachers were aware of this problem and discussed how to teach love of country in what were mainly working class-elementary schools.

This controversy was also recognized while talking about the means of kinship teaching. In 1933, an elementary school teacher from Helsinki, Eino Keskinen, wrote a five-part article in the Opettajain lehti about kinship teaching in schools. He also discussed the reaction of "certain public circles" toward kinship teaching. He emphasized that kinship teaching was not meant to demean anyone. The elementary school was expected to rise above political differences. While talking about kinship issues the teacher should not encourage national hatred or talk militantly about Karelia or extending the Finnish border to the Ural Mountains. By doing so the teacher would destroy the precious goals of kinship teaching and awaken misconceptions. The best way to approach children with different (political) backgrounds was to be moderate and realistic. It takes good will and an open mind to plant patriotic thinking in children from different home backgrounds, he argued, and encouraged teachers to be considerate in their actions. Kinship teaching should not despise peacetime work, which was the basis of life for all nations, Keskinen added. The fatherland and nationality had to be put above politics.[42]

In a book called Suur-Suomen koulu (The School of Greater Finland), edited by Jyväskylä Teacher's college's Karelia Society[43], it was argued that the 'new Finnish national movement' was not only one of national defense but also a social movement. Class divisions and prejudices were to put aside and the people were to be educated to think in terms of society and sense of duty was to be fostered in order to protect the country from Russian expansionism. The future teacher's dreamed of a "teachers kinship union" based on the ideas of Greater Finland.[44] The writers of the book emphasized that the school's task was not only to teach children but also to awaken nationalistic feelings among adult citizens. The school should get close, first, to the hearts of the pupils' and then trough them their parents, revising their characters, and overcoming the existing contrast between school and home.[45] This was the starting point of the elementary schools' citizen education: to get into agrarian and working-class homes via the children.[46]

Not all teachers dared to be open about their political views, partly due to the schools' official task as a "neutral conciliator". In the late 1920s, early 1930s came the depression and radical elements started to raise their voices.[47] Some teachers felt that the neutrality of the schools had gone too far when patriotism was considered as politics. It was declared that the old concept of patriotism should be returned to its former place in the school as well as in the home. Teachers should imprint on the public's mind that patriotism was not a capitalist slogan but a precious and useful instrument for the protection of all members of the nation. In the Opettajain lehti, one teacher advised colleagues to approach the family background of the pupils moderately and without prejudice while introducing the children to an ideology that was different than their own. Only in that way could the education be successful.[48] The statements defending patriotic teaching might have been directed towards the teachers' pacifist organization (Suomen opettajain rauhanliitto), which was established in 1930. It received a lot of criticism from some colleagues, who saw it as a threat to the fatherland. Raising the will to defend the country in citizens was regarded as one of the most important tasks the teachers had, and patriotism in small countries was seen as a matter of self-preservation. This way of thinking was highlighted by a Finnish poet, a docent (later professor) in folkloristics, Martti Haavio under his pseudonym P. Mustapää, in Suur-Suomen koulu:

> But, if your sister, mother, wife is torn by the Russians; if your father-
> land is facing slavery; if the high values of your people and mankind
> are in danger, strike without hesitation, strike by might and main.
> Pacifism is of no help there.[49]

In the Finnish nationalistic discourse of the 1930s pacifism was not encouraged. It was seen as dangerous and threatening for the fatherland. The militarist tone of citizen education could also be seen in schools, and, for example, national defense teaching was given more or less officially to pupils.[50]

Kinship-Teaching in Support of Patriotic Education

The purpose of kinship-teaching was mainly to strengthen patriotic education. Contemporary educators thought that in order to develop national consciousness and love for one's country an instructional base of the life and history of the Finnish family was needed.[51] Patriotic education in elementary schools was very concrete: in becoming attached to their environment, children would learn to love the fatherland, Europe, the western nations and the Christian world, even the whole of mankind. The children learned to separate "us" and "them" based on Finnishness, Europeaness and the Christian faith.[52] The idea of patriotic education was to move from the small and particular to the large, more general level: first the child should learn to love his/her hometown and the local neighborhood, near his/her home. Then the child's love would grow to include the Finnish nation, and finally the whole Finno-Ugrian clan or family.[53] This family consisted of all the areas where Finno-Ugrian languages were spoken. The kinship-movement was considered to be a wider form of nationalism. It was thought that where kinship is regarded as an important factor there also will exist a high national consciousness.

The Finno-Ugrian school convention organized in June 1921 started to promote kinship teaching via its president Matti Pesonen and secretary Alfred Jotuni. The National Boards of Education in Finland, Estonia, and Hungary were informed that now that the most substantial Finno-Ugrian nations had gained their independence, the conditions of these kindred nations should also be taken into account in schools. It was important to create a strong kinship spirit in the young generation. The children should be introduced to the history, literature, folklore, and governmental and geographical conditions of the kinship nations.[54] The Ministry of Education, at the proposal of the National Board of Education, released a circular in 1928 suggesting that when new textbooks were introduced into Finnish elementary schools, secondary schools and teacher seminars, the kinship aspect should be taken in account. Based on this proposal, kinship poems and stories were added to the textbooks. In reality, the amount of kinship teaching depended on the activity and enthusiasm of the teachers.[55]

Elementary schools were regarded as an important factor in the planting of kinship in the public. As one teacher remarked, a kinship conscious teacher could make his school "an efficient reform school for the kinship spirit".[56] Elementary school was – apart from military service for men – the only schooling for many people. That is why it was important to create affection for the kindred nations in the elementary school. It was also considered important to inform the children about the matter as early as possible when they were most receptive.[57] As one article about kinship teaching argued: "precisely in young people's sensitive and responsive minds are most likely to take root the ideas, which in later life will form their way of thinking."[58] Teaching was trying to appeal to the pupils' emotions. By using contrasts and representing the Russians as uncivilized and cruel, the Finno-Ugrian people were made to look like courageous martyrs fighting against an overwhelming enemy. Eino Keskinen put this into words:

> When a child learns to recognize how the Slavic people have for centuries burdened us and tried to fuse our family to them, this clear and cold fact has to have a strong influence on them, right to the bone. It certainly will have an effect on them for life.[59]

The basis of kinship teaching were race-theories, which suggested that only the civilized nations were part of history, the driving force of civilization being the Caucasian nations. The schoolbooks were Eurocentric and emphasized humanity and civilization, which could substitute for the lack of population in small countries. Christian values, which were seen as a mark of civilization, were also emphasized in schoolbooks.[60] Religion was one of the biggest issues where the world of the teacher collided with the world of some working-class families.

Kinship teaching was not an independent subject, but was integrated with other subjects such as Finnish language, history, geography, and singing. History was considered the most important subject in raising the kinship spirit. The shared history of the Baltic peoples and the Finns were to be emphasized instead of idealizing the Swedish past. In history lessons, the Finno-Ugrian peoples' task of guarding against eastern influences and watching over western culture was the main point of kinship teaching.[61]

Finnish lessons were also considered a good opportunity to enhance the national spirit. The significance of mastering the kindred language was emphasized in kinship teaching. The whole idea of Finno-Ugrian kinship was partly based on philological arguments – the similarity of the languages was seen as proof of their common origin. Finding Estonians and other linguistically-connected relatives was part of Finnish nationalism.[62] A good command of the neighboring language, Estonian, was regarded as fundamental to kinship co-operation. Language skills were seen as the key to true understanding and kinship love. Professor of Baltic-Finn languages Lauri Kettunen in a speech to school children argued, that if you can speak Estonian you will not be held as a stranger in Estonia, and added that if the people can understand each other, the nations will stand stronger together against the external threat and will also be able to avert it.[63] Through language skills, "Finland-Estonia" would feel like a common fatherland and cultural area – the two nations will not be competitors or envy each other's achievements but acknowledge each other as co-workers, who have the same goals and interests.[64]

One way of improving language skills was to exchange letters, which was recommended to students as a good way to deepen kinship awareness. The Department of Kindred Nations gave directions for correspondence and teachers were encouraged to help children to write letters.[65] Correspondence between Finnish and Estonian schoolchildren was started, at least in Helsinki. Some children even got to know their Estonian neighbors on class trips to Tallinn.[66] The idea of student exchanges was also brought up, but it met resistance: in Helsinki, the teachers pointed out that most of the elementary school pupils were from poor homes and would, therefore, be unable to travel.[67]

Celebrating the Racial Togetherness of Finno-Ugrian Nations

Special kinship celebrations were introduced into elementary schools in the late 1920s, when kinship themes were included in the program of Kalevala-day, celebrated in honor of the publication of the Finnish national epic. In 1930 a particular kinship day was introduced, which was celebrated at the same time, the third Saturday of October, in Estonia, Hungary, and Finland. The purpose of the kinship day was to dedicate one day to the idea of Finno-Ugrian racial togetherness.[68] The kinship day was also recognized at governmental level when the governments of Finland, Estonia, and Hungary signed an agreement over cultural co-operation in 1937 – there was a request to reinforce the already established kinship day and dedicate one lesson of that school day to the kindred nations.[69] The Finnish Alliance also stressed the importance of the Estonian Independence Day to the Finnish public. At the Fifth Finno-Ugrian Cultural Conference it was decided that the various kindred nations' Independence Days should be celebrated widely; for example, in the schools.[70] This was affirmed in a Cultural Agreement between Estonia and Finland in 1937. This was said to have encouraged this good habit, which at least kinship aware teachers in both countries' capital cities had followed for a number of years.[71]

The Department of Kindred Nations of the Finnish Alliance was the main organization to promote kinship day in schools. It edited and distributed program leaflets to be used in kinship day celebrations and for the festivities on Estonia's and Hungary's independence days. The leaflets included, for example, speeches, plays, poems, and songs handling the ideas of kinship written by kinship activists, among them many elementary school teachers. The tone of the leaflets was very patriotic, even militant. Their purpose was to awaken love of one's country and the wider Finnish clan and also to strengthen the will to defend the sphere of Finno-Ugrian culture. The suffering of the Finno-Ugrian nations was colorfully described in plays and poems.

In the model speeches for the kinship feasts, the kinship connection was illustrated with concepts of family. It was explained how the kinship nations were close relatives in the same way as siblings or cousins and that these relatives should be treated as one's own family members. The kinship brothers should help each other in times of need, celebrate each other on their birthdays and keep in touch with them for example via the exchange of letters. The common factor in the history of all the Finno-Ugrian nations' was the age-old oppression of alien powers. Children were taught that together the oppressor could be overpowered and by joining forces independent Finland and Estonia could maintain their independence. Together the nations could more easily stay free than alone – just as good family members supporting their next of kin.[72] The rhetoric used in kinship teaching supported the national defense teaching given in schools. By learning to love the special features of the "Finno-Ugrian race", the pupils would also be ready to stand up for their clan and protect it from alien (eastern) influences and conquerors. The Finno-Ugrians were the protectors of western civilization.[73]

This defense theme featured strongly in plays meant for kinship day celebrations. In a play called Suomen sillan rakentajat (The Builders of the Finnish Bridge), schoolchildren discuss the meaning of kinship. It is explained that the kinship spirit can be found in songs, music, and folk arts. The people are in good spirits when kinship brothers succeed and experience pain when they suffer. The children refer to history and say that Finnish men were courageous in war, even when they fought in the Swedish army. Now, Finland was independent and would stay that way – but only if the Finnish people stayed united and loyal to their country. Later they say that the Finnish family should be stronger, so it could not be oppressed.[74] A play called Kantele ja risti (Finnish Zither and Cross) is extremely warlike featuring battle horns and sabers. It describes the struggle of the Finno-Ugrian nations. The different Finnish tribes are described as children of a "kinship-mother" and "kinship-father". All the children come to their parents and talk about their lives. All the tribes have encountered suffering and oppression. The independent nations, Finland, Estonia, and Hungary, are presented as the future of the Finno-Ugrian family. Children of the free tribes swear before God that they will be loyal to the land of their fathers, cherish its future, love the Finnish family, and not be ashamed to be part of it and do the best they can for their family. [75]

Both plays mentioned were written by teachers. It is important to notice that in addition to the basic defense-theme, both plays also have another dimension. Between the lines, the writers are trying to convince the viewers that the Finnish tribe is great and worthy of love and respect. The Finnish soldiers' courage in the Swedish army is brought up in order to identify the Finns as forming their own race, which is as good or even better than the Swedish or Germanic one. In the latter play the children are told that they should not be ashamed to be part of the Finnish family. The Finnish people are often said to have a "poor national self-esteem". It might have grown partly out of the theories that they were of an inferior Mongolian race, living on the periphery of, or even outside, civilized Europe. This controversy was also felt in their relations with the Swedes and Swedish-speaking Finns.[76] Towards the end of the 1930s, the will to defend the nation was brought up more openly in leaflets, and, for example, the "Liberation wars" of Estonia and Finland in 1918 and 1919 were described as adventures, where young boys had been able to express their natural will to fight.[77]

In the rhetoric and teaching of kinship images from the Finnish national epic, the Kalevala, which was seen as the embodiment of the high level of Finnish civilization, were used.[78] In an article called Kalevalan merkitys kansallemme (The meaning of the Kalevala to our people), published in the Opettajain lehti in 1935, the Finnish national epic was presented as the crystallization of the centennial life of the Finnish race. The attention given to the Kalevala by European scholars was considered proof of a more widespread realization that the "Finnish race", previously ridiculed by the Russians and the Swedish-speaking upper class, had been capable of creating high culture for centuries. That is why Finland also deserved to survive as a nation.[79] The Kalevala is a perfect example of an invented tradition, based on some real foundation and developed and reserved for nationalistic purposes.

Brotherhood of the Small

The similar features of the Finnish and Estonian languages and cultures were emphasized in the kinship discourse, even though there were significant

221

differences in both the language and culture of the two nations. Their common history was often brought up, but in fact the two had mostly traveled separate paths. Did Finland and Estonia in the end have only one thing in common: the enemy? It could be argued that the Estonians had only instrumental value for the Finnish national movement. The concept of a Finno-Ugrian fraternity was used to strengthen the status of Finnish culture in a European context. On the other hand, it was utilized in the schools' patriotic teaching: exciting stories about the Finnish tribe fighting for its freedom were used in order to awake emotions and, in that way, support patriotic feelings.

The myth of Finno-Ugrian togetherness and kinship can be seen partly as an invented tradition. It made use of epics such as the Kalevala and used them to emphasize the old and enduring civilization of the Finnic people. The teachers were part of the new middle class, and their task was to socialize working-class children in a nationalistic ethos: the children were supposed to put the Finnish nation and the Finno-Ugrian clan above everything else. The Finnish construct of Finno-Ugrian kinship, predominant particularly in the 1930s, was one manifestation of the nationalistic, right wing movements in Europe.

In the teachers case this instrumental value should not be exaggerated. Patriotic kinship feelings were such an important part of many teachers' self-image, and kinship issues required so much of their free time that it must have also had an intrinsic value for them. It was part of their patriotism, and they felt a genuine affection towards their kinship brothers and sisters. The co-operation between Finnish and Estonian teachers also had a professional value; as colleagues of two small and young nations they exchanged ideas and shared experiences. The expectations put on the elementary school as the educator of the masses were high in these two countries, which had only recently reached nationhood and were trying to find their place in the European community. The countries needed a justification for their claim that they were civilized and worthy of their independent status.

The teachers did not have free time in the sense we understand it today. They were constantly on duty and had to live up to their official statements in the classroom through their actions. Though kinship work, some teachers found a rewarding way to associate, travel, make new contacts, and develop their occupational skills. They combined in their kinship identity projects the occupational identity of a model citizen and ways to enjoy themselves. Often their hobbies were shared with friends made in the teachers' colleges. These former fellow-students shared the same moral order.

In their jobs as model citizens of the nation, the teachers tried to spread the good news to those who had not yet understood the greatness of the Finnish tribe and the importance of defending the Finnish cultural sphere. This task was intertwined with the Finnish teachers' interwar mission to unite the nation behind the same patriotic values. They felt a responsibility not only to guard the safety of the Finnish, or Finno-Ugrian, culture but the whole of western culture against the east. Finno-Ugrian areas were seen as a cultural buffer zone on Europe's border, and teachers were the propagators and maintainers of high European cultural values.

NOTES

1. According to Eric Hobsbawm, the principle of nationality, invented in the nineteenth century, triumphed at the end of the First World War. This was partly due to the collapse of the great multinational empires of Central and Eastern Europe, and partly due to the Russian revolution's impact on European politics. Hobsbawm 1990,131.
2. Kemiläinen 1994; Kemiläinen 1998.
3. See, for example, Hietala 1979, 78; Kemiläinen 1994; Kemiläinen 1998; Isaksson 2001, 263–275.
4. See, for example, Klinge 1983; Immonen 1987; Karemaa 1998. About anti-Russian psychological images see, for example, Vuorinen 2005, 255–259. According to Vuorinen the self-image of the Whites consisted of militarism, anti-Russian patriotism, and the idea of maintaining the 'legal' social order.
5. Hobsbawm 1990.
6. Hobsbawm 1983, 1–14, 264–307. The need for this kind of invented concept of nationalism based on the past was according to Hobsbawm, greatest in the rising middle classes, who wanted to distance themselves from the old aristocracy and the emerging working-class. See also Pakkasvirta & Saukkonen 2005, 30–31.
7. Rantala 2002, 15–17.
8. The Fennoman movement was a nationalist movement that aspired to promote Finnish language and literature. As a result the Finnish language achieved official status alongside Swedish.
9. The romantic image of the common people had already started to crumble in the first Russification period, which started in 1899, see, for example, Siltala 1999, 614–630. The general strike in 1905, during which the workers movement became an active and independent actor in society, also affected the images of people in the minds of the educated classes.
10. Alapuro 1973, 45–55.
11. Gellner 1983, 24–38; Paasi 1998, 215; Pakkasvirta & Saukkonen 2005, 33–34.
12. Arola 2003, 223–224; Ahonen 2003, 99; Tuomaala 2004, 70–71.
13. Rantala 2002, 172–174.
14. About the relationship between teachers and working-class children/families, see, for example, Peltonen 1996, 231–237; Tuomaala 2004, 312–333.
15. See for example, Karemaa 1998, 187–188, 197, 213–218; Nygård 1985, 468–470.
16. For the Academic Karelia Society, see Alapuro 1973.
17. In the interwar Europe the so-called Border States were countries, which had won their independence from Imperial Russia after the revolution. The border state-policy aimed to build a defense against communism by co-operation between these nations.
18. Karjahärm 1997, 60; Roiko-Jokela 1997, 67–78.
19. There were several issues that made the relationship between these two young nations cooler. One was the behavior of Finnish volunteers in the Estonian Civil War (Estonian War of Independence). In addition, the Estonian authoritarian government (in the 1930s) and its links with Finnish right-wing activists were a problem for the Finnish Government. Other factors were the smuggling of spirits (*pirtu*) from Estonia to Finland and the situation of the Ingrians in Estonia. The attitude towards Germans was different: for (white) Finns they were liberators, for Estonians oppressors. Alenius 1997, 23–26; Karjahärm 1997, 60–61; Hovi 2001, 11–12.

20. In Finnish *heimoaate*. Literally, the Finnish concept *heimo* means tribe, but by using this concept, misconceptions could arise. The word was used to describe the people who spoke Finno-Ugrian languages and supposedly had the same racial, historical, and cultural background.

21. This article is based on the author's forthcoming doctoral thesis on the relationship between elementary school teachers and working-class communities in Helsinki in the interwar period, which she is preparing with the support of the Finnish Cultural Foundation.

22. Ylijoki 1998.

23. Hovi 2001, 13–14. Some voluntary Estonian lessons were given in the interwar period in teachers' colleges, secondary schools, and even in some elementary schools. The depression in the beginning of 1930s led to their abolition in the schools, but they were reintroduced again after the cultural agreement between the Finnish and Estonian states in the late 1930s. Estonian lessons were mainly given in secondary schools, but in Helsinki a teacher Kerttu Mustonen, taught Estonian in elementary schools, for example, through the school radio. She also gave Estonian lessons to Estonian children living in Helsinki. About Kerttu Mustonen, see Rausmaa 2004, 6–7.

24. The term Finnish Alliance will be used in this article because of the term's compact form although the translation *Association of Finnish Culture and Identity* is a better description of the nature of the association, whose mission was to promote Finnish cultural values.

25. The inspector of Helsinki's Finnish speaking elementary schools (between 1908 and 1935) Matti Pesonen was an extremely religious man, who came from the revivalist religious movement (*herännäisyys*) of Savo (a province in South East Finland). His most important social networks and beliefs were the elementary schools, the kinship movement, religious revivalist circles, and, at the end of his career, also anticommunism. Pesonen was known as "a strong man of conviction" and his personal interests were said to have influenced the educational institutes he was in charge of. See, for example, Tarkastaja Pesonen 60-vuotias. *Opettajain lehti* 31/1928, 552.

26. Rausmaa 2004, 6.

27. Suomalaisten opettajain matka Tallinnaan. *Opettajain lehti* No 27/1919, 366.

28. Virolaisten opettajain vierailu pääkaupungissamme. *Opettajain lehti* No 36/1919, 457–460. These visits led to a brief kinship enthusiasm among teachers. The Estonian teachers looked to Finland for ideas to build their own school system. Many teachers and officials traveled to Helsinki to visit schools. Virolaisten koulunopettajain vierailu. *Opettajain lehti* No 22/1920, 275; Pesonen 1954, 79.

29. Conferences were held in Helsinki in 1921, Tallinn in 1924, Budapest in 1928, Helsinki in 1931 and Tallinn in 1936. For more information on the conferences see Received letters, inspector 1919–1936, Ea:27–Ea:44. The Archive of the Finnish-speaking elementary schools' inspector, Helsinki City Archives. There can be found a great deal of Matti Pesonen's personal material (letters etc.) concerning the Finno-Ugrian co-operation.

30. Pesonen 1954, 80–83; Ensimmäinen yhteissuomalainen koulukokous. *Opettajain lehti* No 28/1921, 425–426. 700 Finns, 442 Estonians, and five Hungarians along with some participants from Eastern Karelia and Ingria attended the conference.

31. Ensimmäinen yhteissuomalainen koulukokous. *Opettajain lehti* No 28/1921, 425–426.

32. Kokko 1997, 310–311.

33. Mitä kansakoululaisen tulee tietää Eestistä, written by Alfred Salmela. Suomen heimopäivä 1935. Ohjelmaa koulujen heimojuhliin, 9–11. Circulars of the National Board of Education 1935, Ec:34. Finnish-speaking elementary schools' office, Helsinki City Archives.

34. Halila 1950, 315. Johan Käis was the head of the Võru teacher seminar and he was interested in the idea of the working school (*arbeitschule, työkoulu*), on which the elementary schools of independent Estonia were based to a considerable extent. The ideas of Käis were described in depth in the *Opettajain lehti*. Johan Käis also visited Finland and gave lectures on his ideas on education See, for example, the following articles: Joh. Käis ja Eestin kansakoulu I, written by Akseli Salokannel. *Opettajain lehti* No 13/1935, 193–197; Joh. Käis ja Eestin kansakoulu II, written by Akseli Salokannel 15/1935, 229–232; Uusi koulu käytännössä, written by Aarne Huuskonen. *Opettajain lehti* No 49/1934, 149–150.

35. See, for example, Suhteemme Eestin opettajistoon, written by K. N. Hanhijärvi, and the counterpart of the editorial staff. *Opettajain lehti* No 6/1934, 71–73 and Koulunäyttely ja kasvatustieteellinen viikko Tallinnassa, written by Akseli Salokannel. *Opettajain lehti* No 51–52/1930, 916–917. Finnish teacher Akseli Salokannel visited Tallinn's pedagogical weeks in August 1930 and stated that Estonian teachers were aware professionals, ready for sacrifices and interested in schools abroad. Only six Finns attended these pedagogical days and Salokannel argued, that speeches and good wishes were not enough in building a bridge between the Finns and the Estonians.

36. About the conference, see, for example, Kutsu neljänteen suomalaiseen kulttuurikongressiin Helsingissä 16.–18.VI.31. *Opettajain lehti* No 13/1931, 227–228; IV suomalais-ugrilainen kulttuurikongressi. *Opettajain lehti* No 24/1931, 441–442; Kulttuurikongressi. *Opettajain lehti* No 26/1931, 489–491; Kulttuurikongressi. *Opettajain lehti* No 27/1931, 504–506; Kulttuurikongressin vaikutelmia. *Opettajain lehti* No 29/1931, 533–534. See also Helsingin Opettajayhdistyksen vuosikertomus vuodelta 1931. Minutes of the Teachers' association 1922–1933, Cb:1. The Archive of the Helsinki Teachers' association, Helsinki City Archives.

37. Suomen Opettajayhdistyksen edustajat Eesti Õpetajate Liidun vieraina. – EOL:n vuosikokous. *Opettajain lehti* No 46/1934, 713–715.

38. Suomen Opettajayhdistyksen 42. vuosikokous. Opettajain lehti No 27/1935, 446–448.

39. See, for example, Eestiläis-suomalaiset opettajain päivät. *Opettajain lehti* No 21/1935, p. 348–349; Virolais-suomalaiset opettajapäivät. *Opettajain lehti* No 25/1935, p. 409–410; Ministeri O. Mantereen puhe Suomen-Viron opettajapäivien avajaisissa 18.6.-35. *Opettajain lehti* No 26/1935, 429–430; Viron ja Suomen opettajat heimosiltaa rakentamassa. *Opettajain lehti* No 26/1935, 435–436.

40. Metsikkö & Oksanen 1943, 163.

41. Somerkivi 1977, 82–84.

42. Heimo-opetus kansakouluissa V: Heimo-opetuksen muodollista perustelua, written by Eino Keskinen. *Opettajain lehti* No 21/1933, 313.

43. There were also other forms of kinship activity in the Jyväskylä Teachers' College. In 1928 the students made a trip to Estonia, and a special Estonia-club (*Eestin kerho*) was founded in 1932. Especially the directress of the seminar, Eva Maria Heikinheimo, held the kinship work dear. Alongside the voluntary Estonian lessons the female students also got to know Estonian literature. Aimo Halila has argued that after independence, the Finnic people and their culture were tried to be taken

225

into account in the Teachers' college's teaching. Halila 1963, 224, 303–304.

44. Suur-Suomen koulu (introduction). Jyväskylän Seminaarin Karjala-Seura 1930 (ed.): *Suur-Suomen koulu.* Jyväskylä: K. J. Gummerus osakeyhtiö, 9–11.

45. Koulumme ja puolustuskunto, written by Lauri Pihkala. Jyväskylän Seminaarin Karjala-Seura 1930 (ed.): *Suur-Suomen koulu.* Jyväskylä: K. J. Gummerus osakeyhtiö, 18.

46. See, for example, Tuomaala 2004.

47. In the beginning of the 1930s (1929–1932) Finland stood on the brink of a right wing coup d'état, when the so called "Lapua movement", dominated by anti-communist nationalists, gained political influence.

48. Isänmaallisuuden ja puolustustahdon kasvattaminen kansakouluissamme. Alustus opettajayhdistyksille, written by Yrjö Suhonen. *Opettajain lehti* No 16/1932, 243–246; Koulun uskonnollis-isänmaallinen kasvatus, written by Eemeli Etelälahti. *Opettajain lehti* No 48/1932, 822–825.

49. Kysymyksiä pasifisteille ja maailmanparantajille, written by P. Mustapää (Martti Haavio). Jyväskylän Seminaarin Karjala-Seura 1930 (ed.): *Suur-Suomen koulu.* Jyväskylä: K. J. Gummerus osakeyhtiö, 312.

50. Metsikkö & Oksanen 1943, 167–159, 189; Halila 1950, 209–211. Vasara 1997, 643. The Teachers' Association sent a presentation about the national defense teaching to all teachers. All the teachers' organizations agreed with the writers that creating love for one's country and a will to defend it was an important educational question, behind which all the citizens should stand. Maanpuolustuksen opettaminen kansakoulussa, written by I. V. Ahonen. Suomen Opettajayhdistyksen Keskustelukysymyksiä XLIX, Helsinki 1936. Conversation questions 1923–52, Db1. Finland's teachers' union's archive, Clerical employee's archives (*Toimihenkilöarkisto*).

51. Heimo-opetus kansakouluissa V: Heimo-opetuksen muodollista perustelua, kohta 1. written by Eino Keskinen. *Opettajain lehti* No 21/1933, 313.

52. Tuomaala 2004, 195–204.

53. See, for example, article Heimo-opetus kansakouluissa I. *Opettajain lehti* No 17/1933, 250–251; Peitsalo 1927, 156–157; Vasara 1997, 640.

54. Kouluhallitukselle 8.12.1921 yhteissuomalaisen koulukokouksen puolesta Matti Pesonen, puheenjohtaja, Alfred Jotuni, sihteeri. Received letters, inspector 1920, Ea:28. The Archive of the Finnish-speaking elementary schools' inspector, Helsinki City Archives.

55. Also optional Estonian language classes were included in the syllabuses of Finnish teachers' colleges and secondary schools provided there were enough participants. Heimo- ja viron kielen opetus kouluissamme. Kouluhallituksen lausunto. *Opettajain lehti* No 5/1928, 65; Heimo-opetus kansakouluissa II: Heimoharrastuksemme, written by Eino Keskinen. *Opettajain lehti* No 18/1933, 265; Halila 1950, 207–208.

56. Eestin ja Suomen kansakoulujen yhteistyö, written by Akseli Salokannel. Jyväskylän Seminaarin Karjala-Seura 1930 (ed.): *Suur-Suomen koulu.* Jyväskylä: K. J. Gummerus osakeyhtiö, 295.

57. Heimo-opetus kansakouluissa V: Heimo-opetuksen muodollista perustelua, written by Eino Keskinen. *Opettajain lehti* No 21/1933, 313; Eestin ja Suomen kansakoulujen yhteistyö, written by Akseli Salokannel. Jyväskylän Seminaarin Karjala-Seura 1930 (ed.): *Suur-Suomen koulu.* Jyväskylä: K. J. Gummerus osakeyhtiö, 294–295. See also Vasara 1997, 640.

58. Peitsalo 1927, 155.
59. Heimo-opetus kansakouluissa IV: Heimo-opetuksen periaatteelliset perusteet, written by Eino Keskinen. *Opettajain lehti* No 20/1933, 297.
60. Kemiläinen 1994, 122–126; Hietala 1979, 79–82; Tuomaala 2004, 195–207; Paasi 1998, 226–235.
61. See, for example, Heimo-opetus kansakoulussa, written by Eino Keskinen. Jyväskylän Seminaarin Karjala-Seura 1930 (ed.): *Suur-Suomen koulu*. Jyväskylä: K. J. Gummerus osakeyhtiö, 123–141; Suomen kansan omavarainen elämä historian valossa, written by Lauri Santamäki. ibid, 54–122; Isoniemi 1937, 83–84.
62. Lehti 1998, 86.
63. Heimokielen opiskelu – hauskaa, hyödyllistä kauaskantavaa työtä, written by Lauri Kettunen. Ohjelmaa koulujuhliin. Eestin itsenäisyyden julistamisen 20-vuotispäiväksi 24.II.1938, 10. Circulars of the National Board of Education 1938, Ec:37. Finnish-speaking elementary schools' office, Helsinki City Archives.
64. Heimopäiväpuhe varttuneelle nuorisolle, written by Leeni Vesterinen. Heimopäiväjuhlien ohjelmistoa. Suomen heimopäivä 1939, 20–22. Circulars of the National Board of Education 1939, Ec:38. Finnish-speaking elementary schools' office, Helsinki City Archives. Vesterinen presented a familiar example from sports when Estonian athletes succeed, for example, in the marathon, the Finns can feel that they have won. An athlete of pure Estonian blood is a representative of our race, she declared.
65. See, for example, Ohjeita suomalais-eestiläisen oppilaskirjeenvaihdon aikaansaamiseksi Suomen heimopäivä 1935. Ohjelmaa koulujen heimojuhliin, 28; Heimokielen opiskelu – hauskaa, hyödyllistä kauaskantavaa työtä, written by Lauri Kettunen. Ohjelmaa koulujuhliin. Eestin itsenäisyyden julistamisen 20-vuotispäiväksi 24.II.1938, 10. Circulars of the National Board of Education 1935, Ec:34 and 1938, Ec:37. Finnish-speaking elementary schools' office, Helsinki City Archives.
66. Heimorakkaus voimakkaaksi! Puhe heimopäivänä, written by J. O. Metsikkö. Ohjelmaa koulujen heimojuhliin. Suomen heimopäivä 1937, 5. Circulars of the National Board of Education 1937, Ec:36. Finnish-speaking elementary schools' office, Helsinki City Archives.
67. Johtokunnan pöytäkirja 17.11.1938 § 21, liite § 21 (pöytäkirja kesävirkistystoimikunnan kokouksesta 19.10.38 § 3). Johtokunnan pöytäkirjat. Finnish-speaking elementary schools' office, Helsinki City Archives.
68. See, for example, Kehoitus yleisen heimopäivän viettämiseen. *Opettajain lehti* No 40/1930, 708; Kouluhallituksen kiertokirje No 682 (508) 11.10.1930. Circulars of the National Board of Education 1930, Ec:29. Finnish-speaking elementary schools' office, Helsinki City Archives.
69. Heimopäivän ohjelmistoa. Suomen Heimopäivä 1938, 2. Circulars of the National Board of Education 1938, Ec:37. Finnish-speaking elementary schools' office, Helsinki City Archives.
70. Ohjelmaa Eestin ja Unkarin itsenäisyyspäivien koulujuhliin 24.II. ja 15.III. 1936. See also Kouluhallituksen kiertokirje 8.2.1937 Oppikouluosasto No 863, Kansanopetusosasto No 647. Circulars of the National Board of Education 1936–1937, Ec:35–36. Finnish-speaking elementary schools' office, Helsinki City Archives.
71. Ohjelmaa koulujuhliin. Eestin itsenäisyyden julistamisen 20vuotispäiväksi 24.II.1938, 2. Circulars of the National Board of Education 1938, Ec:37. Suomenkielisten kansakoulujen kanslia, Helsinki City Archives.

72. See, for example, Puhe, written by Leeni Vesterinen. Suomen heimopäivä 1935. Ohjelmaa koulujen heimojuhliin, 4–6; Mitä kansakoululaisen tulee tietää Eestistä, written by Alfred Salmela. ibid., 9–11; Puhe, written by Niko Oksanen, Suomen heimopäivä 1936. Ohjelmaa koulujen heimojuhliin, 4–7. Circulars of the National Board of Education 1935–1936, Ec:34–35. Finnish-speaking elementary schools' office, Helsinki City Archives.

73. See, for example, Heimorakkaus voimakkaaksi! Puhe heimopäivänä, written by J. O. Metsikkö. Ohjelmaa koulujen heimojuhliin. Suomen heimopäivä 1937, 6. Circulars of the National Board of Education 1937, Ec:36. Finnish-speaking elementary schools' office, Helsinki City Archives.

74. Suomen sillan rakentajat, written by Matilda Sirkkola. Suomen heimopäivä 1936. Ohjelmaa koulujen heimojuhliin, toimittanut Suomalaisuuden liiton sukukansaosasto, 18–23. Circulars of the National Board of Education 1936, Ec:35. Finnish-speaking elementary schools' office, Helsinki City Archives.

75. Kannel ja risti. Kuvaelma nuorison heimojuhliin, written by Ukko Kivistö Ohjelmaa koulujen heimojuhliin. Suomen heimopäivä 1937. Suomalaisuuden liiton sukukansaosasto, 13–23. Circulars of the National Board of Education 1937, Ec:36. Finnish-speaking elementary schools' office. Helsinki City Archives.

76. About self-esteem issues see Kemiläinen 1994, 368–376; Kemiläinen 1998, 276–278. On the race-question of the Finns in the nineteenth century and its connection to the Finnish language-dispute see Siltala 1999, 165–167. The presumption was that only Aryans were able to create culture. Siltala calls the Finnish attitude "self-racism".

77. See Puhe oppilaille Eestin päivänä, written by Maija Väisänen and Nuoriso luo valtakuntia, written by Jaan Rummo and Leeni Vesterinen. Ohjelmaa koulujuhliin Eestin ja Unkarin itsenäisyyspäiviksi 24.2. ja 15.3.1939, toimittanut Suomalaisuuden Liiton Sukukansaosasto, 4–6, 7–9. Circulars of the National Board of Education 1939 Ec:38. Finnish-speaking elementary schools' office, Helsinki City Archives.

78. The Kalevala was compiled and revised by Elias Lönnrot (1802–1884) from poetry in the ancient oral tradition and first published in 1835.

79. Kalevalan merkitys kansallemme, written by O–n. *Opettajain lehti* No 9/1935, 123–125.

SOURCES

Unprinted sources

Helsinki City Archives (Helsingin kaupunginarkisto):
The Archive of the Helsinki Teachers' association: Minutes of the Teachers association 1931
The Archive of the Finnish-speaking elementary schools' office: Circulars of
 the National Board of Education 1930, 1935–1939
The Archive of the Finnish-speaking elementary schools' inspector: Received
 letters, inspector 1919–1936

Clerical Employee's Archives (Toimihenkilöarkisto):
Finland's teachers' union's archive: Conversation questions 1936

Printed sources

Isoniemi, Anna 1937. Heimokysymyksestä äidinkielen opetuksessa. *Me uskomme. Naisyli-oppilaiden Karjala-Seuran 15-vuotisjulkaisu.* Helsinki: Suomalaisen kirjallisuuden seuran kirjapaino.

Jyväskylän Seminaarin Karjala-Seura 1930 (ed.). *Suur-Suomen koulu.* Jyväskylä: K. J. Gummerus osakeyhtiö.

Metsikkö, J. O. & Oksanen, Niko 1943. *Suomen Kansakoulunopettajain Liitto. Piirteitä 50-vuotisesta toiminnasta.* Suomen Kansakoulunopettajain Liitto, Helsinki.

Peitsalo, Ilmari 1927. Kansallistuotantoa herättävien aineiden opetus ja heimoopetus oppikouluissamme. *Kasvatus ja Koulu. Jyväskylän yliopistoyhdistyksen kasvatus-opillinen aikakauskirja* 1927, 153-159.

Pesonen, Matti 1954. *Ystäviä läheltä ja kaukaa. Muistelmia.* Helsinki: Osakeyhtiö Valistus.

Newspapers

Opettajain lehti (The Teachers' Magazine) 1919–1921, 1928, 1930–1935

BIBLIOGRAPHY

Ahonen, Sirkka 2003. *Yhteinen koulu. Tasa-arvoa vai tasapäisyyttä? Koulutuksellinen tasa-arvo Suomessa Snellmanista tähän päivään.* Tampere: Kirjakas Ky.

Alapuro, Risto 1973. *Akateeminen Karjala-Seura: ylioppilasliike ja kansa 1920- ja 1930-luvulla.* Porvoo: WSOY.

Alenius, Kari 1997. Veljeskansojen kahdet kasvot. *Naapurimaa-kuva.* Roiko-Jokela, Heikki (ed.), *Virallista politiikkaa, epävirallista kanssakäymistä. Suomen ja Viron suhteiden käännekohtia 1860–1991.* Jyväskylä: Atena, 13–30.

Arola, Pauli 2003. *Tavoitteena kunnon kansalainen. Koulun kansalaiskasvatuksen päämäärät eduskunnan keskusteluissa 1917–1924.* Helsinki: Helsingin yliopiston kasvatustieteen laitoksen tutkimuksia 191.

Gellner, Ernest 1983. *Nations and nationalism.* Oxford: Blackwell.

Halila, Aimo 1950. *Suomen kansakoululaitoksen historia 4: Oppivelvollisuuskoulun alkuvaiheet (1921–1939).* Helsinki: Suomalainen tiedeakatemia.

—— 1963. *Jyväskylän seminaarin historia.* Porvoo: WSOY.

Hietala, Marjatta 1979. Näkemyksiä eri roduista Suomessa käytetyissä yleisen historian ja maantieteen oppikirjoissa 1800-luvun lopussa ja 1900-luvun alussa. Ahonen, Kalevi, Myllykoski, Matti & Tiainen, Jorma (eds), *Wie es eigentlich gewesen. Aira Kemiläiselle omistettu juhlakirja.* Studia historica Jyväskyläensia 18. Jyväskylä: Jyväskylän yliopisto.

Hobsbawm, Eric 1983. Introduction: Inventing traditions and Mass-producing Traditions: Europe, 1970–1840. Hobsbawn, Eric & Ranger, Terence, *The invention of tradition.* Cambridge: Cambridge University Press, 1–14, 264–307.

—— 1990. *Nations and nationalism since 1790. Programme, Myth, Reality.* Cambridge: Cambridge University Press.

Hovi, Kalervo 2001. Suomen ja Viron kulttuurisuhteet maailmansotien välisenä aikana. Talvitie, Sakari & Modeen, Tore (eds), *Finland and Estonia.* Helsinki: Henrik Gabriel Porthan Institute, 11–17.

Immonen, Kari 1987. *Ryssästä saa puhua...: Neuvostoliitto suomalaisessa julkisuudessa ja kirjat julkisuuden muotona 1918–39.* Helsinki: Otava.

Isaksson, Pekka 2001. *Kumma kuvajainen. Rasismi rotututkimuksessa, rotuteorioiden saamelaiset ja suomalainen fyysinen antropologia.* Inari: Kustannus Puntsi 2001.

Karemaa, Outi 1998. *Vihollisia, vainoojia, syöpäläisiä. Venäläisviha Suomessa 1917–1923.* Bibliotheca Historica 30. Helsinki: Suomen Historiallinen Seura.

Karjahärm, Toomas 1997. Venäjän varjossa. Suomi ja Viro Venäjän naapureina. Roiko-Jokela, Heikki (ed.), *Virallista politiikkaa, epävirallista kanssakäymistä. Suomen ja Viron suhteiden käännekohtia 1860–1991.* Jyväskylä: Atena, 31–61.

Kemiläinen, Aira 1994. Suomalaiset, outo Pohjolan kansa. Rotuteoriat ja kansallinen identiteetti. Helsinki: Suomen Historiallinen Seura.

Kemiläinen, Aira 1998. *Finns in the Shadow of the "Aryans". Race Theories and Racism.* Helsinki: Suomen Historiallinen Seura.

Klinge, Matti 1983. Vihan veljistä valtiososialismiin. Yhteiskunnallisia ja kansallisia näkemyksiä 1910- ja 1920-luvuilta. Helsinki: WSOY.

Kokko, Marja 1997. Heimosisaruutta vaiko vain uteliaisuutta? Suomalaisten ja virolaisten naisjärjestöjen kontaktit 1860–1939. Roiko-Jokela, Heikki (ed.), *Virallista politiikkaa, epävirallista kanssakäymistä. Suomen ja Viron suhteiden käännekohtia 1860–1991.* Jyväskylä: Atena, 309–325.

Lehti, Marko 1998. Suomi Viron isoveljenä. Suomalas-virolaisten suhteiden kääntöpuoli. Immonen, Kari & Onnela, Tapio (eds), *Suomi ja Viro: yhdessä ja erikseen.* Turku: Turun yliopisto.

Nygård, Toivo 1985. Venäläisvastaisuus ja Suur-Suomi-ajatus suomalaisen äärioikeiston ideologiassa. Kemiläinen, Aira & Hietala, Marjatta & Suvanto, Pekka (eds), *Mongoleja vai germaaneja – rotuteorioiden suomalaiset.* Helsinki: Suomen Historiallinen Seura, 459–475.

Paasi, Anssi 1998. Koulutus kansallisena projektina. Me ja muut suomalaisissa maantiedon oppikirjoissa. Alasuutari, Pertti & Ruuska, Petri (eds), *Elävänä Euroopassa. Muuttuva suomalainen identiteetti.* Tampere: Vastapaino, 215–250.

Pakkasvirta, Jussi & Saukkonen, Pasi 2005. Nationalismi teoreettisen tutkimuksen kohteena. Pakkasvirta, Jussi & Saukkonen, Pasi (eds), *Nationalismit.* Helsinki: WSOY.

Peltonen, Ulla-Maija 1996. *Punakapinan muistot. Tutkimus työväen muistelukerronnan muotoutumisesta vuoden 1918 jälkeen.* Helsinki: Suomalaisen Kirjallisuuden Seura.

Rantala, Jukka 2002. *Kansakoulunopettajat ja kapina. Vuoden 1918 punaisuussyytökset ja opettajan asema paikallisyhteisössä.* Historiallisia tutkimuksia 214. Helsinki: Suomalaisen Kirjallisuuden Seura.

Rausmaa, Heikki 2004. *Arkiston kätköistä. Kerttu Mustonen-Hukin arkisto.* Tuglas-seuran jäsenlehti 4/2004, 6–7.

Roiko-Jokela, Heikki 1997. "Reaalipoliittiset edut vaativat rannikkomme eteläpuolelle ystävällisen maan." Baltia Suomen lähialuepolitiikassa 1918–1996. Roiko-Jokela, Heikki (ed.), *Virallista politiikkaa, epävirallista kanssakäymistä: Suomen ja Viron suhteiden käännekohtia 1860–1991.* Jyväskylä: Atena, 65–94.

Siltala, Juha 1999. *Valkoisen äidin pojat. Siveellisyys ja sen varjot kansallisessa projektissa.* Helsinki: Otava.

Somerkivi, Urho 1977. *Helsingin kansakoulun historia.* Helsinki: Helsingin kaupunki.

Tuomaala, Saara 2004. *Työtätekevistä käsistä puhtaiksi ja kirjoittaviksi: suomalaisen oppivelvollisuuskoulun ja maalaislasten kohtaaminen 1921–1939.* Helsinki: Suomalaisen Kirjallisuuden Seura.

Vasara, Erkki 1997. *Valkoisen Suomen urheilevat soturit. Suojeluskuntajärjestön urheilu- ja kasvatustoiminta vuosina 1918–1939*. Bibliotheca historica 23. Helsinki: Suomen Historiallinen Seura.

Vuorinen, Marja 2005. Herrat, hurrit ja ryssän kätyrit – suomalaisuuden vastakuvia. Pakkasvirta, Jussi & Saukkonen Pasi (eds), *Nationalismit*. Helsinki: WSOY, 246– 264.

Ylijoki, Oili-Helena 1998. *Akateemiset heimokulttuurit ja noviisien sosialisaatio*. Tampere: Vastapaino.

LEENA PAASKOSKI

Green Gold in a Suitcase

In the 1990s the profession of university-educated foresters had become one of the most international professions in Finland.[1] Students had good opportunities to get work experience abroad even before graduating and after graduation one could easily get a job in a foreign country, in, for example, a range of multinational forest industry companies. International experience as well as a knowledge of languages was appreciated by Finnish employers, but Finnish forest expertise was also in demand outside Finland. With an academic forestry education obtained in Finland, a forester could in the 1980s and 1990s go, for example, into commercial business in Europe, into consultancy about forest cultivation issues in Asia, or into forestry co-operation work in developing countries in Africa.[2]

Going abroad was not new among forestry professionals in Finland. Before the Evo Forest Institute[3] was established, about seventy young Finnish men studied forestry in Germany, Sweden, and Russia during the 1850s and 1860s. For one reason or another, some men continued to get their education in these foreign institutes and academies even later than this, although most students studied in Finland, at the University in Helsinki from 1908 and at the University of Joensuu from 1982. Relations with foreign colleagues and forestry organisations had always been quite close, especially in the field of forest research. There had also been different grant arrangements for those who wanted to get further experience abroad.[4] Still, at least before the 1970–1980s, the real base for Finnish foresters seemed to be within Finland in its own forests. What was learnt abroad was also taken home.

Towards the end of the twentieth century, the work of a forester was seen in a wider and more versatile context than before. Foresters now found themselves at the center of ever widening circles: not only in multiple forestry, but in the Finnish and European forest cluster and globalized forest related issues.[5] Finnish forest industries had merged with international companies, international research institutes had been established both in Finland and abroad, European Union membership affected Finland's national and international forest policy and Finland was actively taking part in the global discussion about forest issues. Analyses and predictions made about Finnish forestry in the 1990s had shown that international developments would determine Finnish forestry and national forest policy in the future even more. Since the 1990s, the forest sector has not been a leading sector in the national economy either.[6]

In this article, I will focus on the recent history of individual foresters in a period of globalization. I let young foresters, who graduated in the 1980s and 1990s, discuss – and even raise their voice – with their senior colleagues about their profession, and their manners, values, ideas, and identities as university-educated Finnish foresters. These young professionals themselves often saw a line between "the young" and "the old forester generation".[7] I will use these concepts when talking about generations because they correspond to the real experiences and narrations of my interviewees, even if the narrators do not make the line between the generations particularly clear. Reading the oral history material (interviews with foresters) and student magazines, the line between the generations in the 1970s seems rather instinct and opaque, although in individual accounts it sometimes appears to be quite clear and precisely defined.[8] I will pay attention to the gap between these two generations as well as to the bridges between them and in this way analyze the professional culture and identity of present-day foresters.

The article is based on my PhD thesis on the professional culture of university-educated Finnish foresters from the 1860s to the 1990s. The main material for my PhD thesis consists of biographical interviews with university-educated foresters interviewed between 1999 and 2002 in an oral history project called "Forestry Professions in a Changing Society". For this article, I have read the interviews of twenty-seven men and women who were born in the 1960s and 1970s and started their careers in the 1980s and 1990s, and, for the sake of comparison, the interviews of forty foresters born between the 1910s and the 1940s. There are also twenty-seven men and women who studied in the 1970s, who talk about their ideas regarding the professional culture.[9]

Out of Forests

The profession of Finnish foresters was established in the middle of the nineteenth century to cater for the needs of the new Board of Forestry and a developing forest sector. During the twentieth century, the number of employers markedly increased but the Board of Forestry (Metsähallitus), the forest industry and private forestry organisations were for a long period in the twentieth century the main employers of foresters. A lot of changes in the education and work of foresters has occurred especially in the 1980s and 1990s.[10]

The years after the Second World War were an active period in Finnish forestry and for its professionals. Finland had lost 13 percent of its forested area as a result of the war [11] and was then faced with extensive reconstruction and the paying of war indemnities. At the same time, demand for the forest industry's products in Western Europe was increasing. The difficulties and challenges would, it was hoped, be overcome with the traditional force and national wealth of Finnish society: forests and forestry.[12] This property, the green gold of Finland, was more or less in the hands of university-educated

University-educated foresters in the excursion to Lappland 1961. Photo: Olavi Linna-mies/Lusto/Metsähallitus collection.

foresters. Looking after it was their main task. Slogans like "Finland's green wooden wall", "with wood to better days", "saved from shortage by wood" or "Finland has wooden feet" were well known in post-war Finland and for a long time afterwards.[13] Through his poem a forester A. E. Järvinen (1891–1963) wanted to transmit the values of his generation to the association of forest students, which was celebrating its fiftieth anniversary in 1959:

> We protect our forests with enthusiastic heart,
> we clear our forests with hands, callous and hard.
> The forests will raise our land on high,
> the forests will give us strength of mind,
> the gold of the forests will lead us to victory.[14]

According to a younger forester, even during the 1960s Finnish forestry was still seen as "a political choice" and "a patriotic duty".[15] However, the economic value of the forests and the social task of the foresters were ideas that persisted into the last decades of the 20th century. A woman who had

234

studied forest sciences in the late 1970s wanted to find herself "a mission" in the forest sector: "In a way we are guardians of many things: … nature and our society and all big economic issues… this is what the question is about."[16]

Many other young men and women were also proud of their profession and well motivated, but did not have any special emotional tie to their work.[17] They could feel that many other tasks could be just as interesting: "I don't consider this work a vocation – or think that I have a great duty given specially to me."[18] It seems that the difference between the generations was the amount of tasks they had to deal with. At the end of the twentieth century, one could no longer talk about "the task" of the forester but rather tasks. The pluralistic and versatile forest sector had many tasks, values, and aims. Many different people, ideas, abilities, and attitudes towards Finland's forests were needed to carry them out. If the older generation of foresters had, according to a young forester of the 1980s, emphasized the common interest and common good rather than the particular interest of their employers, younger foresters did not think of themselves as guardians of the common interest, but really as the guardians of many things, as the female forester quoted above noted. The profession of university-educated foresters seemed to split into many different groups, each with its own task.[19] Foresters had to come to terms with the idea that perhaps Finland didn't just have wooden feet. The forest sector was important but it also had to develop in, for example, a more ecological direction. "The forest cluster thinking" put Finland in a more positive, extensive, and international context. The future was interesting, but perhaps unstable and difficult to predict in detail.[20]

Since the 1990s, foresters had also occupied more and more jobs outside "traditional forestry". Although short-term and occasional jobs because of the bad employment environment, or the lack of money for research were both considered problems, it was not purely a question of employment issues as has sometimes been claimed [21] – at least, difficulties in getting jobs in traditional forestry were not the reason young foresters gave. For example, very few of the people who had graduated in the late 1990s were working in "traditional positions of foresters" – but this was mostly due to the lack of interest.[22] During their studies, a forest student's ideas of himself working in a forest lost their attraction and "the aims have since then been totally on another level", outside "practical jobs".[23] Another forester had never even dreamed of "the traditional jobs" in forestry.[24] To be able to work in many different jobs, with the university providing the tools, rather than an education for a particular occupation was considered a positive factor. This attitude was based on a change made in 1978 in the Helsinki university: the former official degree (forestry degree), which had been more directly aimed at an occupation, was replaced with an academic degree, a Master of Science (Agriculture and Forestry). "The real work of university-educated foresters" did not exist anymore, thought one of the young foresters.[25] The decline in the number of traditional jobs had led to more opportunities and freedom in the profession.[26] As the range of occupations became wider, the tie between forest education and the profession became looser. More and more foresters were working in the forest cluster, or even in totally different fields, or in other parts of the world.[27] According to a forester who studied in the late 1970s, this internationalization had been the most significant change in the field.[28] Another forester felt that Finland's European Union membership had affected her work "most totally".[29] A young married couple of foresters who had earlier been working abroad, thought that "as soon as there was a tempting offer" they would consider leaving again.[30]

Some foresters felt that they were also dealing more with people than with forests in their work and that this human co-operation was one of the best aspects of their work.[31] When a forester, born in the 1940s, gave his opinion of the work of the university-educated foresters of today he hardly mentioned the word "forest":

> A present day forester is certainly an active leader, or a high-level operator, working in multiple fields, and has an education which gives him/her the ability to lead organisations and control entities. Some of the work may be outdoors in nature, but I would predict that... most of the work is done by a computer, where a forester is making calculations and mailing them all around the world.[32]

A forest was the immediate working environment of university-educated foresters in the past, as all the professionals well knew. The work today, on the contrary, was anchored more abstractly to forest issues, or even to abilities and expertise, an academic education and knowledge that could give foresters access to almost anywhere. On the other hand, others outside the profession now had an access to forests:

> People understand that the forest world is not separate from the rest of world; everybody has a right to talk about and influence how the forests are used, or forest policy. The forest is of concern to ethnologists as well as to students of the Swedish language, or anybody... A forester is only one among many who can consider forest issues. And of course one's own professional skill has an advantage... it helps us to understand many things but... you cannot silence anyone with it... If I think about an alteration in this profession, then it is that the profession becomes all the time more and more heterogeneous.[33]

As the wider world towards the end of the twentieth century offered more opportunities for forester careers, it also forced the profession itself to break down its own walls. In a way, there were two boundary lines to be crossed: the line of a strictly defined profession and the border of nationality.

On the Opening Borders

The discussion about the work and aims of forestry and about the life of a forester that was being held – in a symbolic way – between the forester generations was taking place within a common group, a profession, or a professional circle. In the case of Finnish university-educated foresters, it is

A forest student course of the early 1980s. Lusto/Jukka Sippola's collection.

obvious that this collective culture had been created during their education and been strengthened in the profession. Consequently, a professional culture can be considered as a result of an ongoing process where customs, values, and ideas are consciously maintained by the members of a group. It is both a question of continuity, whereby the culture is transferred from established members to new ones, from one generation to another, and, on the other hand, of alteration, whereby the group, or generation, changes its traditions or adopts new ones.[34] This is a slow process which eventually encompasses the whole group, or profession. The education aims to meet the needs of a changing forestry and society. Young educated professionals, however, become part of a profession that goes back many generations. The oldest might have studied, for example, in the 1930s, whilst the youngest might have graduated at the end of the 1990s.[35] The professional culture is created in a more or less homogeneous study group, but it lives on in a much more heterogeneous group of foresters with diversified values and ideas.

Talking about university-educated foresters, their duties, work, and their common social relationship often leads foresters to talk about a forester spirit, a feeling of togetherness that was born during their studies in a tight-knit student group. Because the concept of a forester spirit has a long history going back to at least the 1930s[36] and is well-known in the profession, it can be used as an indicator of the nature of the common social relationships and the professional culture of successive forester generations. The forester spirit was important in the profession: its deeper purpose was to create a sense of professional pride and to support foresters in their demanding duties as caretakers of the Finnish forests, "the national wealth".[37] This spirit was not

237

just born, it was consciously created as part of the foresters' education by their teachers (university-educated foresters) and the older students. The real forester spirit included good forester manners, like honesty and responsibility, and reached beyond one's own study group to all forestry professionals.[38]

The togetherness they experienced during their studies meant for many of these foresters lifelong brotherhood and friendship – the forester spirit was often described as a network or circle, of colleagues.[39] It was actively maintained after their studies had come to an end. The group of students that had studied together met each other annually, for example, for course lunches or various other meetings like excursions.[40] As a student of the 1950s explained: "And one has to remember, of course, that [the forester spirit] lasts because there are course lunches once a year..."[41] These meetings were occasions for keeping up the group's cultural tradition, which included collective memories, stories, humor, and professional views. In other words, they were occasions for recollecting past experiences and for reminding themselves of their togetherness in working for the greatest common aim, which, as professor Olli Heikinheimo put it in a student magazine in the 1940s, consisted of "constantly improving the forests and the production of forestry in Finland".[42]

Even if the good sense of togetherness was respected among young forestry professionals, the forester spirit was seldom emphasized in their narrations. On the contrary, young foresters often saw it as having little meaning in a personal way, or as a much weakened or negative feature of the professional culture. It might even be associated with the exploitation of the forests for purely economic gain.[43] Increasingly, from the 1970s onwards, more restrained, negative, even ironic attitudes were in evidence towards the forester spirit.[44] At a time when Finnish forestry was becoming more open and pluralistic, there was a danger that the profession was too introverted and exhibited only the negative side of the forester spirit, an "unpleasant good brother spirit" or "we know best spirit".[45] There were also some critical attitudes towards other forms of social co-operation amongst foresters, such as their trade union.[46] A forester who had studied in the 1980s pointed out that unlike in the past, the profession of foresters as part of present-day society deals more with other professions than with its own members. Earlier, there had been more of a need socially to join the profession's circle, because foresters lived and worked in more isolated places in the countryside. Nowadays, social activities within the profession were not even needed as the social side of life was taken care of in a totally different way.[47] The older generation also noticed that times had changed.[48]

The student days of the younger generations, even if they were remembered as a good time, did not seem to create such a tight and lasting social bond for the whole student group that had studied together. Whilst it was nice to meet old fellow students, course lunches, celebrations, or excursions were not considered as important as before. Many young foresters who did not attend their course lunches often referred to the lack of time.[49] The whole student group (that had studied together) did not meet each other regularly but many had a couple of close friends from their graduate days: they could be contacted without old-fashioned institutional course lunches.[50] One could

238

form social ties and communicate much more easily via e-mail, than in face-to-face meetings with fellow students or other colleagues.[51] One could easily, quickly, and cheaply contact each other, especially when so many of one's fellow students were working and living abroad.[52]

It had already been noticed in the 1970s that forest students did not form as homogeneous a group as before. They themselves pointed out the great variety of backgrounds, aims, and values that were to be found among their fellow students. A forester who had studied in the 1970s emphasized that the values of the students on his course were not uniform: there were commercial-minded students, humanists and hard-headed technocrats studying side by side at the university.[53] An attraction to nature and natural sciences was often given as the reason for choosing the profession, as it was for generations before.[54] But still their different backgrounds and ideas meant that the students were quite different from each other and especially from older generations.[55]

> ... times have changed in a way [in the early 1980s] since the generation after the war... young people now are interested in ecology, perhaps in nature conservation... in other things than just intensive forestry. And then there were still some fellow students who considered intensifying forest production as a duty and the purpose in life of a forester, but... they were already quite rare, so that actually an oppositional and questioning mind were surprisingly strong in this student group...[56]

In the mid-1990s, forest students noticed an even more sudden and stronger change, "a cultural shock", in their student group. When the preliminary practise period[57] that was needed for entering the faculty was removed, more and more people without any previous connection to forests and forestry began to study forest sciences: women, people from Helsinki and its environs, and people from other urban settings. According to one forester, her whole student group had criticised the education they were receiving. For example, one described it as "the nonsense of old men" and as "army like activities". It was a complete cultural shock when these students met "the old hands" and when these teachers met students who did not know what a billhook was.[58] This cultural shock became more and more obvious as time went by, according to another forester. He had lived all his life in Helsinki and graduated in the late 1990s:

> The people graduating now [2000] from forest sciences... and those who graduated last year and those graduating next year, they do... differ quite a lot from the people that were here before... The foresters to come will surprise the older professionals.[59]

However, the cultural shock experienced by these students was only part of the picture. The other forester quoted above, talking so critically about her education and "the old hands", emphasized the good feeling of togetherness there had been during her graduate days, the regular contacts with many fellow students, and "a fine tradition" of course lunches.[60] A forester who had studied forest sciences in the early 1980s said that it was nice and easy to contact one's own fellow students, even after a long time.[61] Even if for some "belonging to nothing", as one student put it, or keeping one's distance from the profession, its traditional lunches and other elements that serve to create its professional ethos, meant personal freedom,[62] the forester spirit and belonging to one's own professional group could still give some others "a good feeling" and provide a necessary network within the profession and a changing society.[63]

As with the older generation, not all the young foresters shared the same attitudes towards their studies, work and profession. However, for many of them these attitudes were familiar. Social relations in the profession were not established just with members of one's own student group but among all foresters of different ages working side by side. The oral history of young foresters includes stories about their spirit of rebellion but also about their satisfaction. Change and continuity, as well as cultural shocks and traditions went hand in hand. A forester who studied in the late 1970s, even noticed that many of his fellow students had "drifted" into "traditional" forestry, despite their prejudices and former attitudes towards it.[64]

However, the profession seemed to be living more loosely, voluntarily and "virtually" than before, encompassing the whole globe if need be. More radical change will become more evident with the next generation (as the young forester above predicted) – with more and more foresters noticing and talking about cultural and other changes having worked for some years in the profession. The experiences that these young foresters were talking about were not only personally close to them but also close in time, whereas, for the older foresters, the experiences they were talking about belonged to a more distant past. The time that has elapsed between the events described and the moment of their telling has a bearing on their telling.[65]

In a Magic Mirror

As far as forestry is concerned, the real content of "the national wealth", Finland's green gold, is increasingly to be found in Finland's expertise in forest issues rather than in her physical forests.[66] The future constantly demands versatility from the university-educated foresters. As a young forester of the 1990s said, they have to be able to work as mediators among different actors.[67] The education of forest students increasingly offered different opportunities and branches of study during the 1980s and 1990s. "One could choose commercial or traditional [subjects] or... one could concentrate, for example, on the forest issues in developing or other countries, rather than just Finland's forestry, or one could choose something completely different. There was a really wide choice."[68] In the 1990s, the public discussion of forest issues also made forest students think that there was more than "only one attitude" in Finnish forestry.[69] At the same time they experienced great structural changes in forest industry which affected the whole forest sector. The profession learnt, for instance, to address environmental and ecological issues by itself.[70] For one forester the fact that his fellow students now worked in so many different occupations was evidence of the declining significance of a forest education in creating close bonds among forestry professionals.[71] The University and forest sciences no longer attracts young people with similar aims and dreams, and consequently it does not produce foresters who all think the same way either, according to one student of the 1990s.[72]

The work has changed enormously from the "old golden images of a forester", said a woman who graduated at the turn of the century.[73] "Well, surely everybody has an image of an old forester," noted another forester.[74] Talking about a typical university-educated forester with these interviewees, it became clear that such an image really exists. It is like a distant but permanent reflection in an old and tarnished mirror of the profession. "The real forester" is an outdoor type and hard-working patriotic man, who comes from the countryside, and, as a friend of a nature, feels at home in a Finnish forest, and, as a social and humorous human being, associates with other foresters. "The real work of the forester" takes place in the woods or at least is closely tied to it. This stereotype was recognised and often repeated by interviewees from every generation.[75] This stereotype is also perpetuated, for example, by the historical images of foresters presented in books and articles devoted to the profession's history.[76]

Everybody can look at this mirror. No one really sees himself or herself in it,[77] but everyone can recognise the image of the real forester. Today everything is much more complicated, and the present world is much more open. A man who studied in the 1970s noticed that "there will be big changes with the coming of the next generation of foresters".[78] According to a young forester, who studied at the end of the 1980s, the old professionals have "somewhat stricter attitudes", as the young ones with their various backgrounds, ideas, duties, and jobs do not "necessarily regard themselves simply as foresters".[79] The "typical" features of the profession are not only changing over time, but are totally disappearing.[80] When a young female forester compared her own identity with the image in a mirror, she noted laughing: "But really, I am not sure if I can be called a real forester!"[81] In the eyes of the older generation, young foresters also seemed to be a group that was quite difficult to describe.[82] Realistic descriptions of present-day professionals are extremely rare in oral history stories when talking about typical foresters. Even if the title of a university-educated forester (metsänhoitaja) is appreciated by many of these young professionals, it is, as a name and in meaning, often associated with the past and with a sense of nostalgia.[83]

An identity is said to be born when one's own personal story meets cultural narrations of the past. Identities are constantly created in relation to something else, "the others", and the cultural systems around us. According to Stuart Hall, national cultures create identities by building up meaningful narrations of nations. Some elements of these narrations are, for example, collective experiences that give meanings to a nation, continuity and tradition, and an idea of an original nation. These nations, "imagined communities", have shared memories of the past, desire to live together, and wish to perpetuate their heritage. National identities are, accordingly, placed somewhere between the past and the future. In reality, no national culture is absolutely homogeneous but includes various social classes, ethnic groups, sexes, values, etc.[84]

University-educated foresters – especially in this case those who started their careers in the 1980s and 1990s – could also be seen as an "imagined community", a heterogeneous group of academically trained professionals, with, however, the idea of a forester and a forestry profession. The magic mirror showing the past and a bit of the future has been part of the cultural fortune of an old and traditional profession. It could have helped to build one's own personal identity as a professional, and to strengthen the idea that people who had graduated in forest sciences constituted a profession of foresters. When going to the world, free and open-minded, one could still pack this mirror in a suitcase together with the valuable green gold.

NOTES

1. Hankala 2000, 8. At the beginning of the 21st century, Finnish foresters worked in 40 countries. http://www.metsanhoitajat.fi (Accessed on October 24, 2005).

2. Lusto A02001: for example, 29/m71, 45/f67, 47/m67, 130/m62, 136/f69, 189/f65, 190/f66, 229/m61, Forestry Professions in a Changing Society – Oral History Project 1999–2002, Lusto – The Finnish Forest Museum, Punkaharju. 'M' or 'f' in the signum means 'male' or 'female', and the following number is the year of birth.

3. The education of Finnish foresters was started by establishing the Evo Forest Institute at the beginning of the 1860s. In 1908, the education of foresters was transferred to the University of Helsinki.

4. Leikola 2000, 483–487; Suomen metsänhoitajat 1851–1931.

5. The concept of a forest cluster has been used since the 1990s to mean of a cluster of industrial and production companies and organizations that have grown up around the forest sector in the last few decades. The forest industry, equipment manufacturers, raw material suppliers as well as research and development are parts of the forest cluster. See, for example, http://www.forestindustries.fi (Accessed on October 24, 2005); Lammi 1999.

6. For example, Hetemäki 1997, 113; Rannikko & Lehtinen 2004, 12; Päättäjien metsäakatemia 1/1996, 6/1998, 10/2000.

7. Lusto A02001: 45/f67, 76/f65, 77/m62, 89/f75, 110/m63, 145/f73.

8. Actually, the definitions of these two forester generations are inaccurate or even unreal. Over the seven decades covered by this oral history material, there would have been several generations with their own distinct experiences, at least in some respect. "The young" and "the old" do not refer to the age of people, nor either, for the so-called "young foresters" may be middle-aged by now. About generations and their experiences, see Virtanen 2001, 22–24; Hoikkala 1999, 401.

9. The oral history project of The Finnish Forest History Society, The University of Helsinki (Department of Ethnology) and Lusto – The Finnish Forest Museum was led by Hanna Snellman. The forest sector, its past, present and future, is seen in this article through the eyes of many individual people. There is a lot of discussion and research conducted on the forest sector by its research and other organisations considering almost the same questions: how and why has this field changed? Where does it go in the future? With what actions will it develop and live on? See, for example, Hetemäki 1997; Päättäjien Metsäakatemia 1996–2003. The answers of researchers and, on the other hand, of professionals experiencing these changes may differ – and they can both be right.

10. See Hankala 2000, 8, 10–11. The Finnish historical name of the professional, still in use, is 'metsänhoitaja' (literally 'a caretaker of the forest'). This is usually translated to 'a university-educated forester' or 'a university-qualified forester' as distinct from forestry institute-educated foresters. When I discuss foresters in this article, I mean university-educated foresters.
11. The Finns had to give this land to the USSR in partial payment of its war indemnity.
12. For example, Lindroos 1993, 117–120.
13. LPA, for example, an oral announcement 11.9.2005/m35; Lusto A02001:89/f75, 96/f63, 112/m35, 130/m62, 189/f65; Lindroos 1993, 164; Lindroos 1997, 12.
14. Sitä me vaalimme uhkuvin povin,/ perkaamme kourin känsäisin, kovin./ Metsä on nostava maamme,/ metsistä voimaa saamme,/ metsien kulta vie voittoon. Metsä-ylioppilas 1959, translated into English by Leena Paaskoski 2005.
15. Lusto A02001:155/m62.
16. Lusto A02001:129/f58.
17. Lusto A02001:30/f60, 47/m67, 151/m57.
18. Lusto A02001:77/m62.
19. Lusto A02001:77/m62.
20. Lusto A02001: 136/f69, see also 45/f67, 47/m67, 142/f68, 167/m60, 180/m62.
21. Lusto A02001:33/f60, 76/f65, 89/f75, 183/m63; for example, Kaipainen 1998, 52; Saarimaa 2004a, 114; see also Saarimaa 2004b, 117.
22. Lusto A02001:149/m73, see also 35/m60, 155/m62.
23. Lusto A02001:29/m71.
24. Lusto A02001:145/f73.
25. Lusto A02001:45/f67, see also 21/m73; Leikola 2000, 498. "The traditional work of university-educated foresters" was not usually defined more precisely. It seems to refer more or less to "old time" foresters working in a forest or at least in closely associated taSuomalaisen Kirjallisuuden Seura (like planning and organizing forestry, supplying the forest industry with wood, providing advice to private forest owners, etc). "The traditional work" could also mean three "traditional" employers, the Board of Forestry, the forest industry, and private forestry organisations.
26. Lusto A02001:30/f60.
27. Lusto A02001:35/m60, 37/f63, 76/f65, 191/m60; Hankala 2000, 8–15.
28. Lusto A02001:98/f57.
29. Lusto A02001:111/f51.
30. Lusto A02001:45/f67.
31. Lusto A02001:35/m60, 47/m67, 110/m63.
32. Lusto A02001:150/m48. According to the trade union its members nowadays "typically work as experts or managers in forestry and forest industries in Finland or abroad. The majority (55 per cent) are employed in the private sector; in the public sector the biggest employers are universities and other research organisations, state agencies and state-owned companies." http://www.metsanhoitajat.fi (Accessed on October 24, 2005).
33. Lusto A02001:21/m73.
34. Arvidsson 2001, 16–17; Ehn & Löfgren 1982, 90. For definitions of 'a culture', see Anttonen 1999, 198–210.
35. Considering the professional culture, one also has to include pensioners (who can still be involved in many kinds of professional activities; for example, in the trade union). This temporal dimension is revealed by my oral history material, 226 university-educated foresters who were interviewed in an oral history project in 1999–2002.

36. For example, Metsäylioppilas 1939, 1947, 1949, 1953, 1956.
37. Lusto A02001: 68/m34, 94/m38, 126/m15, 127/m48, 171/m55, 223/m50; see also, for example, Metsäylioppilas 1947, 1950, 1956, 1959.
38. Metsäylioppilas 1947, 1949; Lusto A02001:10/m37, 222/m34.
39. Lusto A02001:1/m47, 2/m45, 14/m58, 31/m43, 33/f60, 34/m47, 40/f54, 46/m20, 56/f56, 66/f21, 83/m22, 124/m41, 137/m56, 154/m32, 175/m48, 209/m44.
40. Lusto A02001: see, for example, 20/f23, 70/m36, 198/m42, 228/f49; Koivisto & Sippola 1997, 31–32.
41. Lusto A02001:70/m36.
42. Metsäylioppilas 1949.
43. Lusto A02001:15/m58, 21/m73, 29/m71, 37/f63, 47/m67, 96/f63, 100/f51, 110/m63, 136/f69, 142/f68, 143/m53, 147/m58, 148/m51, 149/m73, 151/m57, 152/f58, 167/m60, 180/m62, 184/f57, 189/f65, 191/m60, 215/m59, 229/m61.
44. Metsäylioppilas 1970, 3/1973; Lusto A02001: 98/f58, 145/f73.
45. Lusto A02001:17/f46, 229/m61, see also 15/m58, 25/m43, 51/m43, 77/m62, 107/m47, 170/f58, 179/m36, 207/m56, 212/f54, 214/m53, 220/f57; Metsäylioppilas 1978.
46. Lusto A02001:21/m73, 30/f60, 76/f65, 136/f69, 229/m61.
47. Lusto A02001:77/m62, see also 21/m73, 30/f60.
48. Lusto A02001:108/m23, 197/f22, 199/m26.
49. Lusto A02001:180/m62, see also 33/f60, 89/f75, 171/m55, 180/m62.
50. Lusto A02001:29/m71, 30/f60, 33/f60, 45/f67, 76/f65, 96/f63, 97/f57, 130/m62, 167/m60, 180/m62, 219/m61, 229/m61.
51. Lusto A02001:136/f69, 170/f58.
52. Lusto A02001:142/f68.
53. Lusto A02001:148/m51.
54. Lusto A02001: for example, 21/m73, 29/m71, 33/f60, 35/m60, 40/f54, 47/m67, 56/f56, 64/m57, 89/f75, 96/f63, 110/m63, 137/m56, 142/f68, 149/m73, 155/m62, 171/m55, 190/f66, 191/m60, 229/m61; compare, for example, with 2/m45, 154/m32.
55. Lusto A02001:37/f63.
56. Lusto A02001:215/m59.
57. A preliminary practise period in forestry was an old tradition, which was considered useful because it familiarized students with forestry before their studies.
58. Lusto A02001:145/f73.
59. Lusto A02001:21/m73.
60. Lusto A02001:145/f73, see also 45/f67.
61. Lusto A02001:35/m60, see also 48/m54.
62. Lusto A02001:21/m73.
63. Lusto A02001:189/f65, see also 180/m62, 155/m62, 147/m58.
64. Lusto A02001:215/m59.
65. Portelli 1998, 68.
66. See Seppälä 2001, 64.
67. Lusto A02001:29/m71.
68. Lusto A02001:136/f69.
69. Lusto A02001:47/m67.
70. Lusto A02001:190/f66.
71. Lusto A02001:191/m60.
72. Lusto A02001:29/m71.

73. Lusto A02001:89/f75.
74. Lusto A02001:145/f73.
75. Lusto A02001: for example, 1/m47, 2/m45, 5/m18, 10/m37, 21/m73; 30/f60; 33/f60,
    34/m47, 64/m57, 66/f21, 68/m34, 77/m62, 89/f75, 93/m30, 94/m38, 98/f58,
    109/m37, 112/m35, 123/m49, 130/m62, 137/m56, 142/f68, 148/m51, 158/m45,
    160/m43, 165/m37, 175/m48, 180/m62, 191/m60, 201/m36, 204/m57, 218/m48,
    222/m34, 223/m50.
76. For example, Koivisto (ed.) 1997; Kärkkäinen & Toivanen 1995. The trade union
    Metsänhoitajaliitto has had a tradition committee since the 1980s.
77. Lusto A02001: for example, 98/f58, 148/m51, 93/m30.
78. Lusto A02001:171/m55.
79. Lusto A02001:47/m67.
80. Lusto A02001:1/m47, 2/m45, 76/f65, 77/m62, 96/f63, 145/f73.
81. Lusto A02001:145/f73.
82. Lusto A02001: for example, 1/m47.
83. For example, Metsänhoitaja 6/2000; Lusto A02001: 47/m67, 191/m60, 229/m61.
84. Hall 1992, 291–296; Renan 1994, 19.

SOURCES

Magazines

Metsäylioppilas 1939, 1947, 1949, 1950, 1953, 1956, 1959, 1970, 3/1973, 1978
Metsänhoitaja 6/2000

Interviews

Lusto – The Finnish Forest Museum, Punkaharju
Forestry Professions in the Changing Society – Oral History project 1999–2002,
    A02001.
Leena Paaskoski's private archive (LPA), Punkaharju
An oral announcement 11.9.2005/m35.

Internet sources

http://www.forestindustries.fi.
http://www.metsanhoitajat.fi.

BIBLIOGRAPHY

Anttonen, Marjut 1999. *Etnopolitiikkaa Ruijassa. Suomalaislähtöisen väestön identiteettien
    politisoituminen 1990-luvulla.* Suomalaisen Kirjallisuuden Seuran Toimituksia 764.
    Helsinki: Suomalaisen Kirjallisuuden Seura.
Arvidsson, Alf 2001. *Etnologi. Perspektiv och forskningsfält.* Etnologiska skrifter nr 24.
    Lund: Studentlitteratur.

Ehn, Billy & Löfgren, Orvar 1982. *Kulturanalys. Ett etnologiskt perspektiv*. Lund: Liber.

Hall, Stuart 1992. The Question of Cultural Identity. Hall, Stuart & Held, David & Mcgrew, Tony (eds), *Modernity and its futures*. Cambridge: Polity Press.

Hankala, Tapio 2000. Metsänhoitajakunta tänään. *Suomen metsänhoitajat 1987–1999*. Helsinki: Metsänhoitajaliitto ry.

Hetemäki, Lauri 1997. *Metsäsektori 2010*. Pihlaja-sarja nro 2. Helsinki: Metsälehti Kustannus & Metsäntutkimuslaitos.

Hoikkala, Tommi 1999. Suuret ikäluokat ja työ. Parikka, Raimo (ed.), *Suomalaisen työn historiaa. Korvesta konttoriin*. Suomalaisen Kirjallisuuden Seuran Toimituksia 730. Helsinki: Suomalaisen Kirjallisuuden Seura.

Kaipainen, Jaana 1998. Naiset metsäammattilaisina. Ripatti, Pekka (ed.), *Naiset metsäsektorilla*. Metsäntutkimuslaitoksen tiedonantoja 697. Helsinki: Helsingin tutkimuskeskus.

Koivisto, Arvi A. (ed.) 1997. *Metsästä ja metsän reunasta. Metsänhoitajaperinnettä*. Helsinki: Metsänhoitajaliitto ry.

Koivisto, Arvi A. & Sippola, Jukka 1997. Metsänhoitajien yhteistoimintaa. Koivisto, Arvi A. (ed.), *Metsästä ja metsän reunasta. Metsänhoitajaperinnettä*. Helsinki: Metsänhoitajaliitto ry.

Kärkkäinen, Sirpa & Toivanen, Erja 1995. *Uudistusalalla. Naismetsänhoitajien elämää vuodesta 1918*. Helsinki: Naismetsänhoitajat ry.

Lammi, Markku 1999. The forest cluster: An alliance of wood, machines and know-how. Reunala, Aarne & Tikkanen, Ilpo & Åsvik, Esko (eds), *The Green Kingdom. Finland's Forest Cluster*. Helsinki: Otava / Metsämiesten Säätiö Foundation.

Leikola, Matti 2000, Metsätiede. *Suomen tieteen historia 3. Luonnontieteet, lääketieteet ja tekniset tieteet*. Porvoo: WSOY.

Lindroos, Heikki 1993. *Puuta mottiin*. Helsinki: Teollisuuden Metsänhoitajat ry.

Lindroos, Heikki 1997. *Sotametsän perintö*. Helsinki: Teollisuuden Metsänhoitajat ry.

Portelli, Alessandro 1998. What makes oral history different? Perks, Robert & Thomson, Alistair (eds), *The Oral History Reader*. London & New York: Routledge.

Päättäjien Metsäakatemia 1996–2003. Helsinki: Suomen Metsäyhdistys ry.

Rannikko, Pertti & Lehtinen, Ari 2004. Metsät ja yhteiskunta – lähtökohtia ja avainkäsitteitä. Lehtinen, Ari & Rannikko, Pertti (eds), *Leipäpuusta arvopaperia. Vastuun ja oikeudenmukaisuuden haasteet metsäpolitiikassa*. Helsinki: Metsälehti Kustannus.

Renan, Ernest 1994. What is a nation? Bhabha, Homi K. (ed.), *Nation and Narration*. London and New York: Routledge.

Saarimaa, Riikka 2004a. Metsänhoitajanaiset miehisellä metsäsektorilla. Lehtinen, Ari & Rannikko, Pertti (eds), *Leipäpuusta arvopaperia. Vastuun ja oikeidenmukaisuuden haasteet metsäpolitiikassa*. Helsinki: Metsälehti Kustannus.

Saarimaa, Riikka 2004b. Nainen metsänhoitajan ammatissa. *Työelämän tutkimus Arbetslivsforskning* 2–3/2004. Työelämän tutkimusyhdistys ry.

Seppälä, Risto 2001. Metsäklusterin tulevaisuus omissa käsissämme. *Päättäjien metsäakatemia* 12/2001. Helsinki: Suomen Metsäyhdistys ry.

Suomen metsänhoitajat 1851–1931. Suomen Metsänhoitajaliitto: Helsinki 1931.

Virtanen, Matti 2001. *Fennomanian perilliset. Poliittiset traditiot ja sukupolvien dynamiikka* Suomalaisen Kirjallisuuden Seuran Toimituksia 831. Sosiaali- ja terveysalan tutkimus- ja kehittämiskeskuksen (Stakes) julkaisuja. Helsinki: Suomalaisen Kirjallisuuden Seura.

Contributors

Aalto, Minna, PhD, Finnish literature,
University of Turku, living in Brussels

Ilmolahti, Oona, PhD student, history,
University of Helsinki

Kaunisto, Katri, PhD student, ethnology,
University of Helsinki

Kytönen, Tarja, PhD student, history,
University of Helsinki

Louhivuori, Leena, PhD student, ethnology,
University of Helsinki

Lukkarinen Kvist, Mirjaliisa, PhD, ethnology,
University of Linköping

Lähteenmäki, Maria, PhD, history, Academy Research Fellow,
University of Helsinki

Paaskoski, Leena, PhD student, ethnology,
University of Helsinki

Pihlaja, Päivi Maria, PhD student, history,
University of Helsinki

Snellman, Hanna, PhD, ethnology, Academy Research Fellow,
University of Helsinki

Tanni, Katri, PhD student, history,
The Australian National University & University of Tampere

Weckström, Lotta, PhD student, applied language studies,
University of Jyväskylä

Willman, Terhi, PhD student, ethnology,
University of Helsinki

Ågren, Maria, PhD, ethnology,
University of Gothenburg

www.ingramcontent.com/pod-product-compliance
Lightning Source LLC
Chambersburg PA
CBHW081738270326
41932CB00020B/3312

* 9 7 8 9 5 1 8 5 8 0 6 5 5 *